The
EVERYTHING®
Birthday Personology Book

Dear Reader,

Every writing project is a new adventure, and this book was no different. One of the reasons I embarked on this subject was honestly because my birthday had become rather mundane and routine over the years. There were no real surprises, no big to-dos—just normal routines. Now, that's not the way anyone's birthday should progress! But how could that be changed?

One way to solve the problem personally was to first step back and recognize the specialness of the day. From there, it was just a short leap to activating that potential to make the day truly special, moment to moment. With this in mind, you can bet my birthday is going to be different from here on out! I trust that yours will be likewise unique and interesting after reading this book—that it will be more fulfilling, and more fun!

Realistically we have this second—this day—to make our lives different: to think, and see, and be different. Grab hold of that opportunity with all of your heart and spirit, using Birthday Personology as a helpmate. Celebrate Self, and let others celebrate with you. I guarantee your life, and the lives of those you care about, will transform in wonderful ways as a result.

In Service,

Marian Singer

The EVERYTHING® Series

Editorial

Publishing Director	Gary M. Krebs
Director of Product Development	Paula Munier
Associate Managing Editor	Laura M. Daly
Associate Copy Chief	Brett Palana-Shanahan
Acquisitions Editor	Lisa Laing
Development Editor	Jessica LaPointe
Associate Production Editor	Casey Ebert

Production

Director of Manufacturing	Susan Beale
Associate Director of Production	Michelle Roy Kelly
Cover Design	Paul Beatrice
	Matt LeBlanc
	Erick DaCosta
Design and Layout	Heather Barrett
	Brewster Brownville
	Colleen Cunningham
	Jennifer Oliveira
Series Cover Artist	Barry Littmann

Visit the entire Everything® Series at *www.everything.com*

THE
EVERYTHING
BIRTHDAY PERSONOLOGY BOOK

What your birthdate says about your
life, relationships, and destiny

Marian Singer

Adams Media
Avon, Massachusetts

For readers everywhere who adore their books over TV and video games:
May there never be a generation without books to enjoy!
Also, for Dr. Frank, who may never see this (or realize it). You
were the most influential teacher of my life, creatively pushing your
students ever forward in writing. I wish that every child I knew had
dozens of teachers like you to inspire them.

An Everything® Series Book.
Everything® and everything.com® are registered trademarks of F+W Publications, Inc.

Published by Adams Media, an F+W Publications Company
57 Littlefield Street, Avon, MA 02322 U.S.A.
www.adamsmedia.com

ISBN 10: 1-59337-726-6
ISBN 13: 978-1-59337-726-7

Printed in the United States of America.

J   I   H   G   F   E   D   C   B   A

Library of Congress Cataloging-in-Publication Data
Singer, Marian.
The everything birthday personology book / Marian Singer.
p. cm. -- (Everything series.)
ISBN-13: 978-1-59337-726-7
ISBN-10: 1-59337-726-6
1. Birthdays--Miscellanea. 2. Astrology and psychology. 3. Numerology. 4. Personality--Miscellanea. I. Title.
BF1729.B45S48 2007
133.5'4042--dc22
2006028135

This book is available at quantity discounts for bulk purchases.
For information, please call 1-800-289-0963.

Contents

Acknowledgments

My thanks, as always, to Jennie for putting up with an overly head-strong, workaholic author. Having a sure and steady guide is always welcome in this sea of ink. Also to Lisa, my editor, and other members of the Adams Media team who have diligently guided this project since its inception. Working with you all has been a true joy.

Finally, a gentle and warm hug to various people in my mundane life who do not know that much about this facet of my reality, but who inspire me by their tenacity, honesty, creativity, and overall kindness. Without that touchstone, much would never get accomplished, much would go unsaid, and many treasures would be left buried in a mound of red tape. We often forget that our spiritual lives are not islands, neatly sequestered away from daily reality. We also sometimes forget that the greatest examples of true spirit lie in that very reality. May you all, always, be blessed.

Top Ten Personology Tips, Tricks, Facts, & Findings

1. Personology is a wonderful helpmate to understanding the cycles in your life. However, you are still the master of your present and future.

2. Numbers are dynamic symbols. Those that appear regularly in your life send a message. What are your repeated numbers telling you?

3. The phrase "it's written in the stars" reflects the ideology behind personology. The moment you were born, the placement of all celestial objects created a letter of introduction for all that you are, and all that you can become!

4. Each day represents a new opportunity to transform your reality.

5. Numerologically the word "personology" is a number 1. This represents originality, creativity, independence, and dynamic energy.

6. Personology can easily be combined with other divination systems like the Tarot.

7. Personology is gender neutral. The overall energetic effects play out equally in both men's and women's lives.

8. There are many types of numerology and astrology, including culturally unique systems among Africans, Arabic peoples, the Japanese, the ancient Chaldeans, and others.

9. Numerology was used by ancient Egyptians, the Magi, Cagliostro, and Gypsies, just to name a few.

10. Astrology proponents include Aristotle, Nostradamus, Mary Todd Lincoln, and Warren G. Harding.

Introduction

▶ WHAT EXACTLY is Birthday Personology? Effectively it's the rebirth of two ancient arts, numerology and astrology, joined together. Ancient societies used many methods to try to understand people, including interpreting the positions of moles on the body, feeling bumps on the head, and reading body language. *The Everything® Birthday Personology Book* is no different! This book uses the arts of numerology and astrology for similar goals, while also sharing a smattering of lore and other trivia tidbits for every day of the year.

Combining these two systems results in a unique blend of celestial and earthly influences, both of which gently affect your characteristics and destiny. By understanding these subtle influences you can begin to accent the best vibrations in each day, especially birthdays, and neatly avoid or balance out the worst ones. Better still, this system provides greater insight into the lives, feelings, careers, and dreams of friends, coworkers, and loved ones alike.

Each day offers you an opportunity to celebrate life, diversity, individuality, personal vision, family, and community. Seize that opportunity! Most people have difficulty living in the moment. Homes, mates, jobs, hobbies, and a plethora of responsibilities need attention. Just ask yourself one question: have you ever forgotten your birthday or that of someone very special to you? Why is that? It's because you're juggling so many things and rushing around so fast that days and moments slip by unnoticed. This is a pity, and one you can correct starting right now.

This book covers all 366 days in the year (including leap year)—each one different, and each one revealing something about the people born on that day. This daily personology guide could not possibly include all the different permutations that a person's birth year brings. So, instead, it uses the month number (1–12) plus the day number (1–31). In other words, January 14th becomes 1 + 1 + 4 = 6. To this foundation, you can add in any of your other numbers to gain greater insights.

Besides the practical, hands-on aspect of this book, you'll find a brief introduction to both astrology and numerology. It's always good to develop an understanding of the fundamental systems piloting a guide like this one. It allows you to further personalize the material, and use the systems separately for other purposes if you wish.

Remember that you are the master of each moment of your destiny. Those choices you make today transform your tomorrows. Use this book to get to know yourself on a different level. Use it as a helpmate in making informed, aware choices that create the future for which you hope and dream. Ultimately, this book celebrates all it is to be human—growth and transformation. By taking one small step and picking up this daily guide, each day—its temperament and potential—becomes yours for the taking. Carpe Diem!

Chapter 1
Numerology

The idea that numbers have sacred and predictive energies comes from a long line of thinkers, theologians, and philosophers. Numerology is as old as astrology, and it may well be that these two systems developed together, with one supporting the other. Numbers, like words, were important to all forms of human communication, especially travel and commerce. There's no question that they've participated in a great many metaphysical systems in one form or another.

Ancient Systems

The roots of numerology stretch back to Arabia and India. From here we find evidence of numerological systems spanning many civilizations, including those of Israel, China, Egypt, Tibet, and the Mayan and Celtic regions. In many of these settings the goal was not simply to predict personality, but rather to understand nature and fate, and hopefully create a better future by so doing.

QUESTION?

What is the origin of the word *numerology*?
The term *numerology* traces its roots to the Latin word *numerus*, meaning number, and the Greek *logos*, a word, thought, or expression (also a branch of knowledge).

Early systems of numerological symbolism didn't use single digits. In fact, many regarded a series of digits, often repeated, as having value. Folk cures in a variety of settings, including among the Celts, Arabic people, and even in the Far East, were repeated a specific number of times, using a set number of herbs, and even timed to reflect that number according to the date. So, one cure might be enacted three times, with three herbs, on the third day after the full moon (for example): 333.

Chaldean and Kabbalistic Numerology

The Chaldean system emerged as the first one widely used in the ancient world. It began in Babylon, influenced by Vedic and later Hebraic mystery schools. In this form of numerology, each letter of the alphabet had a numeric value assigned that corresponded to the number's energy. The main difference, as you'll see from the Essential Chart, is that the Chaldeans based their numerology on 8 numbers. The number 9 was sacred and kept apart (potentially to honor Deity). Beyond this, the Chaldean system considered double digits as representing the inner, or secret, self. Outer numbers represent surface appearances, or a more superficial nature.

A related numerological system, Kabbalah, originates with the Hebrews and ties in directly to the Hebrew alphabet and Tree of Life symbolism.

Kabbalistic numerology utilizes only a person's name, not their birth date. There is some argument among numerology experts as to whether this omission makes Kabbalistic numerology less accurate than the Chaldean.

Pythagoras

By far the most influential person in the history of numerology is Pythagoras (530 B.C.E.). Called the father of numerology, Pythagoras found a relationship between numbers, celestial objects, and music. From this relationship, Pythagoras summarily determined that the entire universe has corresponding numbers that, once decoded and understood, would reveal great mysteries. In fact, he taught that a person's life had a direct relationship to various numbers.

FACT

According to Greek mythology, Pythagoras was the son of Apollo and a priestess of Delphi. As a child, he traveled with his merchant father regularly, and benefited from the teachings of many learned people, including men of Syria. Thousands of years later there is no question as to the contributions Pythagoras made to music, astronomy, and mathematics.

Pythagoras received teachings from various great minds, including those from other traditions that had numerological systems (like Jewish and Hindu); and this was but one of his studies. Another discipline that Pythagoras blended into his numeric system was astronomy (whose predecessor was astrology). Pythagoras's tradition was carried on by his students and continues to be the most widely utilized system in the West.

Root Numbers

The Pythagorean and modern systems of numerology include nine root numbers from which all else is derived. The sum of any day, object, street name, or whatever, can be reduced to one of these numbers. Simply add the corresponding digits together to get a total. If it's greater than 9, add those digits together. Take the example of a birthday of February 21, 1960. This adds up as follows: $2 + 2 + 1 + 1 + 9 + 6 + 0 = 21 = 3$.

Root Number Overview				
Root Numbers	Keynote	Element	Planet	Lucky Stone & Color
1	Drive	Fire	Sun	Ruby; Orange & Gold
2	Harmony	Water	Moon	Pearl; Green & White
3	Innovation	Fire	Jupiter	Amethyst; Purple
4	Honesty	Air	Uranus	Topaz; Electric Shades
5	Inquiry	Air	Mercury	Diamond; Pastels
6	Social	Earth	Venus	Turquoise; Blue
7	Mystery	Water	Neptune	Jade; Ivory Tones
8	Leader	Earth	Saturn	Black pearl; Black
9	Seeker	Fire	Mars	Bloodstone; Crimson

So, when any day in a month corresponds to a personal number, you can increase the potential energies in that day by wearing a fortunate stone or color! This information might also be used in planning special events. If, for example, you want to use numerology to choose a date for a political rally, number 8 seems the most supportive of that goal.

Year Numbers

If you want to know what to expect in the current year or what the energies were in your birth year, it's easy to do. Simply add up the numbers in the year, reducing them until the sum is a single digit, like this: $1995 = 24 = 6$. Compare this number to this list:

1. A fresh beginning. This year sets the pace for all that will come in the next nine. Be prepared for change. Lay foundations for new projects, and focus on self-development.
2. Peaceful cooperation helps improve everything. Focus on harmony, especially in communications. A good year for relationships.

3. Busy! Life is moving at warp speeds. Opportunity is knocking on several doors at once, and the social calendar is stuffed full. Carefully weigh your decisions, and stash some of the money this year brings for a rainy day.

4. A relief after Year 3's hurried nature, Year 4 is even-paced and calm. Persue personal projects and goals and re-evaluate priorities. An excellent year to ponder a move, start a new hobby, heal any misunderstandings, and breathe!

5. Expect the unexpected. New and interesting challenges and options present themselves. Don't wait too long before acting on either. Release old, outworn ways of thinking and behaving, and be proactive.

6. This year focuses attention on the hearth and home (be it an apartment, house boat, or castle). Think things through completely before acting or talking to avoid mistakes and misunderstandings. Embrace patience, especially in business.

7. Introspection and personal development. Expand mind and spirit rather than continuing to just "go along" with social trends. Renew the relationship with Self, improve self-confidence, and remember to balance temptations with old-fashioned common sense.

8. Year 8 speaks of abundance in some form—be it a plethora of new friends, a bountiful garden, or improved finances. Hard work and diligence bring their own rewards.

9. Completion. Clean up, clean out, purge, organize, and put things into good order so the next nine-year cycle is better than the last.

Name Numbers

It's said that adding the value of the vowels in a name reflects the inner realities. The consonants are what we show to the world, and the whole name is a balanced reflection of the inner and outer life. When added together using the Alpha-Numeric Essential as a guide, a person's name number reveals hidden potentials and dangers. For example, if someone were considering a job offer, they could compare the values of the company's name with their own name number to see if it's a good match. Or, comparing one's name number to that of potential mates could prove very interesting.

Alpha-Numeric Correspondences			
Value	Modern	Cabalistic	Chaldean
1	A J S	A I Q J Y	A I J Q Y
2	B K T	B R K	B K R
3	C L U	C G L S	C G L S
4	D M V	D M T	D M T
5	E N W	E H N	E H N X
6	F O X	U V W X	U V W
7	G P Y	O Z	O Z
8	H Q Z	F P	F P
9	I R		

This modern system is based on the Pythagorean approach, which is the most widely used. However, if a person would like to see what other systems say about personality, add up all the letters in your first, middle, and last names as follows:

Joe X. Smith becomes:

$$1 + 7 + 5 + 6 + 3 + 4 + 1 + 4 + 5 \text{ (Cabalistic)} = 36 = 9$$
$$1 + 7 + 5 + 5 + 3 + 4 + 1 + 4 + 5 \text{ (Chaldean)} = 35 = 8$$
$$1 + 6 + 5 + 6 + 1 + 4 + 9 + 2 + 8 \text{ (Modern)} = 42 = 6$$

The numerological associations for name numbers follow:

1. **Somewhat independent person, likely to be a trailblazer.** Lots of energy for new adventures. A very inventive leader who lets little stand between him and a goal. On the down side, this person may not always think through the consequences of their actions.
2. **Peace-loving individual who would make an excellent diplomat.** Huge personality, amazing charm, and the ability to bring out the best in others makes this person fairly popular. Even so, he may suffer from a sense of low self-esteem.

3. **The number of inventors and thinkers.** People with restless spirits are typically Threes. These individuals feel appearances are important, and may overvalue others' opinions of them. Keynotes include independence and conscientiousness.

4. **Number of a rational mind.** Practicality is the name of the game. These are very orderly and dutiful people. They create strong bonds between themselves and others, value stability, show kindness, and appreciate loyalty. Not always quick to accept change.

5. **Impulsiveness and adventure.** These individuals live in the moment with an intense ferocity for life that's unrivaled. They'll seek out pleasure wherever it can be found, have passionate relationships, and are risk-takers. On the negative side, they sometimes burn themselves out.

6. **A Six appreciates loveliness.** Lovely art, exquisite jewelry, magnificent gardens—all capture the eye and spirit of this person. Sixes are people of high ideals and strong humanitarians. They can be trusted and read others very well. The caution for a Six is not to lean on others too much for a sense of self-worth.

7. **Philosophers and mystics bear this number.** These innovative folk are always trying to unravel a mystery (and often succeed). Sevens are disciplined, smart, and sometimes rather lucky individuals whose only real drawback is a tendency to retreat too deeply into themselves and away from the world.

8. **Dichotomy typifies this person.** Life is filled with amazing success and terrible failure in seemingly equal proportion. Being strong-willed and having strong emotions, Eights often feel like the odd person out and aren't fully sure how to balance the roller-coaster ride of life.

9. **The warrior spirit.** This is a hard worker who knows when to act and when to wait. While Nines may exhibit a fiery temper periodically, they are also among the first to offer help in times of need. The greatest challenge in the warrior's life is knowing how to live once they're done with a quest.

Birth Numbers

To obtain a birth number, add together the month, date, and year of anyone's birthday. As before, reduce this down to a single-digit number. For example, if someone's birthday is April 15, 1965, that becomes $4 + 1 + 5 + 1 + 9 + 6 + 5 = 31 = 4$. Afterward, check the listing that follows for insights as to what that number means.

Birth Numbers	Keynote Energies
1	distinctiveness; uniqueness
2	cooperation; balance
3	charm; luck
4	strength; work ethic
5	liberation; adaptation
6	peace; idealism
7	sagacity; truthfulness
8	leadership; diligence
9	empathy; selflessness

Birth Number 1

This is a strong individual who sets out to maintain uniqueness no matter the setting. Ones are naturally motivated to lead. These people dream of going into space, or into whatever new frontier the latest innovations offer. Personal ideals and morals guide this person's life. There is no room for compromise, and any challenges to that foundation are typically met with negativity and a stubborn sense of indignation.

People with this birth number do not like to lose, meaning they'll often exert high demands and expectations on everyone in their lives. Ones are very dynamic, insistent, competitive, logical, and independent. While they can achieve their goals, ultimately people with this birth number initiate more than they complete. Not likely to mince words and lacking in patience, Ones must take care that their family and friends don't get exasperated by their highly opinionated natures.

Birth Number 2

Similar to the name number, Twos are the mediators and arbitrators of life's ever-changing game. Adaptable and outgoing, yet never overstepping their boundaries, people born with this number will never be loners. Not only are others naturally attracted to the gentle-natured Two, people with this birth number would rather work in pairs or as part of a team anyway! It's a win-win.

FACT

The Hebrew language uses letters for numbers, and Kabbalism (Jewish mysticism) uses those numbers as a way of better understanding sacred texts and teachings. Pythagoras thought the number 10 was harmonic and eternal. The importance of 10 was also evidenced in earlier Greek and Hebrew teachings. To the Babylonians 12 was important because of its celestial connections, and people regarded it as very positive.

When common sense isn't working to achieve a Two's goal, they turn to natural charm and sensual cues to smooth things over. Between their ability to listen, speak, and bring good-natured humor into a discussion, Twos usually manage to resolve whatever problems life presents. However, this desire for order can become an Achilles' Heel for the Two, who may spin out of control when disparagement, disloyalty, or disorder win out. Keynotes for this number include cooperation, service, openness, and harmony.

Birth Number 3

Joy is doubled when shared. So Threes tend to be very happy, upbeat, expressive, and positive people. This person loves the stage; if they can make others laugh all the better. No matter where a Three travels, she'll find her natural knack for communicating, personal warmth, and generosity in even the most difficult situations endears her to everyone.

From the outside, Threes may seem overly lighthearted. That's really not the case. There's an inner core to the Three that motivates them—a three wants to accomplish something, be it in sports, careers, or love. That aspiration combined with the optimistic Three's nature creates a person who can laugh at failure while still striving for great success. Positive keynotes include good humor, playfulness, sociability, and versatility.

One hard thing for this birth number is choosing. These people can do many things well, and are likely to try a buffet of hobbies and careers throughout their lives. It's not hard for a Three to move very quickly to the forefront of anything to which they apply their hands, so long as they stick to it!

Birth Number 4

Fours are the workhorses of the world. There is no job "beneath" a Four so long as it's something he can do well and see through to completion. When something needs to be done once and done right—call on a Four. This aptitude, combined with seemingly unending amounts of energy, makes Four people naturally adept leaders in the business world.

People with this birth number like to get their hands dirty, so they are often expert mechanics and technicians in a variety of fields. There's nothing more satisfying to these folk than watching personal work manifest itself in wonderful ways. Better still, if someone gives a Four good ideas, he can run with them! This number's keynotes include physicality, sensibility, honesty, and even-temperedness.

Fours prefer a structured life. Fast changes and poor planning by others can upset the apple cart and leave this person off balance for quite some time. Even so, the true-blue nature of a Four person makes these rare, uncertain moments easy to bear. Fours rarely break promises, and consequently have to watch that they don't overcommit themselves (and neglect personal well-being).

Birth Number 5

Adaptation and a thirst for freedom wrap up the Five's personality rather succinctly. These individuals are perpetual students in life's classroom. Outgoing and upbeat, they have no problem making friends and often manage to land on their feet even after the worst of circumstances. The Five greets anything unusual, surprising, or outrageous with gleeful anticipation.

Fives make excellent networkers. Their ability to react quickly, and multiplicity of skills, means that when opportunity knocks you can bet a Five is already waiting at the door. The only problem is seeing that opportunity through to completion. Having a gypsy soul, the Five finds it hard to stay put for very long. This number must keep restlessness in check if they're to achieve goals consistently, let alone maintain a long-term relationship.

Other keynotes for the Five personality include lightheartedness, independence, sex appeal, and the ability to multitask easily.

Birth Number 6

The Six personality has strong humanitarian overtones. This person's ideals and emotions guide action with friends and strangers alike. If you want someone who will not drop the ball on a charitable cause, phone a Six. This is also a problem for Sixes. They don't always know where to draw the line (sometimes help is not welcome or wanted).

Sixes love the beautiful things in life, including beautiful concepts. This means they surround themselves with an ambiance that reflects love, romance, artistic insight, and personal passions. The negative aspect here is that the Six may cling to overly idealistic images and risks being disappointed. In turn, this individual may find herself literally or figuratively retreating to a mountain somewhere (as long as it's a beautiful mountain!).

Positive keynotes for the Six include being loving, open, very real (doesn't put on airs), and a dedicated friend.

Birth Number 7

Sevens blend head and heart into a powerful cooperative force. These people can notice a hair or a word out of place, and if they learn to trust their instincts they can seem downright psychic. This keenness sometimes puts others off or makes them uncomfortable, which is just as well because Sevens aren't the best socialites. Most would rather venture out alone, figure out the puzzle, experience the process, and declare the resulting insights with confidence. Keynotes of this number include an eye for detail, trustworthiness, and inventiveness.

FACT

Sevens make good researchers, academics, and craftspeople because they're curious and thorough. They also have a natural affinity for interesting spiritual belief systems. However, all this deep thinking can bring about detachment, hermetic retreats, or a tendency to second-guess oneself. That's a natural drawback to the visionary nature of the Seven personality: visionaries of any time are rarely understood.

Birth Number 8

Since they're twice four, it's not surprising that the people with this birth number are strongly affected by money and security. They may yearn for either or both, which in turn provides a motivating force to be successful in business. Eights make fabulous executives, being diligent, proactive, persistent, and a very good judge of people and situations. Once something's in motion and producing, Eights are also very protective of what they create.

The key problem for an Eight is a tendency to be overly responsible and unwilling to delegate. There's an underlying sense that if something's to be done, the best person for that job is the Eight himself. Additionally, the Eight bears high expectations for others that aren't always reasonable (but rather based on what the Eight naturally knows how to accomplish). The key vibrations for this number include wealth, leadership, tenacity, a very strong work ethic, and loyalty.

Birth Number 9

Nines have the potential to be the world's prophets. They can see through the fog of words and actions and sense potential outcomes quite naturally. While this type of insight could be disturbing, the Nine applies it to good causes so that they'll succeed. In this regard Nine is very altruistic, even to the point of self-neglect.

Nines will rarely be wholly content with life, society, or the global picture, striving ever for that better ideal. This may cause the Nine to get mired in disappointment that can, in turn, spiral into depression. It's important, therefore, for this personality to find a center, something that keeps overly intense mood swings balanced out. Travel is one excellent choice, as is any-thing that engages the imagination or personal passions. Keynotes of this number include romanticism, compassion, bravery, and generosity.

Less-Used Numbers

Some numerological systems include the values of 0, 11, 12, 13, 22, and 40. The values of these numbers (and the respective meanings for each) may be added to basic Personology profiles as desired. For example, if a person's name adds up to 12, you could substitute this information for the traditional valuation of 3, or add it to the value of 3 for greater insight.

0 Zero is an expression of Spirit, primordial possibilities, and intensity. It adds emphasis, power, and greater potential to any number preceding it (the 1 in 10, for example). Taoism—the void. Kabbalism—boundlessness (the Monad).

11 Mystical people or situations. A balance between all forces (good vs. evil, light vs. darkness). A highly inventive, active, intense number. On the negative side, some traditions see this as the number of illegal activity.

12 Fulfillment, completion, and awareness. Buddhism—sound counsel. Celtic—knightly virtue. Hebrew—a person's "fruits" (12 fruits on the Tree of Life).

13 Bad luck, negativity, depression. Mayan—the number of paradise. Aztec—an important number for divination.

22 Enlightenment. Building toward a strong future. The knack of manifesting one's hopes and dreams.

40 Single-mindedness. Tests successfully completed. Processing difficult lessons. Cleansing. Islamic—transformation.

Different Systems, Different Energies

Not all systems of numerology ascribe the same energies to a number. Here is a list of some of the various interpretations:

1: **China**—masculine and celestial. Hebrew—the "I am." Islamic—total completion. Pythagorean—Spirit, the essential spark of all things.

2: **China**—the feminine number. Alchemy—opposites like the sun and moon, or male and female. Plato—a relationship (or partnership). Kabbalism—self-awareness and wisdom.

3: **Aristotle**—beginning, middle, and end (a full cycle). Global mythology—various trinities (diversity in unity). Folklore—number of wishes and frequently important for curing. China—lucky and sacred number. Hebrew—divine intelligence. Hindu—creation, preservation, and destruction (as part of each other).

4: **Western mysticism**—the corners of creation and elemental powers. Buddhism—the tree of life and directional guardians. China—earth and immortality. Egypt—time's passage. Hebrew—kindness and astuteness. Pythagoras—justice.

5: **Eastern mysticism**—the senses. Buddhism—the heart. China—blessings. Greek—love and relationships (a positive omen for both). Kabbalism—fear. Hebrew—unforgiving strength. Islam—the pillars of faith.

6: **Western folklore**—health, beauty, and good fortune. China—as above, so below (axiom). Hebrew—creation. Pythagoras—serendipity, fortune.

7: **Buddhism**—ascension, paradise. Christian—fasting and sacraments. Egypt—the fates. Greece—a number sacred to Apollo, Minerva, and Pan. Hebrew—understanding the mysteries. Islam—perfection. Pythagoras—the cosmos.

8: **Western esoteric traditions**—regeneration, paradise. Buddhism—achievement, conclusion. China—manifestation. Hebrew—perfect mindedness. Hindu—celestial and earthly order. Pythagoras—stability, foundations.

9: **Buddhism**—ultimate spiritual manifestation. China—the wheel of time and life (this also seems to be true in Celtic regions). Greece & Rome—the muses. Kabbalism—foundations. Scandinavian—wisdom.

Use any of these additional meanings to further personalize each day and provide more insights.

Chapter 2
Astrology

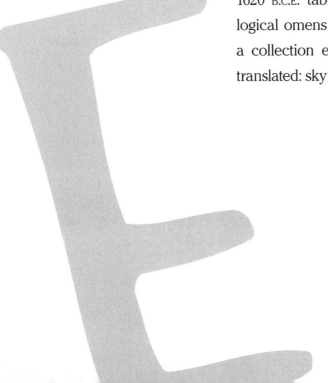

Astrology is regarded as a branch of natural omen interpretation with origins as far back as 2000 B.C.E. Records from around 1700 B.C.E. indicate that the Babylonians believed the gods moved celestial objects to reveal forthcoming events. Around 1620 B.C.E. tablets with over 7000 astrological omens had been assembled into a collection entitled *Anu Enlil* (roughly translated: sky omen collection).

Early Astrology

Mesopotamian priests connected the sun, moon, and planets with specific divine beings, believing that each represented one facet of the universe's order and structure. Slowly these ideas spread into Greece, Egypt, Syria, and India, often carried with merchants and traders along with their goods. The earliest surviving horoscope appeared around 410 B.C.E. on the Cylinder of Gudea from Babylon (currently residing in Oxford). It recounts a dream where a goddess studies a map of the heavens, giving brief positive and negative predictions based on her celestial observations.

By 300 B.C.E. astrologers were already refining their art. Now the sky was divided into twelve sections. During this time, Aristotle developed the principal philosophies for a far more methodical approach to this art. He also encouraged further studies into the art.

Aristotle's efforts were not to be without results. Three centuries later, Greek physician and writer Galen (C.E. 131–201) strongly agreed with Aristotle's ideas and went on to say he believed in the validity of celestial omens including astrology and other observed events like meteors. Alexandrian astronomer Ptolemy (second century C.E.) similarly detailed in his writings, called Tetrabiblos, how celestial objects could affect human life in very complex ways. However, Ptolemy cautioned that this effect was by no means absolute.

Early astrology focused mostly on creating effective sky maps for travel, farming, and folk remedies rather than predicting the future. The concept of natal astrology wasn't introduced until 5 B.C.E. by a Greek astronomer named Eudoxus. Eudoxus's ideas were reintroduced in the fourth century A.D., but somehow did not catch on until much later.

Nearly every culture had is own system of astrology or celestial predictions. In Islamic tradition, for example, the stargazer was known as the Murajjim. It was this person's sacred duty to teach children how to pray for a "true star" that would govern the child's future. To accomplish this, the Murajjim employed the assistance of a complex tool composed of ciphers and degrees, appearing something like a compass. A complete prediction would be finalized by the end of the inquiry.

Astrological correspondences were originally based on a five-planet system consisting of Mercury, Venus, Mars, Jupiter, and Saturn (the visible planets at the time). Astrologers also based their observations on the moon and its phases for things like planting cycles (a tradition that was still common even in 1920).

What does "born on the cusp" mean?
The dates given for a person's sun sign aren't perfectly exact. The time when the sun enters a specific sign changes slightly from year to year. Being born on the cusp means being born on the very day that the sun is shifting into a new realm of influence, say from Aquarius to Pisces. Most astrologers feel that cusp-born individuals often display aspects of both signs in their birthday personology.

Archetypes of Astrology

As with numbers, each sign of the Zodiac has specific energies associated with it. This generalized list provides a quick reference.

Sign	Color	Keynote	Stone	Element	Planet
Aries	Red	Trailblazer	bloodstone	Fire	Mars
Taurus	Green	Realist	sapphire	Earth	Venus
Gemini	Yellow	Raconteur	agate	Air	Mercury
Cancer	Brown	Caregiver	emerald	Water	Moon
Leo	Gold	Leader	onyx	Fire	Sun
Virgo	Orange	Planner	carnelian	Earth	Mercury
Libra	White	Diplomat	chrysolite	Air	Venus
Scorpio	Black	Modifier	beryl	Water	Pluto
Sagittarius	Blue	Explorer	topaz	Fire	Jupiter
Capricorn	Grey	Worker	ruby	Earth	Saturn
Aquarius	Blue-Green	Maverick	garnet	Air	Uranus
Pisces	Purple	Visionary	amethyst	Water	Neptune

There is some disagreement among astrologers as to whether a sign's lucky stone is the traditional month-related birthstone, or these sign-related stones (some of which do match the birthstone). This happens because the timing of birth signs isn't aligned with traditional months.

Our heavens still have twelve divisions, and each sign has specific correspondences. Here are some correspondences that may prove useful in personalizing that information further if a full chart is available for comparison.

Twelve Houses Defined

Just like the sky, a person's chart is divided into twelve equal sections, or houses, each of which is ruled by a sign. The planets that appear in that sector provide information on what that house governs. For example, a person with the moon in the first house might be very intuitive and changeable, whereas having the sun here indicates a rather "hot" personality.

House		Governs
1	Aries	personality
2	Taurus	the material world
3	Gemini	intellect, communication
4	Cancer	home, foundations
5	Leo	children (literal and figurative), playfulness
6	Virgo	service, health
7	Libra	relationships, the arts
8	Scorpio	sexuality, spirituality
9	Sagittarius	learning, travel
10	Capricorn	honor, accomplishment
11	Aquarius	friendship, maturity
12	Pisces	hidden matters, karma

Lunar Influences

Now, here's a good example of adding a planet's influence into a specific house. The typically high-spirited Aries with a moon in their first (Aries) house suddenly becomes someone who climbs over others to achieve, or gets caught up in arrogance. Likewise, a Pisces with the moon in their first (Pisces) house faces being overwhelmed by too much information!

Moon Sign	Keynotes
Aries	dominance, zeal, pride
Taurus	devotion, resolve, equanimity
Gemini	insight, diversity
Cancer	dedication, prudence
Leo	charisma, passion
Virgo	insecurity
Libra	courtesy, ambivalence
Scorpio	emotion, reservation
Sagittarius	imagination, perceptiveness
Capricorn	sensitivity
Aquarius	detachment, anxiety
Pisces	intuition

Pondering the Planets

Astrology is a very detailed art having at least as many permutations as numerology. Knowing what planets are in your chart, for example, can provide increased insights into your birthday personology forecasts. Here's a brief list of each planet's energies:

Sun: abundant energy, power, and self-awareness. Negatively: egocentricity and haughtiness.

Moon: receptivity, insight, psychic aptitude. Negatively: moodiness and changeability.

Mercury: communication, cleverness, conscious thought. Negatively: dependency on mind over heart.

Venus: love, charm, sexuality. Negatively: a "tease" and hedonism.

Mars: courage, assertiveness, accomplishment. Negatively: violent or temperamental overflow.

Jupiter: vision, optimism, justice. Negatively: embellishment, insatiability.

Saturn: self-discipline, responsibility, restraint. Negatively: somberness and cynicism.

Uranus: free-spiritedness, individuality, openness. Negatively: rebellion and stubbornness.

Neptune: sensitivity, creativity, kindness. Negatively: ambiguity and avoidance.

Pluto: discernment, restoration, enlightenment. Negatively: corruption and mania.

Please note that the exact way in which each of the planets plays out in a person's chart depends on the house in which it appears. It's recommended that people interested in having this kind of information get a good chart prepared from a reliable source.

Like any art, it's all in the particulars! The more information you have on hand as you use this book, the more accurate the reading becomes. That's why it's good to get a chart done professionally, if possible. There are several sources online and off that provide astrological charts at reasonable costs (some lucky folks have a friend who's an astrologer!).

Now, those without a birth chart need not worry. Birthday personology will still be useful and interesting! Just bear in mind that the information provided is generalized to suit everyone born on a specific date, without the advantage of the other details to round out the picture.

Decanates

The word "decanates" comes from Greek, meaning "ten days apart," and was originally an Egyptian concept. Each sign of the Zodiac is split into three decanates (first, second, and third), each of which takes up 10 degrees of the zodiacal circle. Each of these has a constellation and planetary subrulers thought to further define and individualize birthday personology.

Date	Sign	Subsign
March 20–30	Aries	Aries
March 31–April 9	Aries	Leo
April 10–21	Aries	Sagittarius
April 21–31	Taurus	Taurus
May 1–10	Taurus	Virgo
May 11–22	Taurus	Capricorn
May 22–31	Gemini	Gemini
June 1–10	Gemini	Libra
June 11–22	Gemini	Aquarius
June 22–July 1	Cancer	Cancer
July 2–11	Cancer	Scorpio
July 12–23	Cancer	Pisces
July 23–August 2	Leo	Leo
August 3–12	Leo	Sagittarius
August 13–22	Leo	Aries
August 22–September 2	Virgo	Virgo

Date	Sign	Subsign
September 3–12	Virgo	Capricorn
September 13–23	Virgo	Taurus
September 23–October 3	Libra	Libra
October 4–13	Libra	Aquarius
October 14–23	Libra	Gemini
October 23–November 2	Scorpio	Scorpio
November 3–12	Scorpio	Pisces
November 13–22	Scorpio	Cancer
November 23–December 2	Sagittarius	Sagittarius
December 3–12	Sagittarius	Aries
December 13–22	Sagittarius	Leo
December 22–31	Capricorn	Capricorn
January 1–10	Capricorn	Taurus
January 11–21	Capricorn	Virgo
January 21–30	Aquarius	Aquarius
January 31–February 9	Aquarius	Gemini
February 10–20	Aquarius	Libra
February 20–March 1	Pisces	Pisces
March 2–11	Pisces	Cancer
March 12–22	Pisces	Scorpio

The effects of each subsign have been taken into account in the birthday personology descriptions that make up this book.

Putting It Together

The energy in your birthday (or anyone else's) has many determinants. In this book we're using the combination of astrology and numerology to highlight the old axiom "as above, so below." Because this book isn't limited to any one year, there aren't the specifics here that one would get from a full astrological chart. Nonetheless, it's a place to start. Think of this as a digest version of each day, and each person born on that day. Other aspects of a chart, and personal life experiences, will impact that digest in some manner, but the groundwork is here—like a cornerstone on which to build and a mirror on which to reflect.

FACT

In the Tarot, the Magician Card—a card that represents control over one's destiny—shows the Magician pointing upward with one hand, and downward with another. This is a reminder that each successful person's path relies on balance, and on seeing the possibilities and potentials both above our heads and below our feet. Birthday personology celebrates those potentials in an honest, balanced way.

While a book of this nature could certainly share only the "good stuff" each day represents, that wouldn't be fair or ethical. Just like with "as above, so below" there is also good and bad, darkness and light, sounds and silences. Life is a unique blend of all these things, a dance, if you will, between what was, what is, and what may be. By taking into account both negative and positive, a person learns to work with their dark side and make it better, while letting the light side shine brightly.

Chapter 3
January

January takes its name from the Roman god Janus, who diligently guards the gates of heaven. He's always shown with two heads: one looking to the future, one to the past. This gives January an overall theme of safety and watchfulness. In the Far East it's the charming Rat that governs this month, offering prosperity, confidence, and the chance to socialize. The first 20 days of this month belong to Capricorn (the Goat), an even-tempered soul with strong convictions. The remainder of the month belongs to the ever-idealistic Aquarius.

January 1

There's a certain spark to New Year's children, a magnetism that makes you very popular. Being born on the first of the year naturally drives you toward success. Note that Taurus has some influence here (see the decanates mentioned in Chapter 2). There's no compromising on goals, no slacking on personal development, no principles that the Goat neglects. You may find you have trouble in relationships because the demands of loyalty and responsibility pull you in several directions at once.

Numerologically the birth number 1/1 (January 1) is a 2. That means when your intentions are misread, you're devastated and seek urgently to re-establish peace and understanding. It's important that you keep a good head about you during this process. Your tendency to forge ahead could only make matters worse! Learn when to approach, and when to wait until the timing's better.

In relationships, you aren't necessarily one to settle down. You like variety and constant challenges. If relationships become too comfortable, you will seek more adventurous ground. However, if you find someone who keeps things interesting, and who also enjoys the peaceful energies that a two craves, it could be a match made in heaven.

Gift idea: anything hip, timely, and fun!

January 2

As with all Capricorns, you are diligent and tenacious. If you trust in your aptitudes, the potential for business success is quite good. You have a strong mind that hungers for knowledge. Feed that hunger, honor it, and appreciate it—it's part of the key to unlocking all of this birth date's potential.

No matter the area of interest, you need goals and frameworks. You have no desire to act unless your energy is used effectively and generates real results. When things don't go along quickly enough, you might get frustrated and push your way forward, no matter the consequences.

There's a unique blending of energies between the numeric value of this date (3) and the Capricorn spirit: Three wants to cooperate as part of a team (share the glory), and the Goat wants to compete (center stage). So you might find yourself naturally attracted to team sports as personal hobbies or even a career, especially if you get to be the leader of the pack!

This divergence between number and sign isn't so positive for relationships and decision-making, however. You might find that your heart and head never quite agree. Worse, that pesky Taurus influence drives you to crave long-term intimacy, but then the Capricorn nature rears up with misgivings. It's easy to see where this can send mixed signals to potential partners! This is where the influence of 3 really becomes helpful. Use that upbeat expressiveness and humor as a coping mechanism when situations tempt a shutdown.

Gift idea: practical items. If it's both beautiful and useful, all the better.

January 3

You have the dominant attributes of both the Goat and the Bull (the symbol of Taurus). Forget retreat on anything—"never say never" is this Capricorn's motto. This makes it very hard for you to give up on a lost cause. As a result, you might spend a lot of time and energy for little in return.

On any given day you can be found out in the community doing something. Sometimes you really want to express yourself artistically in larger arenas, like the theater, and you have real creative aptitude just waiting to be tapped. Nonetheless, usually other people's needs or your personal duties keep you from taking that leap.

That overactive sense of responsibility isn't improved by a date number of four. The unending drive to complete things will be enough to send friends and loved ones into a tizzy periodically. They want some of your time, and tend to rank second on the never-ending "to do" list!

One way to unwind from work is to find something to play with mentally and physically. Direct all that nervous energy toward outdoor gatherings and activities, like playing Frisbee or volleyball on the beach.

Gift idea: things that encourage a little more lightheartedness every day.

January 4

Big ideas and big energy sum up this birthday nicely. You have a sharp eye, diligence, and intense viewpoints—others would be advised to get out of your way once you have a goal in mind. With the Taurus decanate feeding into that headstrong drive, be prepared for people who might want to ride on your coattails. Don't worry, though. That won't last long. The Capricorn intolerance for slothfulness pretty quickly reveals such individuals and drives them away.

Emotionally you are a little reserved. You take your time developing trust. Combined with the restlessness inherent in a birthday number of 5, it can be a long time before you are ready to make any type of commitment to share your mountainside. Once you make that choice, however, it will be a lasting one filled with surprising passion.

The numeric influence of this date also confuses the steady Capricorn temperament. Rather than always looking to the tried and true, you are suddenly struck by whim and fancy. This takes the nearly unshakable Goat qualities and stimulates them in completely startling ways. The good news is that the Five's capacity for quick action blends nicely with Capricorn diligence, and allows you to meet changes with uncanny wit and wisdom.

Gift idea: technological gadgets.

QUESTION?

What flowers are associated with January?
The traditional flowers for the month of January are the carnation and the snowdrop. Originating in the Near East, carnations have been cultivated for over 2,000 years. They were popular in Greece as a flower befitting ceremonial crowns. Snowdrops come from central and southern Europe. Also called Eve's tears, they belong to the lily family. In the language of flowers the carnation represents health and affection, and snowdrops signify hope.

January 5

Don't let outward appearances fool you—this is no ordinary Capricorn. Inside there's a rogue waiting to escape the conventionality of the Goat's framework. The Taurus decanate adds mystery and creativity into this mix, making for a person from whom to expect the unexpected.

In business, focus on jobs that require charm, sensibility, and persuasion. Marketing is one option (which is also a field where this ever-curious personality won't easily get bored). If the job requires travel, that would be absolute bliss!

Numerologically your birth number is 6, meaning that your playfulness can be quickly tucked away if there's a serious cause to pursue. You will give generously to anyone in need. Unfortunately, if you're not careful, this generosity can (and will) be abused by people with less noble aspirations. The rather nonjudgmental, tolerant Capricorn nature often sees the best and overlooks the worst in both situations and people.

More positively, the realness of number 6 endears you to friends, family, and coworkers alike. While the Capricorn energy keeps people in a slightly wider arc, the underlying energies of 6 keep you from being too much of a loner.

Gift idea: good books that celebrate personal interests.

January 6

Hard as nails outside, soft as cotton inside—that's this Capricorn through and through. This creates some challenging situations for the Goat. The ever-confident, able-to-leap-tall-buildings demeanor can be off-putting. You can come across as perfectly content alone, yet you yearn for strong connections.

In work and life, you have a vision, but can't always communicate it effectively. Then in true Capricornish fashion, you simply decide to go it alone if need be. Any disappointment in others or personal insecurity subsequently gets tucked beneath your convincing façade until the vision has either succeeded or failed miserably.

It doesn't help that you have a Taurus decanate adding a relentless stubborn will, nor do the perfectionist energies of number 7 improve matters. You have a highly skeptical side, one that demands proof especially when your personal ideals or goals are challenged. In relationships this means you need detail-oriented global thinkers to be somewhat satisfied. Unusual for a Capricorn, you have an intense romantic side.

Gift idea: flowers, poems, and other tokens from the heart.

In the thirteenth century garnets were worn to repel insects. They were also thought to protect against lightning, ward off disease, change color when danger approaches, and ensure the bearer a cheerful personality.

January 7

A master of staid emotions, you sometimes give the impression of being too serious and regulated. This veneer helps to conceal an over-developed sense of vulnerability, privacy, and timidity. Your cool demeanor acts like armor, keeping all but those you choose to trust neatly at arm's length.

That serious nature serves you well in business or in the arts. As long as you can forge out your own path and follow your bliss, you'll be very content and successful. The difficulty comes when you're constrained by other people's regulations. Usually stubbornness rears its head, and from that point forward there's no end of head butting.

Inside, you have an amazing capacity to visualize and daydream. A quiet voice calls to you, whispering of adventure and freedom, and your active imagination answers that call. The only caution is that you must learn to draw the line between what is truly possible and the stuff of dreams. Thankfully those two sides are neatly balanced by today's numerological overtones. Number 8 strives for keeping both feet on the ground. So while you dream, you also have the power to manifest.

Gift idea: a nicely crafted pen and pencil set or PDA.

January 8

Your significant birthday personology influence can be summed up in one word: potential. Luck has nothing to do with your success; rather, it is your hard work and the ability to use your personal potential effectively. No matter how hard the journey, your tenacity brings victory.

Unfortunately, with Taurus still in the picture, there's a temptation to overdo everything. Today's birth number of 9 accents that tendency with determination. Using up all that personal energy creates dark moods from which it's hard to accomplish all those things that the Goat values. Rather than allow this to happen, refill your inner well regularly so that those projects can continue and relationships flourish.

Speaking of which, today's energies imply that you seek out the whole enchilada in love. You want smart, savvy, creative, and energetic partners. Once the right person appears, you respond in kind with plentiful love and ongoing relationship maintenance. Better still, with the sensitive and insightful energy of 9 to guide actions, this is likely to be a very happy and fulfilling relationship for a long time to come.

Gift idea: the gift of time. Friends should pick up a task that you would normally do so you're free to do something else.

January 9

You have a forceful style that engages life head-on. Fast acting, thinking, and feeling, you are prone to a wide range of behavior even to the point of recklessness. If, in that process, you happen to stumble, just the opposite occurs—you withdraw to avoid re-confronting that apparent failure. This is a direct result of lingering insecurities that, despite your demeanor and actions, still haunt your waking hours.

Danger walks hand in hand with your life. This comes in part from today's birth number (1), which supplies a competitive edge and the desire to be set apart as truly special. If you can learn to fall back on the Capricorn consistency, you can utilize this combination to become very adept in extreme or high-risk sports.

In business the independent nature of Capricorn shines through strongly today. As you are very restless, careers in travel help appease your wanderlust. What's most important is to avoid falling into a rut, as apathy will quickly overcome any initial enthusiasm. You don't mind the hard work, but you crave diversity. Wearing many hats suits you very well.

Being a bit of a perfectionist, deep relationships aren't high on your list. Rather than being constantly disappointed, it's simply easier to keep people at a safe emotional distance and enjoy hot, expressive one-night stands. The birth number of 1 stresses this further: you are not willing to compromise and are always levying hefty demands on those people in and around your life.

Gift idea: a long massage or a night out at a comedy club.

FACT

In order to set the calendar right, the Roman senate, in 153 B.C.E., declared January 1 to be the beginning of the New Year. During the Middle Ages, the Church remained opposed to celebrating New Year's. January 1 has been celebrated as a holiday by Western nations for only about the past 400 years.

January 10

You have an elegant bearing and love the finer things in life. While you know how to handle social situations with a slick diplomatic flair, you have no fear of speaking the truth or sharing honest opinions.

Having this birthday gives you the ability to keep your eyes on the prize while knowing well the road you walk upon; you set your goals high so as to obtain the best. Add to that a pioneer spirit and you will not only reach the mountaintops, but build a luxury hotel once you get there! You never cut corners—everything you do will be started with flair and will end with flair (or not at all)!

In relationships you enjoy being around those who also enjoy the finer things in life. Wine tastings and art exhibits are the types of activities you enjoy. In any of these settings, your natural charm is further aided by the birth number 2, allowing you to offer ideas and insights that get everyone on the same page.

Be forewarned, however. You need companions who are every bit as real as the Picasso on the wall! Those who hide, and those who purposely put on airs, are quickly shaken off like sand from a shoe.

Gift idea: whatever the gift, uniqueness and quality count (the recipient will notice and appreciate the effort).

January 11

Today's decanate moves into the realm of Virgo. This gives you a strong mind and good insights. Add to that foundation a gentle, loving nature and this birthday certainly holds tons of potential for accenting social skills, humanitarian ideals, and family values. This combination would be ideally applied professionally in careers like childcare, education, counseling, or psychology. Conversely, you should avoid jobs that seem impractical or unprincipled.

You love to entertain—sharing your home equals sharing from the heart. That attitude reflects in every corner of your life. There's an organic feel about your furniture and decorations, which are chosen purposefully and with a tasteful eye. No matter who visits, you always try to make that day perfect from start to finish. You are loath to tolerate any negativity or disorder, especially in your personal or family space.

The two numbers that affect today's profile are 11 and 3. The 11 brings a mystical quality to the table (perhaps an interest in esoteric studies), while the 3 supports all the social, upbeat, positive energies you already possess. There is very little chance that you will ever seem boring.

In relationships you need to be careful about how much time you spend pleasing others. Remember to apply the rule that you cannot be all things to all people.

Gift idea: gourmet kitchen goods.

January 12

Charming and always friendly, you give new meaning to the words "hospitality", "good humor", and "cooperation". Even when folks disagree with you, they listen just because you are so engaging! Additionally, you seem to walk with serendipity as a companion. When the worst things happen, something completely unexpected and much better waits just around the corner.

The Virgo decanate brings out a strong sense of personal duty. This blends well with the Capricorn pragmatism and appreciation for order. However, you will never be able to pull off surprises. Steady and sure, you have trouble understanding or appreciating spontaneity.

In business, small environments suit you best. A sea of people is a little overwhelming considering your keen sensitivities. Career ideas include technical writing, cutting-edge arts and sciences, and anything that allows you to apply your impressive communication skills.

Numerologically you have the auspicious combination of 12 (fulfillment) and 4 (foundations). You'll finish whatever you start and rarely complain if the task requires extra effort. Better still, the result is often stunning and financially rewarding.

In matters of love, you are naturally attractive to others—your bearing and magnetism are so natural that everyone feels at ease. Wanting a stable home inclines you toward being fairly monogamous. The chosen object of your passion receives nothing less than warmth, devotion, and intense sensuality.

Gift idea: a month of housecleaning services or a computerized calendar keeper.

ALERT!

Capricorns interested in finding potential partners, friends, and lovers would do well to seek out those born under Virgo and Taurus. In relationships, Capricorn often illustrates fear of getting lost in a sea of emotions. Virgo and Taurus can overcome that and balance those energies. Once Capricorns find what they want, however, just get out of their way! In long-term relationships Capricorns will love deeply and make very committed life partners.

January 13

You often seem consumed with learning new things and then applying that knowledge or skill to real life. Your motto is: forewarned is forearmed (which you take to heart with proactive zeal). There will always be something you want to tackle or try. Stagnation makes for a very uneasy Capricorn. Additionally, the Virgo decanate whispers in your ear: initiate, organize, be direct, move it forward! You don't like to sit still, and may have difficulty relaxing.

For careers, you need something where you can lead the way to wherever your spirit sees a spark of potential. Not willing to be a copycat in the least, you are an original, with the discipline to bring your uniqueness into reality. So, Capricorns, look to jobs that focus on discovery and exploration as one means to achieve soulful satisfaction.

Today's numbers are 13 and 5, which don't play well together. Thirteen has an underlying negative tone that leaves gray clouds lingering around to darken the usually upbeat mood of Capricorns. Meanwhile 5 says, "Hey, get over it already—engage life!" This combination can make for a rather somber or erratic workaholic, and it's something you should guard against.

Relationships can be a dicey affair, since your moodiness and restlessness often overwhelm even the vast devotion you give to a partner. Also, your tendency to launch out on another quest just when things are getting serious makes it look like you aren't interested in a long relationship. Ideally you should find partners who have common interests where you can apply that energy together.

Gift idea: telescopes, microscopes—anything that unlocks a mystery!

January 14

A logical, knowledgeable, and upbeat person who seeks more than just money or prestige, you want to help make the present and future better. Thinking globally and acting locally are definitely part of your game plan. You never run away from difficult challenges, and with a Virgo decanate that's not surprising. Any project you begin gets checked and balanced every step of the way. While some Goats may want to charge directly to the goal, you feel that the devil is in the details!

Being someone of strong ethics and organizational ability, you would do well to ponder careers that focus on supervision, management, leadership, or communications. Your personology profile indicates an uncanny aptitude for persuasive speaking and writing. Couple that with today's birth number of 6 and you are likely to apply those talents in a humanitarian arena (for homelessness, orphans, ecological reclamation, and the like).

At home, you want a well-ordered reality. You keep both your home and body in excellent shape. Guests rarely, if ever, find anything broken or useless in this space. Even things of beauty (that a birth number of 6 added to your life) have some type of practical appeal.

Honest in associations, you can sometimes overpower a partner with unbridled truth. As you learn to use that skill more diplomatically, you make a very affectionate partner as long as the relationship isn't rushed.

Gift idea: a fine stationery set.

January 15

A creature focused on beauty, success, and harmony, you can always be found in a crowd of people who share similar desires and who crave social exchange. When you become enthusiastic—be it toward a person or project—get out of the way! There's no time for compromise or waffling once your mission's begun. You truly believe that to lose the moment is to lose the opportunity, and that's simply not going to happen on your watch.

Despite this determined demeanor, you still have a heart of gold with principles to match. If you perceive unfairness or inequity, all of that intense energy goes toward fixing the problem permanently. And thanks to the highly perceptive number 7 being part of your personology framework, you are likely to succeed even where others have failed. You see things differently, and that unique perspective makes all the difference.

For career goals, look toward positions that have meaning and that engage the finely honed Capricorn mind. Medical and economic research are excellent examples. Music (as a universal language) also appeals to you. Ponder this with the power of 7 to guide your choices—that gut instinct is spot on!

In the rest of your life idealistic views color everything, including relationships. You want romance complete with hearts and violins, but your nature also knows, deep down, that this isn't always possible.

Gift idea: things that appeal to that romantic nature with something totally quixotic, if only for that one day.

QUESTION?

What famous people were born in January?
Betsy Ross (1/1), Mel Gibson (1/3), Diane Keaton (1/5), Kenny Loggins (1/7), David Bowie (1/8), Crystal Gayle (1/9), Alexander Hamilton (1/11), Dr. Martin Luther King, Jr. (1/15), Benjamin Franklin (1/17), Janis Joplin, Edgar Allen Poe (1/19), Buzz Aldrin (1/20), John Hancock (1/23), Wolfgang Amadeus Mozart (1/27), Lewis Carroll (1/27), Oprah Winfrey (1/27)

January 16

This day suggests the attributes of a well-structured list maker. The Capricorn ability to shift direction as the climate changes combined with a Virgo decanate supplies you with impressive organizational skills, almost to the point of obsession. This, in turn, can adversely affect your relationships, especially with dreamier folk who'd rather wait and see what life brings.

All this managerial energy does have a balance point. You have a quiet, sensitive side that sometimes just wants to wander quietly and think about the Universe's plans. Your partner has nothing to fear. You may come home with profound insights or just a nasty sunburn, but you will always return to the space and people that represent safety and emotional comfort. Having a birth number of 8 further indicates that you will set aside any wanderlust or momentary distractions in favor of responsibility and security.

You are rarely conventional in approaching love or any type of ongoing relationship. You have difficulty expressing the deeper aspects of yourself for fear of losing the comfort you have. Deeply vulnerable, you can be wounded almost beyond the point of recovery. However, when you're in a healthy relationship, you are a wonderful and attentive lover.

Gift idea: a trip to a nature resort or spa for that oh-so-necessary private time.

January 17

The personology forecast for today predicts a smattering of sternness, fearlessness, and a strong success orientation that makes you a great supervisor. And don't think small here—you have the capacity to manage ten or a thousand people equally well when you apply your natural ability to delegate.

Your fighting spirit sometimes works against you. You'll run headlong into disaster as quickly as success. The warrior within needs to be tempered with wisdom and a few life lessons. Eventually, you will learn which battles are best left for another day, and when to walk away altogether.

Your hunger for power is obvious to everyone around you. Positions in the military, politics, or high-ranking placements in other stable and influential companies are good choices that feed that yearning. Having a birth number of 9 seems to couple with your ambition. You will never be content as second best. Having to take secondary or tertiary roles is very difficult for the stubborn Goat, but once you can perceive a subordinate position as a stepping-stone, you'll have come a long way to achieving future wonders.

Your partners and friends will need patience. It's likely that you want to protect every aspect of life, including your own heart. Thus, relationships move slowly. Nonetheless, once you make a commitment, it's sure and loyal.

Gift idea: an old-fashioned pocket watch or other timepiece will satisfy your need for punctuality and professionalism.

January 18

Ambition is the name of this Capricorn's game. You know what you want and when you want it, and you will move heaven and earth to make it happen. Others would normally perceive this as bossy and headstrong, but there's a secret underlying all that drive: you treasure the philosophy that there is more to life than just money and power. So, you use considerable amounts of your personal resources for helping others. And thanks to a Virgo decanate, it's easier to communicate the reasons for those actions to everyone!

Professionally you would thrive as a healer, a social worker, or designing life-improving items. Having a birth number of 1 certainly supports this kind of focus with a moralistic and idealistic vision. The only drawback is that you need to develop more patience. Not everything can move quickly, and pressing the issue often backfires.

Humor is your greatest coping mechanism. Sure, it's partially a way to offset hidden personal insecurities, but it also brings everyone onto the same playing field. When you laugh, the world willingly laughs with you, and feels better for it! In love it's best for you to find others who share a charitable vision. Otherwise your partners feel slighted by the time and energy given to your humanitarian causes. When partnered with someone who's challenging and insightful, you become passionate and supportive.

Gift idea: a donation made in your name to one of your beloved charities.

ALERT!

The Capricorn personality is ideally suited to leading, facilitating, administering, and engineering. This practical, smart, and infinitely patient Goat loves to keep things under control. Nonetheless, the Goat doesn't lead with an iron hoof. Rather, he has a way of bringing out co-workers' finest attributes and using them effectively. Capricorns like a small team environment in which they're more than happy to carry a fair share of the work. But, take care. Those born under this sign sometimes neglect personal needs in order to get a task done.

January 19

Coming as it does near the tail end of the Capricorn cycle, a few Aquarian tendencies sneak into this birth date. That roguish playfulness of Aquarius is really good for the sometimes overly serious Capricorn. This is a Goat who knows how to enjoy life and who has an independent streak a mile long!

Sometimes mischievous, you might consider designing toys, working on innovative computer games, or other positions that nurture your inner child. Since you want to see and do everything now, you'll also thrive in an environment where you can open new adventures for others to enjoy.

Having a birth number of 2 and a decanate of Virgo really helps balance you out. The Capricorn is pragmatic, Virgo is methodical, and the new Aquarian influence encourages less structure. The birth number brings those things into symmetry by providing the wisdom to know when and where one can throw caution to the wind, dance in the raindrops, and sing to the trees.

Emotionally you enjoy people and gain a lot of energy and insight from the company of others. You're a little ambiguous about commitments, however, and may not settle down easily. Any long-term partner needs to understand that you rule your roost, which is likely decorated in a style reflecting that self-indulgence.

Gift idea: a season pass to the theater.

January 20

On one hand you have a huge heart, filled with sensitivity and dutifulness. On the other hand, your rebellious spirit aches to make a statement that will last through eternity. Then there's a Virgo decanate trying to bring structure to the chaos. The younger you are, the greater the turmoil. Your saving grace is a birth number of 3 that offers optimism to round things out a bit.

In work, you need to use your sense of responsibility and goodwill in a structured framework. You could be an excellent team player who can wear many hats equally well (and, indeed, you enjoy diversity). You adapt, get along well with others, and have ingenious insights even when your personal inner world seems completely out of whack.

In relationships, you often find you have the deepest (and most volatile) relationships with the women in and around your life. You are not overly inclined to long-term situations simply because they take up time that seems better spent elsewhere. The birth number 3 doesn't help much here, adding indecision and an inability to commit to the picture. Oddly, however, when someone matches your interests and can handle your changeableness, suddenly you transform into a very protective and faithful companion.

Gift idea: a desktop or closet organizer.

January 21

Being born on the cusp, you can't help but feel the lingering influence of Capricorn. While you have the Aquarian aptitude for deep, original thinking, you're also eminently practical and a great communicator. Nonetheless, the Capricorn drive for progress shows up regularly, often moving you forward a little too quickly for anyone's comfort despite frequently ingenious results.

With a blended Aquarius/Virgo decanate, you embrace life dramatically. You thrive in environments that provide a spotlight for your energy, like sales and marketing. Additionally, you might display a talent for theatrical arts that becomes a career. If so, trust that lingering Goat-like diligence and quest for success will quickly bring out a rising star!

This thespian quality either completely engages people or puts them off, because it is both charismatic and peculiar at the same time. One of your greatest challenges will be finding a comfortable balance. The birth number 4 helps foster that balance with a yearning for structure. However, your independent nature might spur you to forge ahead boldly, in your own time, and your own way.

You hesitate to be too committed, for fear it might interfere with an opportunity for adventure. You do best in laid-back relationships with people who understand your constant need for a new conquest. When you do fall in love, it can be intense to the point of distraction.

Gift idea: a certificate for a costume shop or acting classes.

FACT

In Anglo-Saxon tradition, the first month of the year bore the title Wolfmonth. This was because wolves came to villages searching for food at or around this time.

January 22

"Live and let live" are the words you celebrate daily. You have high ambitions and lofty ideals, and you shun anything remotely routine. Essentially you were born too soon, with a futuristic perspective that rattles stodgy, inflexible, and negative minds to the bone. When around other forward-thinking individuals, you share your progressive ideas freely.

It's not surprising to find you in a cutting-edge career. You naturally migrate toward positions that push the mind and spirit into new realms. The birth number of 5 further encourages this outlook with a yearning for anything unusual and astounding.

As with many visionaries, there will be those who consider you odd, quirky, or downright bizarre. This, in turn, may cause self-doubts and insecurity, or the desire to retreat. With a similarly proactive partner, however, you exhibit trust, courtesy, and romance.

Gift idea: your birthstone presented over a great meal with good conversation.

January 23

Individuals born today are the ultimate optimists. A true rogue with a cause, you take your world and turn it upside-down with fresh ideas, startling words, and impressive actions. While some might think you are too idealistic, it is that idealism—and a highly inventive mind—that drives you to succeed where others fail. Combine that with a gentle, kindly demeanor, and it's a recipe for a relatively popular person, comfortable in your own skin even in unusual situations.

The Aquarian decanate's influence adds a sense of perspective. You like to examine history to understand or illustrate the present and future. You are suited to careers in archaeology, art history, or classics. The birth number 6 encourages artistic expression, and the quest for beauty in all its forms may well develop into a hobby like antique restoration.

Your relationships cannot be superficial. They must engage body, mind, and spirit equally. In this setting, you make a highly creative and empathic partner. The only real caution for those born today is not to let the humanitarian nature of your birth number create a distance between yourself and your partners. It's tempting to ride off to the next quest, but sometimes your energy is much better spent focused on heart, hearth, and home.

Gift idea: a rich, fruity wine or some gourmet cheese.

January 24

Friendly but territorial describes this Aquarian succinctly. At first, people find you approachable and chatty. Then, over time, something else surfaces—aloofness and a fierce protectiveness toward your personal turf. Others must be warned: This defensive side is a very sturdy wall.

Beyond that one dark cloud you're very hard working, relatively controlled, independent (yet people oriented), and surprisingly witty. As long as people respect your space, everyone could potentially get along fine! Unfortunately, there's still the birth number of 7 to consider, which stresses aloofness and detachment, making it all the more important to watch boundaries.

Careerwise you would do well to stick with small offices or self-employment to avoid that natural conflict over whose way is the right way. Other alternatives include any positions where you get plenty of alone time (like research). And don't completely overlook the arts—song writing, for example!

Your most difficult lesson comes in love. You want to give and receive love, but don't know how to make a space for others. You often become quiet and removed, feeling overwhelmed. With this in mind, it's best to have a home environment where there's one room just for you to inhabit when you need personal space.

Gift idea: a weekend getaway at a private cottage or cabin.

A number of events happened throughout history during the month of January: Alaska joined the Union (January 3, 1959); Calvin Coolidge died (January 5, 1933); Galileo sited four of Jupiter's moons (January 7, 1610); League of Nations established (January 10, 1919); Henry Ford introduced the assembly line (January 14, 1914); *Hello Dolly* opened on Broadway (January 16, 1938); first presidential news conference filmed for television (January 19, 1955); Vietnam peace agreement signed (January 22, 1973); gold discovered in California (January 24, 1850); slavery abolished by 13th Amendment (January 31, 1865).

January 25

It's hard to get to know you. Your continual focus on whatever engages your mind distracts you from interpersonal communications. It's not that you don't appreciate friends and companions—just the opposite! You love fun, upbeat, and quirky people. But when you grab hold of an idea, you don't let it go until you're completely finished. Add the comprehensive nature of a birth number 8, and it's not surprising that you can get labeled as a nutty professor type—rarely on time, but always interesting.

In both career and relationships, you're a free-spirited being who doesn't fit any mold. A love of mystery, intense curiosity, and strong intuition blend together to ensure that you never limit yourself, or anyone else for that matter. You dabble in many things and encourage similar experimentation in others, leading to some really wild moments in the bedroom!

While in other scenarios your adventurous soul might be dangerous, the birth number 8 provides balance. Beyond the whimsy and autonomy there's a strong sense of responsibility and a healthy portion of common sense. You never ask others to go where you will not. The decanate of Aquarius allows you to see fully into people's motivations. And even when stretching boundaries, your motto is always "safety first."

Gift idea: mental games like Trivial Pursuit or mystery books.

January 26

Your personology profile reveals a lot of turbulence. Your life rarely stays on an even keel, and a somewhat overbearing personality often adds conflict to an already unstable picture. All is not lost, however. You have a lot of tenacity, making lemonade out of life's worst lemons (and sometimes even making a profit at it!). After a while, you learn to look at every situation as an opportunity, and by applying a little elbow grease you usually end up coming out on top.

In your career you like to meet challenges head-on. You readily take to jobs requiring strong commitment and ambition. The military is a definite possibility for you, especially when combined with the bravery and idealism of the birth number 9.

At home, you might be found tucked away in a tidy, well-stocked library reading a good book or tinkering with a favorite hobby. You keep the home in order, along with your heart. Relationships are tricky for you. The on-again, off-again nature of your personology, coupled with a lack of patience, has left some scars that are hard to overcome. You value friendship, as long as you don't get overly sentimental.

Gift idea: antique books or an inkwell.

January 27

Clever, talented, and smart, you have tons of potential waiting to be expressed. Typically your gifts get applied to some good cause, be it helping the homeless, healing the earth, or offering spiritual guidance. There's no question you were a champion of the downtrodden in a previous life, and you loved it! You meet heartlessness and cruelty with the same intensity as you do charity. You're a warrior who won't be intimidated once you're on a quest, and you can actually become ruthlessly overprotective.

Whether wielding words or an actual weapon, you know how to make a point and drive it home. Your aptitude for communication combines with strong organizational ability, so administrative positions are a good option as long as they're applied to a personally beloved ideal (such as education, or facilitating a community center). A birth number of 1 also manifests as a natural aptitude for leading.

Numerology implies that you seek textural touches more so than visual perfection in the home. Fleecy blankets, unique wall hangings, and sturdily upholstered furniture dot the space. There are also likely to be a couple of half-finished projects that had to be set aside for more important matters.

As for love? You like to flirt, but ultimately crave stability. Having a family acts as a substructure and balance to other parts of your life, to which you commit both intelligence and romance.

Gift idea: a meditation CD is a good choice to help calm the combative spirit within.

What are some of the holidays and observances for January?
January is Autism Awareness Month, Blood Donor Month, International Gourmet Coffee Month, National Eye Care Month, and Letter Writing Month. January dates to remember include January 2: Science Fiction Day; January 4: Braille Day; January 8: Rock 'n Roll Day; January 12: Handwriting Day; January 15: Humanitarian Day; January 16: Religious Freedom Day; January 18: Winnie the Pooh Day; January 19: Popcorn Day; January 20: Arbor Day; January 21: Hugging Day; January 30: Carnation Day; January 31: Child Labor Day.

January 28

Zealously independent, you don't worry about other people's opinions. You have a strong sense of self-actualization, like an old soul who's seen and done it all more than once. Consequently you are likely to become a catalyst for forward-thinking initiatives. In the process, you're often misunderstood and misrepresented.

Being in the limelight isn't a problem for you. People and attention feed your energy and stoke your resolve. Additionally, you have charm and a sense of humor that soothe ruffled feathers if people stick around long enough to really listen. No matter what people think of you, it's very hard to simply disregard this personality.

Having 2 as a birth number will be either a blessing or a curse. Either way, you will use it to balance out all that self-determination and work cooperatively with others, or it will leave you struggling with awkward dichotomies. This is especially true in business, where your natural tendency is to go it alone, while 2 screams for teamwork and interaction. Nonetheless, there are a wide variety of jobs where you'll find success, including teaching, writing, and the creative arts.

At home, the environment is playful and relatively relaxed. Life has far better things to offer than housecleaning. Lovers and partners might find themselves exasperated by your never-ending need for variety (you need a very clever life mate).

Gift idea: something that offers a sense of surprise!

January 29

Stubborn and independent yet craving the company of others make for a difficult struggle. Thankfully, you have the number 3 to ease this tension, tipping the scale toward a more social nature. Nonetheless, the Self is never lost to a group or a crowd. You are as unique as a fingerprint or snowflake and like it that way.

The personology forecast for nine implies a generous soul who surprises everyone with an aptitude for listening. You remember odd details of a conversation or situation that everyone else forgets. This aptitude creates fast friends who feel grateful that someone cares enough to pay close attention. Love may not come early in life, but a family of the heart surrounds you. It's just as well—destiny has something up its sleeve, and it's going to require your attention before serious relationships develop.

In work, you tend toward forthright expressiveness. You might find yourself giving legal summarizations, writing the next epic, hosting a TV show, or consulting with world leaders. You are always aware that "to whom much is given, much is expected." That outlook blends well with the birth number 3's giving temperament.

Gift idea: a digital camera for keeping all those memorable moments close at hand.

January 30

The Aquarian superhero—fast on the uptake, fearless, energetic, and zealous. You take up causes like some Pisceans take up hobbies. And our hero's Achilles heel? Having a heart as big as a house. You need a button that says "Stop me before I volunteer again." Otherwise you're likely to burn out very easily.

Your challenge is in trusting your instincts. By paying attention, you can find your way to a pretty amazing destiny.

What do you do in your spare time? Invent! A typical Aquarian spirit, you like to dabble and you have a lot of highly innovative ideas. Get out the patent forms and get busy! Use the extra organizational strength in the birth number 4 to achieve your goals and dreams in a truly distinctive way.

Just like Superman, in love you sometimes hide behind a disguise—trust is a huge issue. Long-term commitment isn't as important as having reliable companions in the moment.

Gift idea: a dream diary to jump-start the process of listening to the inner voice.

FACT

Numerology for January: Adding up the letters in January (1 + 1 + 5 + 3 + 1 + 9 + 7), we get 27 = 9. This is interesting in that the beginning of the year bears a number for completion and truth. Nine tells us to tie up loose ends so we can get off to a fresh start. This bit of numerology also acts as an excellent reminder to focus on finishing those things we promise to do, and stay true to Self in the New Year.

January 31

Psychic awareness permeates your daily reality, sometimes to the point of distraction. Being grounded doesn't mix well with prophetic dreams, object reading, and spirit guides. Be that as it may, that's what you balance in your pitchers. Some Aquarians try to avoid this awareness by staying overly busy. In turn, they tend to neglect other important matters. So, it's best just to accept what is, and work with it. A birth number of 5 becomes a great asset, encouraging the sense of marvel instead of fear and misgiving.

Your environment isn't pristine. It's typically cluttered with odd notes, inspiring knickknacks, and dishes that can wait until the last page of a good book gets turned. Having a decanate in Gemini improves mental keenness, and allows you to integrate information in a truly personal way.

A magpie for collecting information and data, you do well in careers that satisfy the longing for knowledge. Anything that allows you to research a topic (then apply that information) should prove very satisfying and successful. The relationship review is likewise upbeat. You do not like being alone. Even when tempted to pull back, you make an excellent partner for well-defined, strong-willed individuals.

Gift idea: a giant book of crossword puzzles.

Capricorn

Sign: Capricorn
Date: December 22–January 20
Ruled by: Saturn
Element: Earth
Lucky Color: Brown, green
Gemstone: Garnet, onyx
Keynote: Effort
Positive Traits: Dutiful, organized, honorable, practical, pragmatic
Negative Traits: Unforgiving, over-ambitious, insecure
Famous Capricorns include: Isaac Asimov, Humphrey Bogart, Al Capone, Cary Grant, Joan of Arc, Diane Keaton, Martin Luther King, Sir Isaac Newton, Albert Schweitzer

Capricorn, the old Goat, is as stubborn as the animal the stars portray. Typically a very inflexible taskmaster, Capricorns are intimately aware that every action has consequences. The philosophy of this sign is "do it once, do it right, do it my way."

Professionally the Goat often becomes a workaholic, being overly determined and tenacious. People born under this sign don't care how long a goal takes, so long as eventually it's reached. From the outside looking in, this appears self-absorbed, and that is a tempting trait that Capricorn would do well to keep in check.

At home the Capricorn seeks out one really fine item rather than buying three cheap ones. Quality matters, and quality lasts like the mountains. They'll avoid buying any of these items on credit unless desperate, because a Goat should own things, things should not own people.

In social settings Capricorns are honest as the day is long. Sometimes this honesty is brutally harsh. The Goat has no patience for people without a backbone, or those crying over spilled milk. Realism is the name of their game. Additionally, Capricorns don't typically apologize directly, and rarely budge once they've made up their minds.

On the relationship front, Capricorns are fierce about family, and take both their responsibilities and commitments in that space to heart. Loved ones would do well to armor up against the Goat's dry humor, while embracing the Capricorn's practicality and financial acumen. When you need help, and want to trust in promises made, call a Capricorn.

Chapter 4
February

Astrologically the beginning of this month belongs to the Water Bearer, Aquarius. In Greek mythology Ganymede became the constellation Aquarius. He was a young man who Zeus had kidnapped. Who, once with the Olympians, was appointed the gods' cupbearer (and later a god of rain). In the Middle East, Aquarius was a fortunate sign, becausewhen the sun reached Aquarius, it marked the start of much-needed rains. Egyptians associated the sign with the Nile God, Hapi.

February 1

The number 3 influences all your communications in a positive way. Consider working in fields that have a public facet, such as TV reporting, acting, motivational speaking, and other careers that engage an audience to suit your keen mind and quick reactions. Don't even try to catch this Aquarian off guard!

In both friendship and romance, you can size people up quickly. If there's potential there, you'll move forward, trusting your gut instincts every step of the way (rarely have you been proven wrong). On the other hand, you won't endure those who appear imprudent or unmotivated for any longer than absolutely necessary. To some people in your life this attitude seems cold, but intuition is one of the ways you protect all that's dear to you.

In the long haul, your associates know better than to box you into any type of mold or restrict you with "dos" and "don'ts." Freedom is not just another word for you—it's a way of life.

Gift idea: a humorous movie or collection of jokes would be welcome.

February 2

You are friendly, liberated, a bit mysterious, and goal-oriented. More than likely there's a spiritual side to your life that not only influences your thoughts and ideals, but pours out liberally into the work a day world. And as much as the Aquarian soul enjoys the company of others, your sensitive side brings about regular retreats to avoid overstimulation. Without that time, you are prone to burning out. This is doubly true when combined with a birth number of 4 that demands only the best personal efforts.

One of your lessons is learning the value of symmetry. You'll find yourself pulled equally toward land and sea, logic and flights of fancy, and other dichotomies. You must struggle to avoid becoming so engaged in the assessment process that nothing gets done! The birth number 4 adds to this problem and makes you likely to turn decision-making into a very complex matter, even over simple things!

Your air of ambiguity actually creates a good foundation where personal distance improves results. Optimum career choices include counseling, psychology, or anything requiring a combination of talking/listening skills.

However, remember that with a Gemini decanate you are unlikely to stay with one job your whole life. Variety is a healthy spice—use it liberally!

In the arena of love, the need for security struggles with the Aquarian passion for personal freedom. You're probably a better friend than a life mate in that the Water Bearer tends to doubt relationship choices, and struggle with them even after a long, positive period in a relationship.

Gift idea: a divination system to help with those choices where resolutions elude you.

February 3

Your birth date reveals you to be a highly physical being. While one sense (touch, taste, sound, sight, smell) typically predominates, everything you understand of the world comes through the senses. For example, those whose sense of touch is strongest will often seem touchy-feely to strangers and friends alike, while visual people become avid people-watchers. Today's birth number of 5 accentuates your sensual nature, motivating a gleeful zeal to experience those senses fully, especially if it results in something really interesting or unique.

At work, your trailblazing ideas and proclivity for sound research put you at the forefront of success and controversy. You see potential and find inspiration in a wide variety of genres, and you easily adapt to a transforming internal and external landscape. You rarely stumble. Instead, you're often misunderstood or so far ahead of the masses that it takes everyone else a while to catch up to the vision.

For downtime the Aquarian soul with Gemini decanate loves to play with words, or fiddle with highly unusual hobbies. You may be found figuring out a wall-size crossword puzzle, examining tidbits of trivia, or going on an urban caving expedition!

You are similarly eclectic in relationships. Because you're so friendly, folks are naturally attracted to you, but you have a natural dislike of being too engaged or tied down. If you marry, make sure to get regular times alone, which will allow you to regain your treasured sense of freedom.

Gift idea: items to add to your existing collection of oddities!

What is the traditional birthstone for February?

The birthstone for people born in February is traditionally amethyst. The word "Amethyst' comes from a Greek term meaning "precious purple jewel" (purple alluding to a wine-like color). During the Middle Ages many a feast hall cup was adorned with amethyst in the belief that so doing would keep the person who drank from the cup sober. Other amuletic attributes for this stone include protecting the bearer from thievery, plague, headache, and faithlessness. Overall, mystics considered it a stone that fosters peace.

February 4

You're a peculiar person with many grand ideas that may (or may not) get off the ground. The main problem is that your daydreams may occupy so much time that situations in daily life go unnoticed and unattended. In turn, your friends sometimes feel a bit neglected, and rightly so. Try to avoid high-maintenance acquaintances or pets! That's a recipe for disaster.

When considering careers, spending so much time wandering around your own head can be an advantage. If you apply that skill to any analytic or organizational element, there's a chance to bring some of those lofty concepts into reality. In particular, consider humanitarian pursuits, something the birth number of 6 appreciates and sustains. Make sure to balance these efforts regularly with some personal time for refreshment and renewal, otherwise that tendency to get caught up can run amok and you'll burn out before completing the goal.

Intense friendships and romance are definitely in the cards for you, but these interactions are hardly conventional. Expect a unique adventure every day! Aquarians stretch boundaries in life and love, and your partners can't be afraid of experimenting with whole new horizons in Self and in the relationship.

Gift idea: an assortment of gourmet, pre-packaged meals will allow you to keep busy with other things and still get a decent dinner.

February 5

Objectivity and autonomy summarize nearly every aspect of your life. Each situation has several equally valid facets that, in your mind, seem perfectly clear (something the birth number of 7 emulates completely). This is highly frustrating to others, who do not have the advantage of this global outlook. Be patient in your communications, keeping the difference in perspectives in mind, and seek to bridge communication gaps so you're heard and understood.

Sometimes step by step, and sometimes in leaps, you move forward toward a discernable objective. While occasionally the road takes wholly unanticipated detours, for the most part your course is true. The intense mental demands of this process mean that you often work best alone. You're likely to be found in an artist's loft painting, or at a bistro writing the next great mystery novel.

That solitary nature doesn't extend into social settings, thankfully. In fact, this is one place you find balance. You love love, want to give it fully and generously, and receive it gratefully. However, individuals with weak personalities or insensitive spirits will not survive with you as friends or lovers.

Gift idea: a quill and inkwell.

February 6

This Aquarian thrives on drama. As much as you want a good life (and may secretly sometimes dream of a nice, ordinary, calm day), there's something about even the worst situation that provides a stage, setting, and script that feed your very being.

Water Bearers with this birth date are part ham, and part honey (which, thanks to an odd twist of fate, work well together). You have charm, possess a fabulous speaking demeanor, and know how to truly "tickle people's ears" when the need arises. However, dishonesty and manipulation aren't in the program. You are truthful and trustful to a fault, and often rely on humor to soothe over those foot-in-mouth moments. A birth number of 8 grounds your honest nature in protective roots. Once you trust in something, you guard it vehemently.

Labor isn't a word that Aquarians typically like. If you work for a living, you should love what you do. "Follow your bliss" is a phrase definitely written for Water Bearers. So when considering careers, find something playful or an artsy path with the theater, public speaking, or perhaps even local politics where your creative panache shines comfortably.

With lovers, this Aquarian shows an eagerness to please and tease. It's important to you to demonstrate true feeling, and once committed you're very loyal. You tell great stories in bed!

Gift idea: a book of romantic poetry or a dramatic ascot.

February's flower is traditionally primrose or violet. Primroses were typically white and yellow until the mid 1600s, when new varieties were discovered in Greece and Turkey. In the language of flowers they mean "I cannot live without you." Violets are edible and were often used in decorative cuisine through the ages. In folk remedies violets were typically part of curatives for coughs.

February 7

This Aquarian's inner child interacts with everyday life regularly. From taking pleasure in a newly blossoming daisy to looking for pictures in the clouds, you have a youthful exuberance that captivates everyone you meet. With the Gemini decanate you catch the little details others often ignore, and revel in them!

You're much happier jumping in a rain puddle and singing to the trees than attending that board meeting, and often make excuses to do just that (if you can get the board to join you at the puddle, even better!). Each day, each moment is like one part of a buffet that you intend to sample fully. Having a birth number of 9, however, confuses this zeal a little bit. Normally it would go wholly toward acts of pleasure (for self or others), but 9 wants to take a healthy portion of energy and apply it to saving the world.

The great part about having an active inner child is that you are very open to learning new things. You can use that openness to become a sponge for whatever skills you need to learn. From language to law, it's an abundant field ripe for harvesting. In turn, your career needs to challenge and inspire you. It also has to offset your naturally restless spirit.

As a lover—wow! There's no end to your creative energy. The only problem is making sure you know what's serious and what's play, otherwise you might get hurt deeply.

Gift idea: playful bedroom goodies, like edible chocolate body paint, are perfectly acceptable gifts.

February 8

Talk about a huge shift in personology! Today's astrology and numerology create a far more serious person than those born the day before. This Aquarian is staid, with little patience for nonsense. You'd much rather work through the night solving a problem than take a break and come back to it the next day. After all, time is valuable!

A decanate in Gemini helps balance that rather stern demeanor with a little whimsy. When given the opportunity, your personality can shine with humor or ingenious ideas equally well. But afterward you want to get right to work, and not revel in that "ah ha!" moment. Additionally, a birth number of 1 brings in a craving for uniqueness that could turn the brilliant idea into a risky venture. Don't sacrifice the Aquarian vision for the quick fix, as so doing typically attracts trouble in all forms.

When looking for a job, it's a good exercise for you to work as part of a team. Being part of a nursing outreach cooperative is one good example. Alternatively the Aquarian knack for communication could lead to a career in the public sector as a spokesperson.

Your friends and partners will need patience. Many times, you put your present projects and ambitions ahead of all other duties. So long as your inner circle understands this (and refuses the temptation to get jealous of that time), all will be well.

Gift idea: a good tool kit for the home or car.

February 9

The most difficult aspect of today's personology forecast is the need to discipline the stubborn Aquarian's free-spirited outlook. A birth number of 2 definitely becomes a helpmate here, providing some sense of order and timeliness when you want nothing more than to throw caution to the wind. You have a soul with great courage, charisma, and power, and it's hard to put a bridle on that!

You are sometimes prone to flashes of anger and instantaneous decision-making, but they pass quickly. This may leave you feeling regretful, but with Gemini in the picture, there's always going to be a clever idea for damage control. The birth number 2 comes to the rescue here in that it always seeks the most harmonious, stress-free path.

Your independent nature attracts you to multifaceted careers that require as little supervision as possible. Being a travel agent or money manager are two examples. Avoid anything too static or that requires you to answer to administrators. Following the chain of command is alien to your thinking.

With friends and family, you are kindly and empathic. When other people get too close, however, it can disrupt your course and take you in wholly unexpected directions (for boon or bane). Consequently, you may remain somewhat aloof until you can establish real trust in the relationship.

Gift idea: a calming CD of music or meditations.

FACT

Ancients sometimes called February's full moon the Snow Moon or Hunger Moon, especially in northern climates where weather was harsh, and food scarce. Other names for the lunar sphere in February include Trapper's Moon, Cleansing Moon, and Light Returns Moon.

February 10

This is a birthday filled with extremes. Some born today work and live at warp speeds 24 hours a day, 7 days a week. Others have all that drive, but no place to apply it! In either case, you exhibit tremendous inventiveness, and a vibrant will to match. Once there's a project or goal into which you can pour all your energy, there's little stopping you. Unfortunately, sometimes you might run roughshod over associates without realizing what's happened until later. The birth number of 3 creates even more zealous aspirations, but inserts a soothing sense of humor and goodwill that acts as a salve to fix those faux pas.

At play, you're likely to be biking in the park, jogging the beach, racing cars, making complex artistic creations, or enjoying other activities that illustrate movement in some sensual way. Alternatively, you might be putting up the backdrop for a huge charity function, organizing a food drive, or busily handling several goodwill tasks at once.

There's never any question about your motivations. You always lay all the cards on the table with total honesty. That propensity for honor means you should avoid any work that requires even the slightest amount of secrecy. Instead, consider being a mediator or envoy. That way you can present both sides of any situation equally—without coloring the truth to suit someone else's agenda. Your birth number of 3 stands ready to provide necessary communication skills in these types of situations.

Romantically, this Aquarian has very strong feminine aspects. Your intuitive nature shines through, as well as a tendency to nurture others. Love must be a true partnership—it is essential that you are able to both talk and listen.

Gift idea: cases of energy drinks or healthy munchies.

February 11

You like staying close to home. That space is truly sacred, and reflects you in very intimate ways. Throughout your house there are little touches that sing with the Aquarian soul, reflecting a creative and artistic eye. All that tranquility doesn't mean you lack energy or drive. You just want the home to have a cozy, welcoming ambiance.

At this juncture we've moved into the Libra decanate. That exerts its influence by encouraging social interaction, particularly at home. Consequently you are quite the home entertainer—thoughtful and sensitive to all your guests' preferences, needs, and pleasures. Having a birth number of 4 can sometimes make this passion into a nearly business-like obsession, or it could simply give you culinary and domestic skills that rock the world.

For careers, something that focuses on people's homes would be ideal. There's plenty of Aquarian originality here, so a job in interior design, upholstery, or something similar would be ideal. Other than making your own home beautiful, there's nothing you enjoy more than seeing other people's spaces shine.

That concept moves into relationships in the form of nesting. Once you find a good partner, heart and hearth become integral to expressing that around the house.

Gift idea: a stained-glass sun catcher or hanging flowers.

February 12

You are all business. Work is a true joy, and you have strong potential for moving quickly into leadership positions. Be forewarned, however. Having a birth number of 5 can somewhat undermine all that drive with restless distractibility.

When the time comes to consider careers, find either a position with "many hats," or one that doesn't tie you down. Go on the road giving classes, travel as a consultant, become a high-end personal assistant, or go to the far reaches of the world to support a good cause. The last option really feeds that overactive sense of responsibility that's always quietly held your heart in check.

The only real caution is to avoid taking on too much. People naturally trust your go-getting talents, but they forget that you have needs too. You can potentially change the world, but even Rome wasn't built in a day. Allow your Libra decanate some space to breathe and offer a more equitable balance between business and pleasure.

While you enjoy being around a variety of people, typically business and other goals take too much time to allow you to become overly involved in an intimate relationship.

Gift idea: a leather-covered day planner.

QUESTION?

What are good hobbies for an Aquarian to consider?
The Aquarian creativity and love of diversity can lead to exploring a wide variety of personal hobbies. Being outdoors holds great appeal, so perhaps consider hiking, nature photography, garden design, and mountain climbing for starters. Inside the house, look to things that engage the ever-active Aquarian mind, like tinkering with new-fangled gadgets or brain-teasing crossword puzzles.

February 13

This Aquarian is a unique person, with truly individual designs and enough ambition to turn the world on its ear. The problem with being a visionary, however, is getting other people to comprehend your ideas. The idealism in today's birth number of 6 does nothing to assist the communication process. Instead, it just creates yet more amazing notions that occupy your waking and sleeping hours.

If today's your birthday, you never use the word "conform." While you have a shrewd mind and loving heart, love must to be on your own terms. Tradition and conventionality have little value to you unless they are important to someone you hold dear. Then, maybe (only maybe) can you find ways to tame the inner rebel-with-a-cause, and then only for a short time.

With that in mind, it's best for you to be self-employed or work where there's plenty of room for personal expression. Draw political cartoons, create educational video games, write art critiques, or seek out the source for a new spiritual path—but avoid being under other people's thumbs if you want to succeed.

In love, things are similarly free-spirited. Combine Aquarius with a birth number of 6, and you've got someone who falls in love with love, but doesn't want to settle down.

Gift idea: a dream interpretation book or a mind-teasing toy.

February 14

Today's personology keynote is problem solving. There's no end to the complexity that you comprehend, let alone that which you can fix. Normally this propensity would make for a good diplomat or mediator. There's only one problem: You are direct, frank, and completely truthful. Delivery is everything in communication, and your words are often delivered with a sledgehammer. Unfortunately, the birth number of 7 provides highly attuned perceptions upon which friends and family alike depend. Nearly everyone in and around your life wants you as a confidant and advisor.

You started out life sitting on the sidelines and slowly found your voice. All that watchfulness paid off in spades. In fact, if you find a career (like astronomy) that allows you to use those keen observation skills, you've got the work ethic to achieve greatness. No matter your life path, avoid anything that smells of dishonesty and indecision—you have no patience for either.

You like to take your time in relationships. Unlike the romantic air under which you were born, there's no need to rush things, but that doesn't mean you can't flirt. In the right social settings you wrap both men and women into your spell equally well.

Gift idea: a highly personalized perfume or cologne.

February 15

In the book of naughty and nice, you've been a very mischievous Aquarian. There's enough enthusiasm, innovation, and charisma in one of your fingers to turn the most tedious of tasks into something fun. Your dynamic personality takes people's breath away, and sometimes you find yourself tempted to overdo it. This is especially true with money, thanks to the birth number 8. You have a tendency to take unusual risks in the hopes of "making it big." On the other hand, 8 also strives for security, responsibility, and protection, which may prove to be your true saving grace—it can help you avoid rash decisions.

You would never consider any type of "everyday" job. Not only would it bore you to tears, but it would bring out even more roguish tendencies than normal. You walk on the wild side and are attracted to the oddest of jobs, from performing at Cirque du Soleil to performing marriage ceremonies for dogs!

As one might expect, your relationships are likewise on the outer edge of societal conformity. Nothing is plain, nothing is simple, nothing is dull. Your natural charm is endearing, but you're not one to stay with one lover. Often you are attracted to alternative lifestyles that allow more sensual exploration.

Gift idea: a collection of prankish stories.

We know that Romans had a hearty festival that celebrated the spirit of love, but how did our modern Valentine celebrations get started? Legends say that Valentine lived in Rome during the third century. As a priest, he disagreed with Claudius's ruling that single men had to go into service as soldiers (to the point of outlawing marriage for them). Valentine continued marrying young men, for which he was imprisoned. While in jail, people say, our priest fell in love with the jailor's daughter. Before dying, Valentine wrote her a love letter signed simply, "from your Valentine." And thus the first "Valentine's card" was created.

February 16

Nearly the complete opposite of those born on 2/15, you are the strong and silent type. You are constantly engaged in thought, usually about a specific situation or person you are sizing up. Make no mistake: when you finally come out of your shell, you have lots to say, including good advice. Your pragmatic, insightful approach borders on genius.

You may find yourself fascinated by mystical matters. You have rational thinking that measures everything, but behind those grinding gears there's also strong gut instincts that rarely lead you astray. You often suffer from internal struggles—between thought and action, between mind and heart, between restlessness and the desire for stability. In many ways, you truly live in two worlds—mind and spirit—but you also need both, especially with a birth number of 9 cheering you onward toward enlightenment and self-actualization.

The idealism inherent in today's personology forecast implies that you might have a spiritual vocation. Alternatively, only something equally noble will do. Examples include a quality-control inspector, time-management advisor, and social worker.

Love may not have been kind to you, and you bear a lot of wounds that need healing. This may come across to partners as being overly needy, but you cannot give wholly of yourself until those past issues are resolved. Partners need to understand this, or the next relationship will prove similarly unhealthy.

Gift idea: passes to a social club.

February 17

You enjoy pushing the boundaries and opening new frontiers every day. A birth number of 1 agrees with this perfectly, giving you a passion for challenges and very high personal expectations. There's no slacking off in your life, and you cannot tolerate indolent attitudes from others. That's not surprising considering your vibrant passion for justice, achievement, and problem solving.

Persistence is your middle name. Everyone knows that you don't commit to anything unless you can see it through to completion. Sometimes that attitude comes across as officious or heavy-handed, but thankfully the decanate of Libra smoothes things out. When pressed to the wall, fall back and depend on your charisma, as it rarely fails to tip the scales in your favor.

This mix of attributes makes for a very strong Aquarian leader, with a talent for logic, delegation, and technicalities. There are very few jobs at which you could not succeed; however, that doesn't equate to bliss. Some careers that might appeal to you include defense lawyer, college professor, and not-for-profit manager.

One of the difficulties in blending the Aquarian heart with a birth number of 1 is the pressure you place on everyone you know and love. As much as you might like a long-term relationship, it's hard to find anyone who measures up to your high standards, let alone who can cope with maintaining that standard. Nonetheless, if you can keep your expectations more reasonable, you make a very considerate companion.

Gift idea: a stain removal and sewing kit.

February 18

This Aquarian has the heart of a gambler. Risk taking, challenges, and anything out of the ordinary capture your attention far faster than the flash of gold or a pretty face. This over-indulgent attitude may be subdued by the birth number of 2, which encourages you to respect boundaries. The problem is that you feel you have none! Instead, you use the energies of 2 to adapt to the constant chaos you create to keep things interesting.

You are drawn to work in dangerous jobs. You might be fishing for king crab in Alaska, racing cars, cleaning up a biohazard, or doing stunt-double work. Add to this the birth number 2's dynamic, and you may well show up as a correspondent on a war front, revealing those stories "the public needs to know." Your hobbies are likely to be equally showy and original. But all this flash and fanfare isn't without some sense of calling and sincere determination. You have an insatiable hunger for action and activity (the words "apathy" and "sedentary" have never appeared in your dictionary).

If today is your birthday, relationships probably don't work very well. People think you're too "out there" and fear that you'll take their heart along for the ride. What they don't realize is that you have passion and would love to share your adventures with a like-minded soul.

Gift idea: a parachute and some skydiving lessons.

ALERT!

Being an air sign that plays regularly with water, there's a strong desire for movement in most Aquarians. That means extreme sports with lots of energy naturally attract this Water Bearer. Look to sports like snowboarding and surfing to satisfy that adventurous yearning.

February 19

Today is cusp territory (depending on the year), which means that the Piscean insightfulness influences you. You're likely to see people for what they are, and tolerate no disguises. You also have a little Piscean insecurity that motivates your quest for perfection in every corner of life. When in a social setting you want to be the life of the party, something a birth number of 3 appreciates. Professionally you recognize and seize opportunity. The only downside here is that this effort comes from a timid space in your soul that never feels it's quite good enough.

You can think globally and even universally if so motivated. That means at both work and play you need to seek something that resonates with that vision. There's purpose to this plan, and it often ends with you at the center of attention, even if unwittingly (the birth number 3 nearly guarantees this happens regularly). Friends and coworkers alike may feel like you've stolen their thunder, but that's really not the case. This Aquarian had it all along and waited for an ideal time to let it rattle the rafters. And when you're given your second in the spotlight, you will inevitably share it and give credit where credit is due.

The person or people that you welcome into your heart want to be there and stay there. While you are picky about your partners, you're generous with pampering them and offer great amounts of rather surprising romance.

Gift idea: an antique map or globe.

February 20

You're idealistic and romantic, but also relatively goal-oriented and socially aware. This can lead to being overly sensitive to nearly everything and trying to satisfy every demand in life equally well. Stop being so worried about everyone else and start figuring out what you want to do—who you are in the depths of your being. Unlocking that awareness is your greatest challenge and your greatest means of success.

Routines make you crazy—if your life is a river, you're always swimming against the current—not to make some radical gesture, but rather to appease a personal sense of rightness. You never do anything half-heartedly, and you'll do everything to make the best of any situation! That determination (augmented by a birth number of 4) can sometimes be an anchor that keeps you from seeing what's truly a lost cause. The phrase "there's always hope" is like a mantra for you. You must be careful in career choices so as to not embrace start-ups and other iffy propositions that could destroy your valued security.

You are likely to want calm relationships with high-caliber people. You avoid confrontation, often sacrificing true happiness to maintain harmony.

Gift idea: a certificate for a self-assertion course where you can learn to communicate your needs without fear.

February 21

There's little that life could conceivably hand you that would completely leave you floundering without a backup plan. You take to change, challenge, deadlines, and duty like a dog to a well-loved bone. It may take time, but the bone doesn't stand a chance.

It's likely that you were a shy, uncertain youth, more interested in books than socialization. That would not last, however. Inside was an incredibly complex butterfly waiting to spread its wings and fly! Be it hovering the winds of spirituality, resting on the flower of social interaction, dancing with a creative breeze, or focusing on life's nectar—every moment of every day holds potential. You are not one to die for want of living, nor are you afraid of taking on responsibility. There's a sense of pride and assurance that comes with a job well done, and even when weary you'll keep up the good fight. Just try to avoid the martyr syndrome. Take care of yourself as well as you do others, and life will improve dramatically.

This Piscean vocation could be nearly anything, but there's typically an affinity for something creative (minimally as a hobby to balance "real" life). Where many Fish only dream of fulfillment, those born today can own the ocean when they apply skills and good business sense effectively. One word of warning: protect the rewards from these labors, putting some away for a rainy day. The Aquarian tendency for charity ekes into this Piscean regularly, sometimes without thought of the bigger picture.

Family isn't always defined by blood; you want a tribe of the heart. Those this Fish calls friend will never feel neglected. Commitment can be another matter altogether. Swimming and spawning with more than one person is part of the natural code that may lead to a non-monogamous lifestyle.

Gift idea: something that's both thoughtful and useful.

What famous people were born in February?
Clark Gable (2/1), Norman Rockwell (2/3), Babe Ruth (2/6), Zsa Zsa Gabor (2/6), Jules Verne (2/8), Marie Curie (2/9), Jennifer Aniston (2/11), Charles Darwin (2/12), Jimmy Hoffa (2/14), Jane Seymour (2/15), Robert Frost (2/16), Yoko Ono (2/18), Albert Einstein (2/21), George Washington (2/22), Victor Hugo (2/26), and John Steinbeck (2/27).

February 22

Empathic and highly psychic, you may prove a bit moody and reclusive. Being around too many individuals at once causes emotional overload, and then you must retreat to sort out your thoughts. Those periodic hermetic moments prove very helpful to people in your life, as sometimes your knack for knowing becomes unsettling.

You're probably giving to a fault. You have a huge heart and a friendly personality, but sometimes there's a temptation to try and fix the whole world at once. The humanitarian drive inherent in the birth number of 6 adds to that enticement geometrically. Don't spread yourself so thin. Narrow down that "to do" list to two or three reasonable goals and focus on them until completion. Overall, you'll be happier with the results.

In business this Fish swims well in jobs that utilize all that sensitivity while maintaining some emotional distance. This doesn't mean being uncaring, but rather allowing the inner professional to take over. Examples include counseling, career guidance, and possibly even the clergy.

The intensity of feeling in the Piscean life means that you don't take love lightly. If it isn't exactly the ideal you want, the preference would be to go it alone and wait for just that absolutely right someone. Meanwhile, having periodic small social outlets suits the Fish just fine.

Gift idea: a psychic self-defense class.

February 23

You are a highly communicative Piscean who uses words to champion the underdog (whether a person or a situation). You have tremendous drive, coupled with an idealistic nature that's always seeking a new cause. The problem is that you dive into a lot of figurative pools without checking for water. Thankfully your birth number of 7 comes to the rescue and offers a bit of caution and a moment's rest to self-check those ever-useful instincts.

Your living space tends to be traditional but includes periodic flashes of color and the odd piece of art that only you truly understand. Your social life centers around people who have even tempers and sturdy minds. Additionally, you have a strong attraction to affluent individuals. This Fish isn't wholly driven by money, but it does offer some serious appeal.

With the financial end of things in mind, you would do well in positions where your work pays off quickly with both raises and promotions. You tend not to be very patient, but you are talented, especially in sales or other areas where your negotiation abilities can shine through. That aptitude manifests in group environments too, where you can get everyone thinking on the same page.

If today is your birthday, your heart seeks true partnerships with friends and lovers alike. You don't want someone too dependent or wishy-washy (the latter would drive you crazy), and for long-term success you need to be matched with someone that keeps up with (and appreciates) your quick wit.

Gift idea: collectable coins in a nice display case.

February 24

A financial overtone continues into today's personology forecast. You enjoy nice things, but aren't afraid to work hard to get them. This nature finds a strong, supportive co-pilot in the birth number of 8, whose practical, tenacious nature colors every effort. You want stability no matter how muddy the waters get, but not necessarily at the expense of others or a personal ideal. That struggle sometimes comes across to others as "contrariness," but it's not. It just takes a while for you to weigh the options.

Around the house, you are likely to have an odd assortment of high-quality items. You prefer to save up for one excellent kitchen knife than buy ten cheap ones that need replacing in a year. That weighing of quality comes out in relationships too. The combination of being slow to commit, moody, and desirous of gushy emotions doesn't work out for this Fish very well in love's pond. Friendship isn't quite so complex, except that you hold others to the same standards by which you live. Friends, be ready to be challenged!

The birth number of 8 indicates that if today's your birthday, you're likely drawn to jobs that offer both security and a reasonable income. Both are significant to decision making, but you don't jump for the "fast buck." It's more important to find a long-term situation that's likable and pays the bills than to live with uncertainty (even if it means some short-term benefits).

Gift idea: a budgeting program for your computer.

FACT

Besides being Black History Month, National Cherry Month, and American Heart Month, the following are some interesting observance dates for February: February 2: Groundhog Day & Candlemas; February 4: Thank a Mailman Day; February 5: National Weatherman's Day; February 8: Boy Scout Day; February 10: Umbrella Day; February 11: Make a Friend Day & Inventor's Day; February 12: Lincoln's Birthday; February 14: Valentine's Day; February 17: Random Acts of Kindness Day; February 20: President's Day; February 22: Washington's Birthday; February 26: Carnival Day; February 28: Public Sleeping Day.

February 25

You have a Piscean's natural aptitude for intuitiveness combined with the visionary powers of a birth number 9. As a result you might seem puzzling and somewhat disconnected to acquaintances. The average individual may find your mind so vast that it's hard to understand you when you speak (especially in your area of expertise). However, the zeal and passion in those words come through clearly.

For a career path, you would thrive in any intellectual environment where you can focus wholly on uncovering and understanding those things that elude others. Forensics is one excellent example. If there's a way to apply one's talents to better humankind, that would be the icing on the cake! No matter what the field, you will be set apart and recognized for your achievements.

You enjoy clever hobbies like stage magic and illusion. This mirrors your personal conviction that life is far more than what you experience through normal senses. In some cases, you might be inexplicably drawn to seemingly "illogical" arts like divination, hoping to find answers to some of those things that have plagued humankind forever.

Love may not be in the cards for you. You're rather bashful, feeling a bit inept when it comes to social graces.

Gift idea: dance lessons.

February 26

If you were born today, you are one of the gentle giants of the Piscean reality. You're kind yet strong, optimistic yet opinionated, hungry for stability but fidgety, and overall a bit larger than life. There's a good chance even unexpected situations feel familiar, as if you've lived many, many times. But even with all that experience upon which to draw, there's still a real struggle between logic and instinct. The birth number of 1 doesn't really help that struggle, in that 1 wants whatever's unique (and with this Piscean it could be a moralistic display or a truly stunning mental achievement).

You have an artistic edge, and it may come out in humorous ways—an outrageous tie, mix-n-match clothing, or completely varied dinnerware at a formal party. For work, this might manifest as following a career in satire or comedy. If you have chosen a more serious-minded livelihood, you're likely a clever prankster on and off the job.

This creative aspect allows you to have an adaptive nature. While you'll tend to want to swim in your own stream, you aren't without the capacity to compromise, especially for people you love. Speaking of which, while this

Pisces loves very deeply, you sometimes hide emotion. There's an underlying fear of being too vulnerable or having your motivations misunderstood.

Gift idea: a surprise party might be ideal.

February 27

Dance to your own tune, sing your own song. If today's your birthday there's a very strong thirst for freedom combined with a propensity to engage life with spontaneous abandon. When you love, it's completely. When you work, you're wholly engaged in the task at hand. When you play it's outrageous, and when you work in teams it's all-out cooperation or nothing!

There's a lot of intensity here, to which the birth number of 2 offers a vital balancing effect. While this Fish exhibits a powerful attraction to "out there" concepts and activities, 2 comes in and whispers of common sense. You will always have a lot of varied interests, frequently a variety of jobs, and a very diversified group of friends. Nonetheless, 2 allows this individual to bring everything on life's buffet onto a harmonious and functioning platter.

Careerwise, find a job with tons of facets or a way of appealing to your creative Piscean soul. Look to design, or create with rich words those images that inspire others to greatness. In love, avoid overly needy or weak partners. These Pisceans enjoy a sense of laissez-faire in relationships; clingy people need not apply.

Gift idea: a desktop Zen sand garden.

QUESTION?

When the letters of February are added up, what does it represent in numerology?

Using modern numerological values, February is a 6. This combines well with its order in the calendar (month 2). The number 6 indicates that people born in February will be very focused on their home lives and relationship building. Add to that the peaceful qualities of the number 2, and you have a month well-suited to inspiring harmony in any situation, especially with family members.

February 28

You have charm, good humor, and a dynamic personality that appeals to many. Ah, but there's more—a bit of mischief, sex appeal, and an appreciation for honest competition simmer under that sparkling smile. You have aspirations but also know how to have fun, and if you can mingle these two together, it makes for a very happy Fish.

Today's birth number is 3, which mingles with your Piscean upbeat energy with absolute ease. You enjoy making others happy, and especially revel in good surprises delivered with savoir faire. Additionally, you are nearly fearless in the face of adversity. If someone has a problem, you'll try to help and keep pounding away at that wall until either it gives up, or a solution presents itself.

This optimism toward life manifests in career choices in various ways. Some end up traveling, feeling the world is there for exploration. Others delve into curiosities like antiques or anthropology. Others still apply problem-solving skills to jobs that require formularies. No matter what the choice, this Piscean's natural passion for life typically yields success.

For love, there's a touch of fickleness. Our Fish enjoys a handsome or beautiful partner with similarly attractive ideals and manners. Once in love, you make a very fun, romantic partner.

Gift idea: Trivial Pursuit.

FACT

Every 4 years there's an extra day added to the calendar. Having only 365 days in a year results in an error of .24 days (6 hours) per year. In 100 years that means the Gregorian calendar would be 24 days ahead of natural seasons. To align the calendar, one day is added to February every four years. The rules for leap year go as follows: Every year divisible by 4 is a leap year. If a year is divisible by 100, it is not a leap year unless it is also divisible by 400.

February 29

Being somewhat of a "kid" yourself, today's Piscean has a good-humored and youthful outlook on life. Combine this with measurable social skills and you've got the potential for making friends, attracting sensual lovers, and influencing people in truly unique ways. About the only drawback to the Leap Year baby is that sometimes you're too optimistic. When "life happens" in ways that don't bring a smile, it can really cause a tailspin. In this, look to your birth number of 4 as a good partner. The concrete nature of 4 can be depended upon to keep at least one foot on terra-firma.

For hobbies, try out expressive things—various ways of communicating ideas and visions to people with an eye to see what you're saying. Getting involved in a drama club or pottery class are two good options. Don't be too constrained by convention here. Listen to your spirit's voice and create!

Work should be similarly inspiring. Pisceans have an aptitude for visual, verbal, and other arts. You might end up as a great painter or writer, or might combine several skills by performing poetry at an out-of-the-way coffee house.

Unfortunately the confidence exhibited in the arts isn't mirrored in relationships. This Piscean walks with uncertainty as a constant companion, which may cause overdependence on a partner for a sense of self-worth.

Gift idea: toys (like an Etch-A-Sketch).

Aquarius

Sign: Aquarius
Date: January 21–February 19
Ruled by: Uranus
Element: Air
Lucky Color: Yellow-green
Gemstone: Amethyst, sapphire
Keynote: Novelty
Positive Traits: Dedicated, independent, creatively intellectual
Negative Traits: Indecisive, procrastinates, lacks backbone
Famous Capricorns include: Famous Aquarians include: Francis Bacon, Sonny Bono, Lewis Carroll, Charles Darwin, Zsa Zsa Gabor, Galileo, Mozart, Yoko Ono, Princess Caroline of Monaco, Ayn Rand

The first word that comes to mind with Aquarians is "unpredictable." This sign has the capacity to shake things up, change the rules, and transform reality in the most unconventional way conceivable. There's a rebellious, liberal soul here—someone who proactively challenges outmoded thoughts and ways.

At home, it's laissez-faire. Nearly anything can, and does, go, depending on the mood. No white picket fences here, no sense of conformity. Weird takes on sacredness in the Water Bearer's home. The Aquarian sense of order is highly personalized, and often guided by those things that provide them with mind candy (computers, books, etc.).

Aquarians make good friends, because they have an aptitude for emotional detachment when the situation warrants. Better still, they can listen to differing views without feeling insulted (if anything, the conversation engages them further), and they often come up with that brilliant idea that others couldn't quite uncover. This aptitude is sadly unpredictable, but wonderful when it happens.

As life mates Aquarians can find themselves restless. The sense of independence often overwhelms all else. If a Water Bearer hasn't found a long-term relationship by their thirties, they may discover contentment in the single world where they can be alone with their freedom, adventurous hopes, mysterious dreams, and thirst for people-watching.

Chapter 5
March

March gets its name from the Latin word *Martius*. Originally it was the first month of the year, but when the calendar changed it became the third month. It's named after the Roman God of war, Mars. In Anglo Saxon tradition it was called Hlyd (stormy) or Hraed (rough). Astrologically the first part of this month comes under the unconventional rule of Pisces. Come March 21st, the fire of Aries moves in. This naturally heats things up and brings an air of authority and renewed energy.

March 1

Pisceans are dreamers, but those born today are liable to take those dreams and make them into realities. You find challenges tempting, inspiring, and intriguing. Just don't let unnecessary challenges lead to similarly unnecessary distractions. Additionally, you can be a tad moody, and those moods can cloud good judgment.

You have the advantage of the birth number 4, granting a measure of stability to a life that could otherwise get off course in daydreams and wistful thinking. Here, the number 4 couples with the Fish's ideals and provides the drive necessary to defend those beliefs and utilize them in achieving long-term success. Additionally, when you dig your tail into the sand, you're not likely to budge (especially on subjects like liberty and equality).

Around the house you're likely to have added splashes of color nearly everywhere. You love well-lit rooms, preferably with many windows covered by only the sheerest of curtains. Sharing this space with a life mate may prove difficult. There's a sense of ownership, and many times you like being alone in that watery cave. Friends are another matter altogether. People find you very easy to be around—creative, admirable, and intelligent.

Gift idea: a huge art set and paper.

March 2

You likely have a knack for social graces. There is little room in your life for rude, inconsiderate, or willfully ignorant people. That outlook developed from rather turbulent personal experiences, but it serves you well nonetheless. Daily reality is much happier and more productive when others who share your discretion and intuition surround you.

Your Piscean nature manifests in a tendency to allow others to steal your thunder. Your biggest life lesson is not simply discovering your power, but keeping it. Opportunists see your abilities and hope to take advantage of them, without giving you any credit!

People find you very charming, with a definitive bearing that seems to imply "take no prisoners" even though you have a heart of gold. The external reserve acts as a safeguard not only for your sensitive emotions, but also against those unhealthy things (or people) that cause you to flounder. That means it takes a while to get to know you. Anyone wishing for a long-term relationship needs a little patience and a willingness to give to that relationship as much as they receive.

Gift idea: savings bonds.

March 3

There's no question that you see the world through optimistic, and sometimes overly rose-colored, glasses. This, in turn, creates the recipe for having your feelings hurt and dreams dashed when reality doesn't measure up to that vision.

In your own home, you don't sweat practicality very much and can become downright disorderly. Sharing space with this Piscean means setting limits as to where that mess can land, or it will be everywhere. This isn't because you don't care about others' feelings or doesn't value that space. Rather you are simply distracted by other things (usually some type of business or personal engagement). A birth number of 6 might not be much help here, as it will inspire you to juggle even more projects, never wanting to say no to anyone with a real (or perceived) need.

In relationships you need something to feed your mind and heart, and a good sense of humor is absolutely essential. Additionally your partner needs to be aware that you are prone to being distracted easily and have relatively iffy self-esteem.

Gift idea: a personalized mug reading: "World's best _____."

FACT

Historians tell us that daffodils came to Britain via Roman travelers. In Rome, daffodil sap (called Narcissus) was used for healing. The word daffodil didn't come into popular use until the 1500s, as a corruption of the Greek *asphodel*, the field where ghosts walked freely. It was here that Persephone was seen wearing a crown of these flowers, representing the hope of renewed life come spring. It's said if you walk carefully and avoid stepping on daffodils, you'll have good luck!

March 4

Your head and heart are constantly at war. The Cancer decanate stresses the intuitive nature and lofty goals, and the Piscean nature adds in tenacity. Now add the birth number 7 with its creative, nit-picking talent, and its no wonder that these Fish often feel like they're swimming in circles. Nonetheless, when you get all the facets of your personality working cooperatively, it translates into success.

All this diversity makes for an eclectic living space. At first glance, a newcomer might think our Fish has no sense of focus, but just the opposite is true. You have wide personal/hobby interests, with far narrower professional goals. In particular these Pisceans may excel in fields that allow them to utilize mind and heart, such as fund raising for charity.

Your relationships probably have been bumpy at best. You can go from zero to sixty mentally in a flash, and you expect others to make that leap with you. Partners must be brilliant and artistic, but never jealous. You cannot be "owned" by anyone, and will run quickly at the first sign of possessiveness or dependency.

Gift idea: a book on astrology would be welcome, as would a gourmet ice cream cake!

March 5

You're like Curious George—if there's a mystery to unravel, you will be there in full detective mode. And just like Scooby Doo, you love to share adventures with family and friends alike. Beyond intense inquisitiveness, you're also a social butterfly, but underneath all that seemingly impulsive activity is the desire to create long-standing relationships (both personal and professional). Once you make someone part of your circle, they're "in" for life. About the only thing that takes this Fish out of the social pool is people who are purposefully cruel. Once betrayed, this Piscean will never return to that figurative pond.

It's strongly advised that you create a sanctuary for yourself. Single Pisceans, focus on your bedroom, making it as calming and peaceful as possible. You'll find you appreciate this on those nights when all those clues keep you up late. If coupled, perhaps you can make a special office space into which you can retreat. In business, you could become a professor, researcher, or even a detective!

Gift idea: a mystery novel.

March 6

You like life to have a sense of order and beauty, with just a little bit of sparkle to keep things interesting. You thrive on independence, but also love to be around others who value autonomous thinking and collective sophistication.

The Cancer decanate speaks of someone with an aptitude to spot both quality and value (this translates well for those who choose careers like appraisal and art dealing). Unfortunately, with the birth number of 9, this aptitude may create a difficult conundrum. Does one buy the most expensive piece, or the piece that's better in price and value?

Your home is decorated with elegance and good taste. Even the closets look like a picture from a cutting-edge home design magazine! Your partners need to be just as polished and cultured in their outlook and character.

Gift idea: a certificate for one of your favorite stores.

QUESTION?

Why is it said that if March comes in like a lion it will go out like a lamb?
Typically the first days of March hold tumultuous weather, but by the end of the month the skies clear and the winds calm. By the way, the first three days of March are considered most unlucky. It's said that when rain falls on these days, harvests will be slim.

March 7

Intellectual, shrewd, and resourceful, you love to test limits. Sometimes it seems that the fates constantly tinker with your life, and the oddest things happen at completely unexpected moments. Combine that with birth number 1's propensity for inimitability, and it's certain this Piscean never gets bored. If anything, you have learned to swim in all manners of weather and still manage to make headway.

You probably crave the company of rivers, oceans, and waterfalls. This is the best place for you to process all the information the world tosses your way. In business, use Fate's attention in unique ways; perhaps open a high-end casino, teach people about investment, or study chaos theory!

In relationships, your lovers and mates are nearly as unexpected as every other part of your life. It doesn't matter how long the relationship lasts, as long as there's an equal exchange of tenderness.

Gift idea: a surprise party, of course!

March 8

The normally liberal-minded Piscean mold gets broken in today's person-ology forecast. You are anything but footloose and fancy-free. Instead the terms "overly practical", "calculating", "impatient", and "verbally critical" come to mind. What happened? In part, it's the Cancer decanate energies that make you far too aware of other people's feelings and motivations. Having a rough demeanor pushes people away and allows you mental and psychic breathing space. There is also the birth number 2 that pushes you right back into rough empathic waters, craving company and a cooperative atmosphere.

As one might expect, this makes relationships difficult. You back off quickly if you feel too vulnerable, yet may rush ahead when lonely or wanting some gentle attention. Rather than seek out challenging relationships, you may become wishy-washy and say yes to the harmless lover, while ducking the exciting one.

Work is one space where that serious, staid side is totally at ease. Your ability to stay on task, remain committed, and manifest concepts in practical ways builds a strong foundation for long-term stability and ongoing accomplishments.

On the flip side, home is far more relaxed and cozy than one might expect, complete with at least one space for a beloved, creative outlet such as pottery or gourmet cooking.

Gift idea: something that celebrates your private space and pleasures.

March 9

In an odd dichotomy for a water sign, your personology is filled with fire, passion, and zeal. Every moment of life represents a new adventure, a new challenge, and an opportunity for self-expression. Nonetheless, for all that bravado your intuitiveness simmers under the surface, matching all that outward energy with inward, emotional sensitivity. Harsh words cut you like a knife, but you'll never let it show. Happiness, on the other hand, is shown and shared gleefully, as we'd expect from the birth number 3.

Your home likely reflects all your intensity. It wouldn't be surprising if you designed or built at least one part of that space from the ground up so it was "just so." In fact, that creative process proves highly addictive and slowly extends to every nook and cranny. You'll undertake this transformative process several times in your life, wanting your space to reflect personal growth and vision every step of the way.

For a career, you excel at jobs that offer movement. Look to jobs like dance instructor, athletic trainer, or life skills coach. These types of positions engage body, mind, and spirit into harmonious action, pleasing the inner perfectionist.

In relationships, seek out an honest, creative lover. There's no question that trust is a huge issue for longevity, but you also need periodic surprises to maintain sexual interest.

Gift idea: a personalized set of tools (for maintenance and upkeep).

ALERT!

March 8th is International Woman's Day. The entire United Nations commemorates this day, and in many countries worldwide it's a nationally observed holiday. The purpose of this celebration is commemorating everyday women who gave extraordinary things to society and fought to establish equality with men. The concept for this festival came about in the early 1900s, as the industrial revolution, war, and a growing global picture began changing women's roles dramatically. The date was observed in the United States regularly from about 1910–1920, dwindled for a while, then reappeared in the 1960s alongside the women's liberation movement.

March 10

You are the clownfish of the Piscean school. You love a good joke, are socially outgoing, and have a dramatic flair that's a mile wide! You care deeply about people and use humor as an equalizer, especially in stressful situations. This, in turn, attracts a wide variety of people into your life, and you couldn't be happier!

Outgoing in public, at home you'll often be pursuing much quieter things. The Cancer decanate adds a passion for daydreaming, so reading fanciful novels is one possible pastime. The décor of your home is personally pleasing, a little offbeat, but also tasteful. You want others to feel welcome and comfortable in your home, and probably do a fair amount of entertaining.

Work is a different matter yet. Whether performing at a comedy club, writing a screenplay, or using humor to cheer the elderly, professionalism finds a gentle balance with this person's caring and humorous outlook on life. Your partners must have similar lightheartedness. You don't like gloomy people and nay-sayers!

Gift idea: an aquarium with playful accoutrements.

March 11

You thirst after the spiritual or mysterious aspects of life. Deep in your heart you know that Fate has called you to something different, challenging, and yet utterly wonderful. As a child you mystified your parents and teachers alike by being too otherworldly, intuitive, astute, and/or wise beyond your years. Later in life these same characteristics inspire trust and confidence from associates and loved ones alike.

The energies inherent in the birth number 5 mingle well with your natural sense of purpose. In business this may manifest in things like creating a wholly new gadget, developing a fresh idea for reforming an outmoded structure, or implementing a highly successful mode of adult education (just for starters). Honestly, you can do nearly anything, so long as the foundations are already in place for that project.

Your interpersonal relationships are as dynamic as your concepts. You'll surround yourself with brilliant, spiritual, sensitive souls who feed and inspire others.

Gift idea: a copy of *Jonathan Livingston Seagull* or the Dali Lama's writings would be apt.

March 12

You have a sense of playfulness and whimsy, and even the most tumultuous waters don't seem to faze you. But be careful about being too reckless and wild. Thus far life has taught you that you can overcome a lot, but that doesn't mean it's okay to toss out common sense. You don't need to be bizarre to get attention. Unfortunately a birth number of 6 does nothing to equalize that tendency, so it's up to you to take the reins.

At home, you surround yourself with lovely things, especially items with a touch of whimsy. A Victorian painting of fairies might be on one wall, while a glass-art flying pig coaster sits on a tabletop. And somehow it all works together (thank the birth number 6 for that help)!

In relationships, you play an odd game of push-me-pull-you. One day you're needy, the next day wholly independent and stretching boundaries to the max. Your partners need patience and the ability to see through the ruse.

Gift idea: some fun gag items and one serious touch like a brightly colored daisy in a delicate bud vase.

QUESTION?

What did the ancients call the full moon of March?
The most popular name for the full moon of March seemed to be Worm Moon. This was likely due to the fact that the ground was finally thawing, and the robins returned to waiting food. This also often marked the beginning of fishing expeditions and farming efforts, adding the other titles of Fish Moon or Seed Moon.

March 13

You are a mover and a shaker. This is wonderful when projects stagnate, but not so great when you take on whale-like ferocity and cause all-out earthquakes personally and professionally. Thankfully the birth number of 7 may temper this explosiveness with forethought and logic.

Professionally, your birth number provides an awareness of those small details others miss completely. Combine that with natural potency and you could discover the next cure for cancer, explore new reaches of space, or design an effective weight loss plan! Anything that requires research, determination, and a willingness to think out of the box is perfect for you.

Your personal life tends to be a little wanting. Folks aren't quite certain what to think of all that compulsion, and some are frightened of getting run over during one of your sleepless, driven tangents. You get moving too fast and become too focused, and all else goes by the wayside. If you can learn to slow down and breathe, allowing others to catch up with your ideas and progress, personal relationships will go much more smoothly.

Gift idea: a game of laser tag.

March 14

A spark of Aries fire is sneaking into your personality. This provides balance between the emotional and rational, between instinct and knowledge. Pisceans tend toward procrastination and a quiet voice. Adding a little Aries heat creates stronger motivations and convictions.

While you often feel as if you were born in the wrong era, the waning of Piscean influences provides a smidge of practicality and a sparkling air of mystery. Much to the delight of friends and lovers, this is not a predictable Piscean, let alone someone who can be boxed in! When these strengths are applied to the naturally creative nature of Pisces, there's no end to the wonders they can create, especially if loosed in an unconventional setting. Better still, there's money to be made from independent artistic pursuits when you learn to focus and follow your bliss.

Numerologically this date adds up to 8, which really helps give you stronger foundations. You have the capacity for genius, especially at the outset of a new project. Just don't forget to put foundations under those dreams. Today's numerology also creates a difficult conflict. You have a strong distaste for structure, while 8 cries out for a functional framework. You need to balance those extremes. In love, while you often strive too hard to please mates, you also recognize your personal needs and aren't shy in sharing them.

Gift idea: a dream diary with an interpretation book.

FACT

Julius Caesar was assassinated during the Ides of March in 44 B.C.E. This is the date to which Shakespeare alluded in his famous writing, "Beware the Ides of March." What most people don't know, however, is that the Romans had no great fear of March 15th. In fact, the word *ides* was a commonly used designation on the Roman calendar. The beginning of the month was marked as *calends*, from which we get the word calendar"! The *nones* came at the 5th or 7th of a month, and the ides were the 13th or 15th. These three points in each month became a point of reference for the remaining days.

March 15

When the word "alluring" was first coined, it defined people born on this day. No matter the outside packaging, there's something innocently sexy and subtly erotic that lies just under the surface. There's no question that passion plays an important role in your life—be it toward a person, a group, or a beloved project. Couple that desire with the visionary birth number of 9 and there's no doubt that you will produce something of lasting value both personally and professionally.

One caveat: You may go to unnecessary extremes (something the overly idealistic birth number of 9 does nothing to allay). Learn to find a balance between zeal and reasonable pacing and expectations. Otherwise life proves disappointing, which squelches the Piscean creativity and leads to depression.

The key to success in your life and relationships is variety. Professionally this manifests as having several careers throughout your life, or more than one job to keep things diversified. While you're not great at fixing your own love life, you'd make a great relationship counselor! To engage in a long-term affair you need someone who's inventive and as changeable as a chameleon to keep your interest.

Gift idea: a soft blanket, a bottle of wine, and a roaring fire.

March 16

It's natural for you to feel overwhelmed by emotion; it's typical of your birth sign. You need to dig deeper, look longer, and adjust your perspectives to control the sea of feelings that threatens to drown you. Turn to your birth number of 1 for a new perspective and the determination to stick to a more global outlook. Release the things you don't need so you can embrace a more positive lifestyle.

You have the capacity for truly proactive vision and enough charisma to put it into action. When in this mode, you get on swimmingly well, especially in fields like advertising and design, where timeless appeal or futuristic innovation really sells the product. The birth number of 1 is a great helpmate here, offering all kinds of unique, creative insights.

At home you are rather private. Being home calms emotional turmoil and encourages a renewed sense of purpose. You are not likely to be a great housekeeper or entertainer, but you make a wonderful housemate, often putting the needs of others first. This is also true in long-term relationships, if you can overcome past scars that inhibit deep commitment, and can refrain from being overly philosophical about everything.

Gift idea: a CD of nature sounds (like the ocean or waterfalls).

March 17

You have a big heart and compassion to match. You are a consummate comforter and nurturer who needs to say "no" periodically—otherwise you'll burn out on other people's problems or during the pursuit of the next great, idealistic quest. This is where the birth number of 2 offers some control, wrapping all that goodness into a sensible package that can extend and retract as needed.

You caring nature leads readily to paths like nursing, care-giving, counseling, and other outlets where people reap the rewards of your wisdom and insightfulness. You have a strong work ethic, fabulous discipline, and high standards, alongside a natural ear for sympathetic listening. People can't seem to resist talking to you, and once engaged in conversation, trust grows rapidly thanks to your intuitiveness. A Scorpio decanate strengthens this aptitude.

You have no patience for deliberately flaky people. You prefer genuine individuals who are dependable and forthright. This is doubly true in relationships where your thoughtful nature might otherwise get abused. Once you mate, it's usually for life with someone who is just as devoted as you are.

Gift idea: a massage.

St. Patrick was born in Wales around 385 c.e. He started out life as a pagan, but found himself drawn in a different direction after being captured at the age of 16 by Irish invaders. Six years later he escaped and traveled to Gaul. There he entered the monastery and determined to help other pagans find their way to Christianity. Eventually he was able to return to Ireland, where over a thirty-year period he established schools and churches and won many converts. He died on March 17th, 461 c.e., which later became a holiday in his honor. The first St. Patrick's Day celebration in the United States was held in Boston in 1737.

March 18

Forget about boundaries and obstacles, there's no stopping you. You live each day as if it were your last, and enjoy each moment with impressive zeal. Just watching you makes everyone else feel tired, and leaves a lingering question as to where you find the time to accomplish so much. In truth, part of the talent comes from multitasking. The other part is sheer, unadulterated willpower. Combine that with the humor afforded by the birth number 3, and you accomplish even the most difficult of tasks with a smile and a song!

People find you appealing but also somewhat of a mystery. While friends or loved ones plan and ponder, you act and achieve. In fact, you sometimes get frustrated with people (or a whole society) who cannot keep up with you. This is a good time to use your birth number as a touchstone. Laugh daily, and realize that most people can't maintain those warp speeds, which is also what makes you so special! As for changing the world? You could do it, but not necessarily as quickly as you'd like.

With love you enjoy a challenge, so partners should let you do the pursuing. You are as imaginative with courting as you are in lovemaking. Lovers should be prepared for surprises.

Gift idea: a well-aged bottle of wine for those rare "down" moments.

March 19

You are very professional and career oriented, but it has to be in the best position where you can use all your charisma and persuasive power. The determination and work ethic present in a birth number of 4 nicely complement these wonderful traits. People see you as graceful, vividly present, and talented. The stage or something that provides a hint of glitz is terribly appealing. A career in theater, TV, or radio might be just the ticket!

Your home always includes theatrical touches. A playbill from a beloved musical, posters of *Singing in the Rain*, or a Mardi Gras mask are among the eclectic items one might find here. This ambiance gives you a space in which to explore all facets of yourself. Eventually, usually around the age of forty, you'll find the perfect starring role, possibly by marriage.

As with most stagehands, you are a little insecure and often hide behind various facades until trust builds. The person who gives you love and loyalty will receive just as much (if not more) in return.

Gift idea: a makeup kit or movie memorabilia.

March 20

While you are very kind and compassionate, you struggle to be understood by others. In part that's because you typically don't self-actualize until close to midlife (meaning there's no clear identity that's easily communicated to others).

You often act with good cause, but end up doing all the wrong things. That's somewhat normal for cusp-born individuals, as the energies from two different signs pull equally. The quick reaction time provided by a birth number 5 isn't a great ally either. You jump quickly, but usually right into trouble.

You have aptitude with organization, but worry that you're not good enough. This, in turn, leads to accepting positions that truly are beneath your talents simply because they provide a comfort zone and a reasonable income. That impulsiveness can lead to dead-end jobs that you'll end up hating but will stay with in order to feel secure.

Impulse and security issues rear their heads in relationships too. Don't be so clingy, and don't think that every affair is the last! You're very worthy of love and loyalty and owe it to yourself to find what makes you truly blissful, not merely content.

Gift idea: an incredibly bright skirt or tie to appeal to the birth number 5's sense of whimsy.

March 21

The celestial wheel has turned again, and now the Ram arrives: sure footed, socially appealing, totally upfront, and achievement-oriented. For all this good-natured appeal, Aries doesn't want to tread the path alone. All good things, especially adventures, are so much better when shared with another.

Today's birth number of 6 matches your friendly and upbeat demeanor beautifully, especially if you apply some of that drive to good causes. Career-wise you might become a décor specialist or personal trainer. Six is also a very lucky number, and sometimes luck comes to you effortlessly. Serendipity will always be part of your life.

You will develop a strongly autonomous nature by the time you're in your thirties. Part of this independence is driven by your unconventional ideas and outlook on life. Part is simply a lack of tolerance for dependent people. You prefer the company of other bright, free-spirited individuals who can find their own paths, or share yours for a while without losing any independence.

Gift idea: a lottery ticket.

ALERT!

Sometime around March 19–21, winter officially ends and spring begins. This date is determined astronomically by when the sun sits directly above the equator. In four-season environments, this is about the time when hibernation cycles end, and early-blooming plants start showing signs of growth.

March 22

Lady Destiny has something in Her pocket for you, and no matter what it is you can trust that reality will rarely (if ever) seem dull. A sense of synchronicity surrounds each day, and often touches those you bring into your karmic circle. Be careful about taking kismet for granted when it should be embraced, celebrated, and appreciated fully.

You are a person of firm convictions, some of which come across a little harshly. It's not that the Ram intends to butt heads, but your upstart spirit can't help but be honest, sometimes brutally so, especially if you detect any mismanagement or fruitless efforts. This can make partnerships with you challenging to say the least. Those without backbone and firm convictions would do well to steer clear of where angels fear to tread!

At work, you are a charming natural-born leader. Your audacity is even endearing and motivational! You can see potential in others and apply it effectively. That quality receives an extra boost from the symmetry of birth number 7.

Of all the areas in life, love is one road that you find difficult to travel confidently. If you find someone who can break down your barriers, the result is a strong, committed relationship that grows and flourishes.

Gift idea: a strategy-oriented game or a power tie.

March 23

You are experiential and sensual. You want to gather in each tidbit of life like part of a treasured harvest, especially those people and experiences that feed mind and soul. The birth number of 8 gives you a strong yearning for security, but this cannot be in the conventional sense of the term. You are far too independent to stay tied down to one place or one situation overly long (unless it provides a lot of variety).

Your home is laid-back and cozy. Nothing speaks of starch or stress. You want to feel totally at ease in your own space. At work, you seize control, using wit and wisdom to overcome hindrances. Here the birth number 8 provides a strong work ethic that blends with the natural Aries drive. Great careers to consider include stunt double, explosives expert, or a sport where a coarse personality is a great advantage.

In love, well . . . you're great in bed, but monogamy isn't strong in today's forecast. A variety of lovers, perhaps one in each city, is more your style. Friends, however, find in you a wonderful companion who is generous and thoughtful.

Gift idea: a little black book (maybe several).

March 24

Your inner child runs with scissors. Externally you appear very youthful, naïve, even innocent. You take pleasure in simple words and simple beauties, and have abundant amounts of energy to explore both. So what's the catch? A dark cloud of malcontent and sense of entitlement. This is where the stomping, whining, belligerent child rears a very ugly face, spewing harshly and using all the sensitive information and righteous indignation that the visionary nature of a birth number 9 provides. As much as the rant might sometimes be deserved, the delivery hits home, and hits very hard.

Your relationships run the complete spectrum. One minute you're in heated discussion, the next you're giving the cold shoulder. In other situations the Arian is peaceful then confrontational, cold-hearted then obsessed (often moving from zero to sixty in ten minutes or less). And don't even think about an open relationship—this kid does not share!

Business is likely to be similarly bumpy for our Aries, in that the child wants to play rather than work. Consequently you'll gravitate toward jobs where you can tinker (computer repair, toy design) or where work feels like recreation (golf caddy, exotic dancer, entertainment, etc.). In these settings you can actually fare relatively well.

Gift idea: toys, of course! In particular, light-up yo-yos, Legos, and toy train sets.

On the Christian calendar, March 25 is Lady Day, also known as Feast of the Annunciation. It is also the first of four Irish Quarter Days. According to tradition, this is when Gabriel told Mary she would bear a son. This holiday falls close to the vernal equinox for good reason. It ties into the earlier pagan beliefs that this was the time when God and Goddess enacted the sacred marriage that continues life's circle.

March 25

For an Aries, you have strong Piscean overtones that leak through from the last celestial cycle. Where most Rams focus on the present, you sometimes allow your daydreams to interfere with what you might otherwise accomplish. Why? Because you want the happy, peaceful images your mind creates as an escape. There are advantages to this rich imaginative life if you learn to apply it in a career like fiction writing and screenplays, but you cannot live in your imagination to avoid the pressures of daily reality.

Around the house you surround yourself with mementos, either personal or historical. There's something to be said for all these trinkets. You actually see human and personal lessons reflected in each—lessons that should be integrated and applied to make a better world (the world in your dreams).

Take care that your fantasy life doesn't ruin promising relationships. It's perfectly normal to have unspoken desires, but you don't want your mates feeling like they have to measure up to some mythic and impossible ideal. Instead, share stories with your lovers; weave them into your dream! Read poetry together, learn dirty dancing, and generally find ways to express a little of that rich inner vision. That will keep your life very exciting and spicy, indeed.

Gift idea: sturdy shoes so you can keep one foot in the real world.

March 26

Welcome to the world of the undaunted. You have all the intensity and power of a full-grown ram, complete with the horns to back up that claim. Some may take you as a bit of a bully, but that's really not your style. It's just that drivel has no place in your life. Projects require sensibility, people should have depth, and a civilized society has order.

In career pursuits this outlook on life may lead to a military career, especially as a diplomat, or another profession that stresses organization and measuring all sides of an issue (like time management). People may not always like what this Ram says, but your opinion is always measured equally and delivered honestly. A birth number of 2 helps round out any Aries rough edges by providing a little adaptability and insight (offsetting that concrete logic and structure).

You are attracted to competitive games ranging from chess to gymnastics. Such activities need to somehow improve your body or mind for you to consider them worthy of your time. Things that challenge you to refine toward ultimate perfection are ideal.

In love, you need to learn gentleness. You are accustomed to giving orders and being obeyed. That, of course, is not the way to maintain a balanced partnership. The partnering aptitude of birth number 2 assists in this transformation, especially with an equally structured partner who honors boundaries, but also offers a surprise now and again.

Gift idea: *The Art of War* by SunTzu.

March 27

You are the impetuous, impudent rogue of the Zodiac. If your life were a movie, it would take place in the Old West, where you'd be either the Sheriff or the Bad Guy, and in either role people would love you! It's odd to see such a thorny figure find such acceptance, yet there's something about you that's completely endearing.

At the workplace, there's little that can stop your charismatic energy, and even a rogue knows when it's time to apply a little elbow grease to accomplish goals. You definitely have the gift of gab and can use it successfully in careers such as news anchor or public relations person. Any employer to whom you give your loyalty will be very well served to have you at the forefront of any storms.

You home is filled with lush trappings, sometimes bordering on foppish and frilly. You love a little drama, a little romance, and your environment reflects that with almost gaudy richness. Nonetheless, it's a comfortable kitsch—no plastic here (rather lots of overstuffed pieces with soft fabrics).

Gift idea: something like a toilet-seat warmer or a very dramatic scarf!

ALERT!

Being the third month, March has a lot of curious energy to sort through. There's some remaining vibrations from winter that focus our attention on health. There's also the whispers of spring that excite the senses and motivate renewed hope. The wheel turns, and with it March's name number of 7 implies that many individuals find themselves pondering personal development. To receive the greatest benefits from this number's attributes, one would do well to consider both long- and short-term aspirations and not simply leap into the unknown. Work on what's possible and let other things simmer until a better window of opportunity presents itself.

March 28

Where yesterday's personology report read a bit like a party, today you become more serious. You tend to have a strong sense of responsibility, toward yourself and others, that grows throughout life. We can thank the Arian determination for part of this, along with the birth number of 4 that strives to complete every task with pride.

Where some people see drudgery, you see opportunity to shine. Being a homemaker, stay-at-home dad, maid, butler, or worker in any service-oriented job suits you just fine. In your mind it's not so much what you do, but how you do it.

In work and life there's nothing shallow or one-dimensional about you. You have a sense of sincerity that's rarely matched in the Zodiac. These are what you might call "salt of the earth"—truly good human beings upon whom you can depend in a pinch, who remember every special day (even if they don't know you well), and who always have a good word and a smile to offer. The only time you'll ever lose your cool is with pettiness. It's the one button that sends up a surprising inner warrior ready to use those horns to defend the little guy.

Love for you is a very serious matter and something you consider "for life." You seek out a partner who can appreciate life's simple pleasures and beauties, who revels in a job well done, and who extends love to family of blood and of heart/choosing. Tenderness is a keynote in this relationship, as is a gentle voice.

Gift idea: something made by hand.

March 29

When the Velveteen Rabbit speaks of being "real" you know exactly what it means. You are wholly genuine in every aspect of life. Not to be so implies some sort of trickery, which is simply not acceptable. Your pride, intellect, and sensitivity won't stand for anything less than "just the facts, ma'am!" Additionally, as a pathfinder and leader, this Aries has manners! The words "please" and "thank you" are never forgotten or overlooked. You are polite almost to a fault.

Even with all this control, there's certainly a spark of enterprise just beneath the surface. This typically manifests in career choices, especially those where you can help other people achieve and self-actualize. In particular career counseling and job placement assistance suit you very well. The outgoing, networking aptitude in a birth number of 5 serves this goal perfectly. You can spy opportunity for someone else easily, and help direct them toward opening that door.

Moving from the office to the living room, you surround yourself mindfully and tastefully. There's certainly an order to this world, but also sensitivity to your friends and family in each décor choice. You want a harmonious home, and work every touch of ambiance accordingly.

What about the bedroom, you ask? You don't go to bed on the first date, and maybe not even the tenth. You take your time in choosing a mate, wanting it to be a responsible choice based on that person's authenticity. It takes time to figure out who's being real and who's a flim-flam artist. When someone is lucky enough to pass the test—Wow, talk about steamy!

Gift idea: a book on Feng Shui or a potted bamboo plant.

FACT

This Month in History: Congress authorized Yellowstone National Park's creation (March 3, 1872); Texas became independent of Mexico (March 2, 1836); Vermont became the 14th state in the Union (March 4, 1791); Alexander Graham Bell patented the telephone (March 7, 1876); Girl Scouts of America established (March 12, 1912); Planet Uranus discovered (March 13, 1781); Julius Caesar assassinated (March 15, 44 B.C.E.); Congress ratified Daylight Savings Time (March 19, 1918); U.S. Mint produced press-made coins (3/23) 1836; first long distance telephone call initiated (March 27, 1884).

March 30

If today is your birthday, you have an uncanny aptitude for development and facilitation. But you are never boring! If anything, just the opposite is true. You have strong social cravings and love being the life of the party. If you can design and execute that party it's really a big "whoo hoo!" since it marries both aspects of your personality into a successful whole. With this in mind, wedding or event planner definitely rank as good career options.

This date brings good fortune and an upbeat disposition on its heels. You prefer focusing on the bright side of life. That outlook finds support in the birth number of 6, which treasures beauty, optimism, and romance. You're likely to find this Aries enjoying hobbies like hiking on a sunny afternoon, grilling for friends and family, or strolling through art galleries.

That generally upbeat presence naturally attracts long-term friends and lovers. This Ram rarely walks alone, and honestly prefers not to. The company of others makes the path less long, and if that person turns into a mate, they'll discover a very tender partner, filled with passion.

Gift idea: a sun catcher or mirror ball for the garden.

March 31

Quick minded, fast acting, and very masculine describe you whether you are a man or a woman (please understand that "masculine" here refers to generally accepted archetype traits including leadership, logic, and fierceness). To balance this out, you have a highly creative and intuitive side, supported by the psychic birth number of 7, but it takes trust and time to see this aspect.

You're typically drawn to highly complex careers such as those in astrophysics, microbiology, and if you're feeling whimsical, string theory! You have a ravenous mind, and whatever you do in life needs to keep feeding that hunger regularly or you find your drive peters out. As you study or work, it's important to build professional relationships with various institutions that could support grant requests and future research.

Privately friends and family sometimes have difficulty understanding your intelligence, but they don't question your sincere enthusiasm. However, these same people may not always be so understanding about the time and effort our Ram's studies require. This translates into relationship difficulties—the sense of being overlooked or ignored emotionally for an intellectual possibility. Whomever you choose as a partner needs to have a life outside the relationship, preferably one similarly dedicated to research.

Gift idea: scientific equipment with a side order of gourmet food (brought to the lab, of course).

Pisces

Sign: Pisces
Date: February 20–March 20
Ruled by: Neptune
Element: Water
Lucky Color: Violet, blue
Gemstone: Aquamarine, amethyst
Keynote: Reverie
Positive Traits: Kindness, compassion, thoughtfulness, sensitivity, intuition
Negative Traits: Escapist, secretive, weak-willed, overly malleable
Famous Aries include: Elizabeth Barrett Browning, Chopin, Albert Einstein, Jennifer Love Hewitt, Michelangelo, Dr. Seuss, Sidney Poitier, Sir Elton John

Being ruled by Neptune and water, Pisceans are often typified as dreamers and idealists with the aptitude to change with the waves, on a moment's notice. Those changes can be emotional or mental, ranging from despair to joy, feeling powerless to taking charge, and lacking creativity to suddenly gushing with ideas.

In their natural surroundings Pisceans have a taste for beauty and refinement. History and modern times find a comfortable meeting ground here, like an old oak roll-top desk housing a computer. No matter what, Fish adore their homes, and if they can use water in that space they will—from fish tanks and blue colors to bathtubs suited to a mermaid.

Among friends Pisces has a very tender, giving heart. This sign empathizes with others, is psychically inclined, always has time to listen or help, and offers charity even if that means setting aside personal needs.

In relationships a Piscean has the ability to change to meet a variety of circumstances—both logical and intuitive (note there are two fish in this sign's imagery). This allows people born under this sign to fit in fairly easily no matter where life or love takes them. Nonetheless, the watery nature of Piscean emotions leads to insecurity. This naturally ends up expressing itself as introversion and shyness, or collecting as many friends as possible to prove one's worth. In the end, however, the Fish's capacity for love, seduction, and compassion eventually leads them to some type of long-term commitment.

Chapter 6
April

The Roman name was *Aprilis*, a word that means "opening." Depending on where you live, this can be the beginning of the planting or harvesting season, and also a favorite month to begin that annual bout of spring cleaning. April's flower is a daisy, and the birthstone is diamond. Astrologically this month begins with Aries the Ram, a strong and willful personality that drives the next 20 days forward with assurance. It ends with Taurus, who balances a little of the Ram's masculine overtones with feminine earthiness.

April 1

You are the crusader, advocate, and campaigner of the Zodiac. While you may not have school smarts, street smarts are more than abundant. Life has been your classroom, and you use every morsel of that knowledge to achieve goals.

The birth number of 5 indicates a person of strong beliefs who responds very potently to sensual input. If something can't be defined by sight, sound, touch, taste, or smell, it has no real place in your world. That means you are probably not spiritually oriented and might consider yourself agnostic. Every moment is already crammed full with a variety of projects, none of which require faith in anything but oneself, which the Leo decanate ensures in abundance.

You'd make a great leader in business, but typically not the arts. You prefer to put your hands into projects from which you can see the results relatively quickly. Teaching or accounting are two good options. Relationships also require structure. Someone who is messy, distracted, or lacking in ambition will not be a good mate for you; such people are probably relatively disastrous as friends as well, in that you want to direct their lives. You're much better off in the company of individuals who can keep up with a high energy output and lofty expectations.

Gift idea: gold or yellow items (especially of a practical nature) appeal to the solar Leo sneaking into this personality.

April 2

Fresh, youthful outlooks inspire you. There's a playfulness about you, curiosity about even little things, and an appreciation for life that's contagious. About the only thing you can't muddle through is disharmony. It's very important that you don't become entangled in other people's problems, especially with the birth number of 6 that demands kindness, peace, good will, and high ideals.

Your charming nature shines even more brightly thanks to the Leo decanate, but take care as this influence can also manifest in foot-in-mouth syndrome. The Leo in your chart is very talkative and loves showing off. The Aries is a little impetuous, so make sure to engage your brain and think through what you say. Double those efforts in the workplace; you might be drawn into positions that require a lot of verbal or written skills, including negotiation.

Your home is a whimsical environment complete with all manner of toys. And thanks to the birth number 6, everything has an ambiance of splendor that you enjoy sharing with friends. Speaking of which, you'd be hard pressed to find a more sincere companion. While not the best listener, you really care and want to make friends and family happy. About the only issue is a tendency to try too hard to please, something a good partner can easily overcome.

Gift idea: a long, leisurely drive through a naturally beautiful area (bring a picnic!).

April 3

You have several keynotes, including desire for social acceptance, personification of changeability, convincing bearing, and a somewhat surprisingly patient demeanor. On the social side, the Ram needs to be a little more reserved about jumping into situations and conversations. The Leo decanate whispers of center stage, but the Aries's more subtle energies can rein in that tendency nicely. As for changeability, this is actually a positive trait. It allows our Ram to roll with life's transitions more easily. And, of course, being tolerant and credible typically help in all aspects of life!

The birth number of 7 implies that this Aries does well in positions that provide mental or spiritual challenges. Not being overly interested in physical exertion, sports like football or track rarely enter the picture even as hobbies. On the other hand, anything that allows emotional expression, offers a hint of romance, or suggests voyeuristic excitement attracts you. Taking this into consideration, you do well in education, religion, social planning, or cultural photography.

In relationships, it's easy for you to fall in love, and not always with someone who can hold your attentions for the long haul. You should seek out someone with fire, creativity, and playfulness for the best match. Even then, sometimes you get overly caught up in your partners' desires, forego-ing your own in the interest of meeting even unrealistic fantasies.

Gift idea: *The Tao of Pooh.*

ALERT!

No one really knows for sure how April Fool's Day began. Some believe that it started in France when the New Year moved from late March to January 1. In France, the people who were slow to acknowledge the change were sent silly gifts. Alternatively there's a chance it heralds back to a Roman spring festival called Hilaria, during which laughter was considered healthy and lucky!

April 4

Individuals born today are the bards of the Aries cycle. You're a natural weaver of yarns (both true life and fiction), and have that magical presence that keeps people engaged. Like the troubadours of old, however, you aren't afraid of hard work (that's what it takes to refine your skills and become a remarkable talent). And the Leo decanate loves having lavish amounts of attention (thankfully this doesn't manifest as ego, but rather as genuine appreciation).

Having a birth number 8, today's Ram has a good work ethic, and takes personal responsibility seriously. To whatever this Aries applies those horns, be prepared for movement! In careers, this determination along with effort-less inventiveness frequently resonate with the performing arts. Alterna-tively you might engage in a position that allows you to make admirable things from the ground up (like architect).

Around the house, you show both caprice and practicality. For example, you might have a wonderfully sturdy coffee mug that portrays a favorite story character, and soft, comfortable bed linens purchased on sale from the Dis-ney store! Your entertaining takes on a similar flair. Food will be diversified and rich in flavors, while still being appropriate to each person's diet.

In love, you need a quirky, fun partner—someone who appreciates your zany ways and lighthearted outlook.

Gift idea: Bully Hill wine.

April 5

Hollywood, watch out! You are about to saunter in and show off your style with flair that marks you as a classic in the making. There is no role too difficult, no part too "out there," and no aspect of the business that's beneath you. In order to make it to the top, you must understand the industry from inside out—and that's exactly what you intend to do.

The birth number 9 stresses your insight. It may also, however, diminish your desire for a flashy career and turn you toward something you consider more dependable (like teaching drama or classical poetry, or writing the next great screenplay). With 9 in the picture, take care not to be all seriousness and no whimsy.

That desire for capriciousness extends into your love life too! You don't care for the company of static, tedious people—you might tolerate them in family, but not in friends or mates. Once the right person gets snagged on your horns, you'll hold on tight, always being honest and real (sometimes too much so).

Gift idea: an antique book or classic movie reel.

April 6

Ever the champion of the little guy, your naturally charitable heart and hands are always open to giving a little more, especially if the outcome envisioned by birth number 1 rings true. Don't take on lost causes or burdens that aren't yours to bear; otherwise, you'll have no energy left for situations or people with real potential.

A birth number 1 emphasizes two things: desire to be outstanding and striving for a better world. You're likely to dedicate your life to groups like Unicef or Doctors without Borders. You love being around others, and if you can be healing and helping during that time, your life will be complete.

Constantly on the go, you might not buy a house; instead, you might opt for a motor home out of practicality. The interior of that space tends to be cluttered, like the whirlwind of the last trip (or the next) hasn't completely settled yet. Even so, you know exactly where everything is—it's an organized mess!

Relationships are difficult unless your partner is involved in the same humanitarian efforts. Even when your partner joins you on the road, you struggle to balance time for each other against the needs of others. It will take serious commitment and awareness to make love last.

Gift idea: a chef for a day or a week of housekeeping.

Each culture celebrates birthdays differently. In Japan it's best to give a collection of ten items for good luck. If you cannot give ten, absolutely avoid any sets of four or nine, and don't use white gift wrap (it represents death). Also, the celebrant often gets a whole new set of clothes for the occasion. Muslims often use green gift wrapping to encourage good fortune. In the Far East eating rice on your birthday is similar to eating cake in the Western world. In China eating noodles assures the birthday celebrant long life. Russian tradition dictates that the celebrant receives a pie with good wishes baked into the crust.

April 7

Brassy, courageous, and forthright, no one would ever suspect that yours is the heart of a dreamer. The biggest difference between you and other dreamers is that your dreams are precognitive. You see the naturally unfolding patterns in life and various situations in which you find yourself and can follow them outward to their conclusion. In this process, life weaves a network of very interesting and unusual acquaintances into your life, many of whom prove valuable to future goals.

Thanks to the birth number of 2, you've never questioned that something wonderful would come of your life (especially with good friends to help). You'll watch destiny's hand pointing, dance that way to your own tune, and end up in the lap of happiness. That means that you might not find your career (let alone bliss) until midlife or later, but the waiting is well worth it!

You adore a good, stimulating conversation sprinkled with just enough levity to keep things from getting maudlin. In love, the beginnings of your relationships have a lot of heat and intensity. Once you feel secure, however, that fire cools into something that won't easily burn itself out.

Gift idea: a palm reading chart.

QUESTION?

When does Daylight Savings Time start?
Normally Daylight Savings Time begins on the first Sunday in April and lasts until the last Sunday in October (thus the saying, "spring ahead, fall back"). However, starting in 2007 DST will go from the second Sunday in March until the first Sunday in November, adding a full month. Note that some states choose not to recognize this clock-shifting.

April 8

You run the risk of spending a little too much time inside your own head. Emotionally, gray clouds seem to haunt an otherwise bright mental and physical life. Part of the reason is the zeal with which you approach each moment. Thanks to the solar influence of Leo (who doesn't like to lose), and the birth number of 3 offering a tripod of balance, sincerity, and regulation, you can learn to avoid those downward spirals and stay on an even path toward success.

Your home reflects cautious optimism. The colors are warm but not outrageous, with periodic bursts of bright, lively hues that speak of hope. There's a fire extinguisher in the kitchen, safety latches on the door, but also a stuffed animal in the bedroom! You like being alone, yet yearn for company.

Careerwise you fare best alone or in small business environments. The birth number 3 may influence those choices a bit with a focus on taking chaos and making order. Thus, being an independent time-management consultant or mediator would suit you well. In your love life you will seek out the "perfect" person to spend the rest of your life with. There's no chance of infidelity here; however, you can be too possessive. That's an expression of personal insecurity that can be overcome with a little TLC.

Gift idea: broad-spectrum light bulbs to offset the blues and a trip to a tanning salon.

April 9

You are a charismatic softie! Incredibly social and likable, you have a presence that enters the room ten minutes before you do. Rather than putting people off, however, that bearing acts like a magnet—especially for overly needy people. While your kindness is a charming attribute, you often get used. Your life lesson is learning how to say no. It won't be easy.

Your birth number of 4 indicates you love making people happy and fashioning a firm foundation. Thus, you often conceal personal pain with a joke or total withdrawal. The latter may be a better course of action—giving to yourself and letting yourself heal are very important to the world's caregivers. As a caregiver, you are likely to choose teacher, facilitator, motivator, or something similar as a career.

A relationship is the one place where you let down your hair. You want to be fed with lots and lots of touching, holding, and verbal affirmations. But you're not "needy" in the traditional sense. It's just that because you have given so much to so many, your partner represents the one safe haven for refilling your inner well.

Gift idea: a day of pampering at a spa or beauty salon.

April 10

You were born to be wild and enjoy a hint of danger in nearly every aspect of your life. You seem to have an excess of drive, magnetism, childlike optimism, and hospitality. This can drive you to take unnecessary risks just for that endorphin thrill ride. However, your birth number of 5 could keep you out of trouble if you learn to listen to that small voice within.

At work, your Sagittarius decanate gives you high aspirations and plenty of stubborn fortitude for seeing your goals through to completion. A good financial flow decreases some of your drive to achieve greatness (especially if you can be part of someone else's spotlight).

Love is the one area where you take no risks. There's no rushing friendship, sex is rarely "casual," and you never want to feel like you are out of control emotionally. That can make it hard for partners unless they have a pliant, somewhat submissive nature. Even so, once this individual trusts, they become romantic, and a lot more physically adventurous.

Gift idea: how about an evening together at a casino?

FACT

Diamonds (this month's birthstone) are very strong and durable, made of crystallized carbon. Most of those that exist today are at least one billion years old, and 80 percent of those cannot be used for jewelry making. It takes moving over 200 tons of rock to obtain one carat of usable diamond. The value of the diamond is ultimately determined by its size, color, clarity, and excellence of cut. And while white diamonds seem favored among consumers, colored diamonds are actually rarer and more valuable. Yellow is the most common, but blues and reds have been discovered.

April 11

Outwardly you seem brassy and bold. If there's a good cause or a difficult task, you're the first to volunteer to help, especially with a birth number of 6 exerting humanitarian overtones. You are very empathic, sometimes to the point of being overwhelmed.

You have strong morals and visions, and may even discover an aptitude for clairvoyance (through dreams or hunches). The key is learning to trust that voice within. It's rarely wrong, especially when it comes to healthy situations and people. Speaking of healthy, you also probably enjoy a healthy lifestyle—exercise, nutritional (but tasty) food, and lots of fresh air.

In relationships, some may consider you a bit of a tease. Even so, once you commit to a relationship you remain monogamous (at least for the duration). Finding potential mates isn't difficult—you have tons of charm and a great heart, and do well when coupled with other intuitive people.

Gift idea: a vegetarian cookbook or vegetable steamer.

April 12

You start lots of things but rarely finish them because you lose interest or something else catches your eye. Maturity will help with this, but it will never take away your sweet wit. You use comedy to your advantage in life. Trust in your birth number of 7 to help with this, giving you the instincts to time everything just right.

Your procrastination bug sometimes manifests as wanderlust both professionally and personally. You may go from job to job or country to country, following that elusive "something" for a season, then moving on again. While this would prove disastrous for others, it actually works for you because you find success and good fortune no matter where you end up!

Your good fortune doesn't end with business and travel. You are also quite lucky in love, always stumbling into the best situations at the best time (much to the envy of others!). This is the one area of life where you do not hesitate. You will, however, hold back certain parts of yourself and want a level of independence in any relationship.

Gift idea: a collectable coin, or frequent flyer miles.

April 13

You have a fidgety nature and don't like sitting still for too long. You live each day squeezing activity into each precious moment. A lot of your drive comes from the overly responsible birth number of 8, which demands diligence. The rest comes from your passion for reaching toward those elusive brass rings. This naturally attracts others to join your quests, and puts you at the forefront as a leader. Unfortunately, you'd rather walk alone, so be careful that the gruff Aries nature doesn't push away potentially very good friends and allies.

Around your home, you love clever, challenging items. Puzzles, mental computer games, and self-assemble furniture often dot the landscape in any manner deemed interesting.

In business, while you could lead, it's probably best if you don't. You tend to be a little too pushy and grumbly if things don't go exactly as you dictate. Nonetheless, you are a very good decision maker with astute insights, which could translate very effectively into a career in investment management (as one example).

You are a good lover, but not always a dedicated one. You have to work to slow down enough to get really close to anyone. If you find another person who keeps your pace (perhaps a strong-minded Leo), there could be some impressive sparks there!

Gift idea: a certificate for hang-gliding lessons.

ALERT!

Arians love fashion! The fresher, more exciting, and bolder the style the better. In fact, these people often create styles that catch on, or at least catch the attention of appreciative eyes. If this is your birth sign, it's likely that you tried clogs and denim jackets before anyone else, along with those bright, tie-dyed leggings. Don't be afraid to explore, accessorize, and express yourself!

April 14

You seem out of place no matter the era or setting, which isn't surprising with a visionary birth number of 9. You are determined to sink or swim with your personal visions and boundaries intact. While this lands you in a lot of hot water, you also have a knack for communicating concepts and sponsoring causes effectively, as long as they're cutting-edge and proactive.

Thankfully you have a cheerful outlook about all this awkwardness, and a great aptitude for speaking powerfully about things you believe in. Consider pursuing writing or public-speaking careers in those areas that match your ethics.

You love music (of many varieties) and decorate with a touch of judicious class. You like beautiful things, but only if they're practical too (no waste!). There's no question that your space reflects your freedom-loving personality, but there's room for others to relax and be themselves there too.

In relationships, your need for independence can cause problems. Seek out similarly independent lovers and the relationship can blossom.

Gift idea: a portable MP3 player.

April 15

The birth number 1 inspires you to be truly unique and creative—to do something amazing. Nonetheless, especially at a young age, you aren't so certain of your footing. Ever striving for harmony no matter the situation, moving to the forefront of the pack isn't high on your wish list.

You like to be with people, especially those who understand you. Take care, however. You may seek the approval of others a little too much. One way to balance out that tendency is by bringing people into your own space and dealing with them in your territory on your terms. It's likely that you enjoy entertaining.

In relationships, you tend to be a little immature and may not settle down until midlife. You like whimsy in love, but you're also strongly dependent. A Libra partner might balance this out nicely.

Gift idea: items that are suited for guests, like a nice china party platter.

April 16

If people didn't know better, they'd swear you're a Gemini with all that changeability. Your transitions from introspection to gregariousness, from logic to emotion, and from boldness to reserve confound people. But there are two very good reasons for this behavior. First is the birth number 2, which is totally adaptable and very aware of life's dichotomies. Second is the fact that your mind and spirit battle for supremacy. If you could get those two cooperating, what wonders would result! On the other hand, all that angst has tremendous potential for expressing itself in the arts, where you'd feel at home.

Others find you endearing (kind of like a wounded puppy that also happens to be very talented). You're generous with friends and companions (sometimes too much so—yours is a life of extremes).

Your giving nature, along with the typical Arian romanticism, certainly extends into love. You aren't interested in flash-in-the-pan relationships. A Piscean might be a good empathic partner.

Gift idea: a perpetual-motion paperweight.

In terms of travel, there's no question that Aries love adventure and risk-taking. They're always up for some action, and don't sit still well for anyone or anything. The Arian curiosity may manifest in globe trotting, seeing the world's wonders on your own schedule and in your own way. However, if that trip can be combined with some good cause, then this Ram becomes exuberantly happy. He becomes the white knight and experiences all of that life he so dearly craves.

April 17

No matter how many times the path to the top gets bumpy, or how many times you stumble, you pick yourself up, dust yourself off, and just keep going with a smile. The upbeat character of birth number 3 certainly helps maintain that sunny demeanor. Unfortunately it does nothing to help improve your lack of patience. Sometimes you run right into trouble, confounding friends and pleasing enemies. In a career environment it's best if you apply for positions where you can get observable results quickly.

At home your impatience manifests in a slight mess. Your house has a definite "lived in" look, yet there's also a sense of propriety. Even when the house isn't perfect, you are an excellent and thoughtful host, bending over backward to make sure everyone has what they need.

You're not quite so accommodating in love as in your living space. You probably enjoy the challenge of finding and wooing the right lover more than being in a long-term relationship. Truth be told, you're a bit of a flirt, and enjoy the attention that brings from a variety of people. Consequently, seek out creative, multifaceted individuals to share your life.

Gift idea: a closet organizer!

April 18

Ever a guardian to anyone in need, you have to be careful about volunteering too much time and attention to others (while neatly avoiding problems in your own backyard). You certainly have the physical aptitude to finish projects, but you can become overconfident and cocky because you feel invincible. In part, you're right! When you apply yourself, there's little that you can't overcome (thank the birth number 4 for part of that overwhelming drive).

Today's personology report reads a bit like a superhero's portfolio: You're strong, brave, bold, inventive, hard working, and always defending some good cause. The main problem you face is learning personal limits. The structured nature of your birth number 4 may help a little in establishing guidelines, but it also stresses hard work.

As for love, all that toughness completely disappears once you find a suitably challenging mate. In fact, you become downright schmaltzy (think hearts, flowers, and violins!). While you need someone who is an individual, you also love a romantic.

Gift idea: a weight-training set.

April 19

You might initially seem rather shallow. You love wealth and power, and want to position yourself in a space to enjoy both. Luckily you have enough personal allure to pull that off, along with a birth number of 5 that allows you to adapt to any situation. Thus, by midlife you have typically achieved some level of leadership and financial security.

There's no question you revel in beautiful things. The rare piece of art, a crystal bud vase, and designer furnishings dot your home. These things are not merely decorative; they represent everything you've worked for, and they're also an investment that provides the security you need. You also have a hunger for exhilaration and plenty of creative ideas to go with it!

Your sex life is every bit as sensational as every other part of your reality. In order to remain faithful, you need a partner with enough pizzazz to keep you from getting bored.

Gift idea: a sports car, of course!

April 20

After yesterday's flash and fanfare, today's personology report seems quite staid. It is the first day of Taurus, and you exhibit the typical loyalty and stubbornness of the Bull as well as the Ram's determination. That actually makes for a very fine blend, especially in careers where tenacity pays off.

You're Mr. or Ms. Sensibility—everything in and around your life speaks loudly of pragmatic thoughtfulness. You plan, ponder, and peruse things thoroughly before jumping into the fray (especially if it's a business deal). After that point you're wholly committed, and you'll be successful as long as there's a good plan in place.

In business, you remain steady and firm even in the most chaotic moments. In relationships you are quite the opposite—you want to play a little, love a lot, and toss caution to the wind with a trusted lover.

Gift idea: something that appeals to this person's organized nature, like a new address book.

QUESTION?

What does April's numerology predict about this month?
April is a month perfect for starting something new. With a month number of 2, there's plenty of cooperative energy and positive attitudes to support this effort—just remember to tie up any loose ends first so you begin on a fresh note. The order number of 4 only improves this forecast, providing accomplishment and the promise of rewards for honest personal effort.

April 21

Your nature is an interesting mix of loyalty, ethics, nervous energy, and an air of inscrutability. There are not a lot of people who know you well, and that's the way you like it. You'd much rather run with a small circle of honorable people than expose yourself to hordes, many of whom can't be trusted. Understanding this is vital in your career choices—you'll want to focus on jobs that reflect strong morals, and may even be drawn toward religious callings. A birth number 7 indicates that you may want to apply that loyalty in careers that require research or academics.

At home, you typically have a large, bright, and well-equipped kitchen. That hearth is truly the heart of your social life, from which you serve many meals with insightful conversation. Superficiality is a foreign word to you, which is another reason for keeping close to only a few key people.

You are faithful to a fault. Even when a relationship proves detrimental, you'll hang in there until the last vestige of hope expires. In healthy relationships, however, you're incredibly affectionate and sensual.

Gift idea: a chef's knife.

April 22

You're not the least bit dull, but you are sure and steady, calm and focused . . . and totally immovable when necessary! Your unruffled demeanor is a disguise; you're really a powerhouse waiting to be tapped. In psychological terms all that composure hides a very driven Type A personality, one that completes what they start (usually early and usually with a personal flair). The birth number 8 supports this quality, offering even greater persistence and responsibility.

Anything that's not here-and-now holds little interest for you. Your living space is likewise practical, and organized in such a way that you can find what you want, when you want it—quickly!

Even the spirit of love cannot ruffle you; you're not prone to showing feelings easily. It takes a while to crack the surface and see what's really inside. However, with diligence a good lover can discover a very compassionate and often surprisingly sensual mate.

Gift idea: a desktop Zen sand garden.

Your home is lovely and strongly reflects a passion for the arts (something stressed by the birth number 6, which appreciates beauty in all its forms). You may have even chosen a career in music, dance, or art. You're generous with friends and family alike, offering dinners fit for kings.

Partnering with you is an intense affair. You feel things very deeply, very early into a relationship. Once you're committed that eases a little, but you still love to pamper your mate with breakfast in bed and periodic surprises.

Gift idea: something kitschy.

ALERT!

The Month of April is Alcohol Awareness Month, National Autism Awareness Month, National Child Abuse Prevention Month, National Garden Month, Humor Month, Keep America Beautiful Month, Poetry Month, and National Welding Month.

April 30

You are a very popular and well-respected Taurus, heavily involved in your neighborhood or community. You're active on school boards, ecological cleanup campaigns, and volunteering at the local YMCA. This is also what you expect from the birth number 7.

Your giving nature can be a detriment sometimes. Remember that all those causes you love cannot get your time and attention if you're weary. Additionally, because you put yourself out there so much, you're exposed to a lot of tagalongs. Don't allow other people to take partial credit for your inspirations and efforts. You may not like confrontation, but this is one area in which you should not compromise.

You have a social, outgoing nature, but also periodically need a break from all that. Partners may not understand this and wrongfully interpret it as an internal relationship problem. Therefore, it's important to be very clear about your intentions in love, and seek out someone who isn't overly clingy.

Gift idea: a day planner.

Aries

Sign: Aries
Date: March 21–April 20
Ruled by: Mars
Element: Fire
Lucky Color: Red
Gemstone: Ruby, diamond
Keynote: Initiative
Positive Traits: Bravery, pioneer spirit, go-getter attitude
Negative Traits: Inflexibility, self-centeredness, possessiveness
Famous Aries include: Leonardo Da Vinci, Hugh Hefner, Harry Houdini, Loretta Lynn, Debby Reynolds, Diana Ross

Aries is among the most active signs of the zodiac. Winning is the name of the game, as is the quest for new adventures. The world is theirs for the taking. These people are never wallflowers—in fact, the more exciting something is, the better.

Arians love leading and offering creative ideas that will not only fix a problem, but improve upon what's already there. They're an endless source of ideas and inspiration in both business and the home.

While their idealism can sometimes seem daunting, it's more than offset by passion, a forgiving nature, and the ability to support those they love 150 percent. They don't hide the true self from lovers, friends, or life mates: What you see is what you get. However, the Ram will want partners who can keep up, and who will also provide the TLC that the Ram needs. All that outward confidence shields a very sensitive soul.

On the downside, the Ram is fast to act, often before thinking things through. Patience is not this sign's virtue thanks to that stubborn iron will combined with an unconventional outlook on everything. The Aries truly believes that spontaneous action can be its own reward.

No matter their age, Arians tend to wear the pants in the family. Children born under this sign show unnatural maturity, focus, and drive at an early age (mind you, that can make for quite a parental challenge!). As Arians mature, they become generous to those they care about, very playful, and focused on pleasurable people and pursuits, and whatever it takes to achieve success.

Chapter 7
May

According to tradition, May is named after the goddess of spring, Maia, who inspired the earth's reawakening. Her Latin name literally means growth. The first twenty days of May belong to the astrological sign Taurus. The Bull's keynotes include being somewhat aloof, artistic, and very "earthy." Characteristically, Taureans are not what you'd call morning people (they do much better work in the evening hours). The remainder of the month belongs to the sign of Gemini, the twins.

May 1

The old saying about walking on   bright side of life was probably penned with you in mind. Like a ty͟   Taurus, you have a strong sense of structure, but also a lot of creativi͟   he birth number of 6 helps by giving you reliable gut instincts and p͟   ͟n through which that creative spirit can manifest.

Structure manifests in you͟   he environment too. You like things in a specific place, and a house r͟   a timely schedule. Overall, this isn't really a negative unless your roor͟   ͟'s sloppy or a perpetual procrastinator!

In a committed relatior͟   you unwind a bit. You appreciate a partner you can relax with totally, ͟   ͟cially if that person is bright and quietly optimistic, with a kind-hearte͟   ͟emeanor. You far prefer slow-and-steady individuals to flashy ones an͟   ͟y.

Gift idea: a certificate ͟ a tanning salon.

May 2

You have a soft vo͟   good ideas, and an approachable demeanor, so people see you as a͟   ͟urer with whom they entrust their deepest secrets. If allowed to go tc͟   ͟, this can become problematic. Look to your birth number 7 to provide ͟ ͟u with an instinctive awareness of when you're coming close to overstepping a boundary.

Taurus has a good work ethic to begin with, and that certainly holds true for you, but dull, dead-end jobs really zap your spirit. If you have no choice but to work in that type of setting, your home will renew you. There, items that elevate the spirit and mind abound with sensuality and color.

In love, your counseling, empathic, and caregiving nature may overwhelm your partners. Rather than a 50/50 partnership, you end up trying to mother your mate (or maybe "smother" is a better word). That is very hard to control, but control is necessary for long-term commitments.

Gift idea: a decorative diary.

Externally you exude confidence, but internally you're like gelatin. You have a lingering sense that something isn't quite right, but you can't figure out where the problem lies—it's like an itch you can't scratch. Sometimes the resolution is finding another focus for that restless spirit, like meditation or yoga. Additionally, make sure your living environment resonates with a sense of calm order that puts you at ease. Otherwise you're likely to turn into a very tightly wound spring, waiting to go off.

Where others find themselves more exposed and self-conscious in relationships, you fall into a comfortable partnership, and happily so.

Gift idea: some sandalwood incense and a decorative burner.

May 6

Whether personal, domestic, or professional, you focus on people-to-people skills. You don't like discord among individuals or groups and will strive to become a bridge in those situations, in both word and deed. The birth number 2 accents this flawlessly, providing grace and empathy in even the most difficult of situations.

Professionally you're likely to be in caregiver positions where you can apply those people skills. Alternatively you might become a moderator or counselor. No matter the work environment, however, the home front is where you shine brightest. You love hosting parties or casual gatherings that focus on improving the group dynamic (typically through conversations or cleverly chosen games).

In your intimate relationships, you seek perfect love and trust, and as wonderful an ideal as that may be, people aren't perfect and never quite measure up. If you can adjust your expectations, you can settle into a wonderfully deep love that lasts.

Gift idea: a brass flower vase for the table, or gourmet goodies.

May 7

You're far dreamier than most Taureans. In some cases, daydreaming can be helpful, as it fuels your rich imagination. However, you have to be careful to keep one foot in reality or you'll find daily life rather disappointing compared to your visions. Having a Virgo decanate becomes a huge blessing here, as it provides a logical balance to your reverie.

You might have trouble in your career. At first a position seems exciting, but then the repetitive work starts to whittle away your enthusiasm. So, you look for something new, which also can't measure up unless it's a position in which you can use some creativity. Because of its upbeat demeanor, the birth number of 3 may help in providing some satisfaction and a little more longevity on the job.

As for love, there's no question you want to find your soul mate. Nothing less will do. Consequently, you should seek out other spiritually minded individuals who aren't afraid of that kind of intensity (perhaps those who have the Moon as a strong player in their charts).

Gift idea: a huge pad of drawing paper and set of colored pencils.

May 8

You put the "bull" into bull-headed. Once you commit to a goal, task, battle, or ideal, there's no turning back. On one hand, this tenacity is great for productivity. However, you need to learn which struggles can be won, and which really aren't any of your business. Your birth number of 4 prods you to dive into projects with both feet, but remember to pause first and make sure that pool has water in it! Trust your Virgo decanate when it whispers of caution.

Despite a rather gruff exterior, you have a very soft side. It's not something you share with just anyone. That part of your heart is kept for only close friends and mates, neatly hidden behind a wall of power, strength, and conviction that seems impenetrable. Thus, part of your life lesson is to be more adaptable, lighthearted, and tender without feeling vulnerable.

In love, you take things a little too seriously. You would do well to seek out someone more playful, who can help you loosen up and enjoy love fully.

Gift idea: workout tapes and sparkling water.

May 9

You have the mental fortitude to overcome the many traumas that life throws at you. You also have a touchy temper that's easily set off by any form of waste (be it time, energy, or resources). Thankfully having a Virgo decanate cools that hot head rather quickly, and your birth number 5 then jumps in, adapts, and turns the situation to your favor.

Typical of this birth sign, you are a hard worker with plentiful drive and follow-through. However, because of your desire for prompt, refined results it might be easier for you to work with a small group of highly trained individuals, or branch out into a private business. Examples of good career choices include architectural design, musical scoring, and microbiology.

With friends and family, you give generously of whatever you earn in life. You love to lavish surprises on others, and find it hard to refuse any request. You are also very protective of the people in your personal circle, even to the point of standing in harm's way.

Gift idea: a punching bag or martial arts classes.

ALERT!

May's birthstone is emerald, which also happens to be the traditional stone for celebrating a couple's 55th wedding anniversary. Folk tradition tells us that wearing emeralds improves clairvoyance, encourages good health, and improves love prospects. The stone originated in Egypt, but was often mistaken for peridot (and vice-versa). As a result, historians often have trouble unraveling exactly which stone was being written about in early texts.

May 10

You have an exaggerated focus on self-image and probably work out regularly. Unfortunately, you don't always know your own strength, which can prove damaging in relationships. This is where the gentle, compassionate nature of today's birth number 6 comes to the rescue.

Your body isn't the only thing that's strong; you also need to watch your words. Your Virgo decanate is very communicative and logical, but sometimes your words come across as too logical, too pointed, or too critical. Just as with your muscles, you need to think through the potential effects of what you want to say before blurting it out. Once you've honed that skill, you'll make an excellent teacher who can explain complex systems in simple and immediately applicable terms.

In relationships your physicality cannot help but come out. You want to be with someone equally beautiful. You also love to hold hands, touch, and cuddle.

Gift idea: a sheepskin rug.

May 11

You can multitask and organize amazingly well, and you make a natural leader. No matter how many things fall in your lap at the same time, with a flick of your wrist, a phone call or two, and a moment of planning it's all fixed. Having a Capricorn decanate stresses that fast-acting zeal, and adds a heaping helping of personal responsibility into the equation.

One would think you would be rooted in the real world, but that's not always true. Inside you have a spiritual or philosophical bent that's hungry and inquisitive. This develops out of natural curiosity toward the most ancient of mysteries, combined with the visionary birth number 7 that loves a good puzzle.

Relationships are about the only area of your life that moves more slowly. You want to savor friends and lovers like a fine wine. Once you find the right partnership, you nurture that relationship with a balance of playful social interaction and private TLC.

Gift idea: *The Mind of God* by Paul Davies.

May 12

At first glance, your life seems rather unremarkable. You hold a mid-level position at a local company, have a dependable routine, a nice home (that's not ostentatious), and a neighborly smile when passed on the street. Those

Taurus traits are partnered with a birth number 8, reflecting security, and a Capricorn decanate, which is highly dutiful. Overall, nothing terribly exciting or unique—but we're missing something! A very witty, engaging, and insightful person comes out once you get past the small-talk stage in interactions. In fact, you have a lot of very intelligent perspectives that take people by surprise.

You must take care to avoid getting mired in the ordinary. There's no reason to disparage a commonplace career—it serves the Taurean's craving for structure perfectly well, and in truth you like the simple, dependable nature of it. You're equally well liked by coworkers and respected by administrators.

As for a love life, your partners will always wonder if they know your whole heart. There's something always tucked away, a carefully guarded secret or weakness.

Gift idea: a few shares of the company stock.

QUESTION?

Why was hawthorn chosen as the May flower?
White flowers are often associated with the youthful goddess, who is pure and whimsical. They also dominated the landscape of Europe throughout the month of May (even being called the May tree by some rural people). Since the flowers were readily available, they were made into garlands for May Day festivities. However, none of those flowers was ever brought indoors—to do so was considered inviting bad luck.

May 13

You don't go out of your way to be the center of attention, it just happens. Sometimes this causes you to retreat, feeling overexposed. Be it around a campfire or with a pen, you have a bit of the bard inside—you thrive on in weaving stories. Combine that imagination with a quick wit, sound wisdom, and charm from a Capricorn decanate, and you'll find you can open doors and improve nearly any work environment.

Since friendships come easily, you may sometimes forget little maintenance matters. Your partners must create a routine of touchstones to gently remind you to be an active participant in a relationship, not simply a content bystander.

Gift idea: an inkwell.

May 14

A incurable bookworm and thinker, you sometimes get caught up in your own head. Try to remember to feel once in a while too. Not everything in life can be analyzed, nor should everything be dissected, especially people. You need to give friends and family the room to simply be.

In the workplace, you have the slow, determined pace common in Taureans. In terms of social interactions, you march to the unique beat of your own internal drummer. You might seem a little odd and totally distinctive, something that a birth number of 1 also emphasizes.

The same slow-paced attitude goes into relationships. There's no rushing you into love's arms. You want to really know a person before committing to more than a friendship (and even that isn't taken lightly). Your partners should remember to be patient. Once you trust, you are a very passionate lover.

Gift idea: a subscription for *Scientific American*.

May 15

One thing that may hold you back in life and love is possessiveness. The green-eyed monster is something that dwells predominantly within and regularly threatens to run roughshod over situations and people. Be aware that part of the solution to this shortcoming begins with recognizing personal insecurity and the role it plays in your reactions. Additionally, many individuals who share this birthday have control issues, especially when life pushes you out of a comfortable space. Trust in the cooperative, gentle nature of your birth number 2 for a little assistance in achieving that goal.

People who share this birthday have a strong tendency toward calculated careers like science or accounting. However, most of your life's important lessons have manifested through hands-on situations. Your hobbies may reflect that by veering toward clay, carving, and other highly tactile experiences. With that Capricorn decanate lending diligence, these arts can prove quite impressive.

The highly structured nature of Taurus becomes a downfall in love. You love routine, and forget sometimes that "same old, same old"—while comfortable to you—gets boring to lovers. Your partners should be ready to add a little spice to your life, but in very slow, steady measures.

Gift idea: an air-filtering system.

FACT

Famous people born in May include Catherine the Great of Russia (5/2), Golda Meir (5/3), Audrey Hepburn (5/4), Orson Welles (5/6), Robert Browning (5/7), Harry S. Truman (5/8), Candice Bergen (5/9), George Lucas (5/14), Debra Winger (5/16), Sir Arthur Conan Doyle (5/22), Drew Carey (5/23), and Ralph Waldo Emerson (5/25).

May 16

The Bull's need for caution seems to color today's entire personology report. Being impulsive isn't high on your list of aptitudes. Every choice, every move in your life is carefully metered to ensure security. Unfortunately that tendency can make success elusive. You may hold back at the wrong moment, when opportunity knocks and you have to answer quickly. Sometimes just trusting your gut works better. Take baby steps in that direction.

For recreation, you'd much rather enjoy simple pleasures like a board game, cards (no betting!), or a stroll in a well-known park. Not surprisingly, your career is also pretty staid. You're likely to be content working at a desk job. You value stability over money. On the other hand, having a birth number of 3 may provide just enough motivation for more notoriety and interaction (like lead customer-service representative for a bank).

Relationships can prove difficult. Personal lingering insecurity (not feeling good enough) typically fuels ambiguity with lovers. It takes a very steady, supportive, and determined partner to get past that barrier. Once they do, however, you are incredibly faithful.

Gift idea: a collection of daily affirmations.

May 17

Making a plan and sticking to it, you push ever forward with a specific framework in mind. Would that life were so simple! When that plan doesn't work out, all hell breaks loose emotionally. You might be unable to cope with anything unanticipated. The birth number of 4 only accents the desire for firm foundations—so there's not going to be a lot of assistance here except perhaps from the Capricorn decanate that understands the value of prompt action.

If you share this birthday, you have a strong stubborn streak. If there's an ideal in which you believe or a project that you want completed, there's no changing your mind. Some people find that uncompromising nature frustrating, but the majority of your acquaintances like your integrity. Others never have to second-guess your motivations, and that's actually something in which you take pride. Honor is an important part of your makeup.

As for love, it's not something this Bull gives away without good cause. Love is earned, trust is earned, and our Taurus sometimes tests friends and partners in unrealistic ways. Once that confident foundation is firmly in place, however, these individuals provide a lot of intimate support and reliability.

Gift idea: an embroidered handkerchief.

May 18

You have strong humanitarian overtones, and the typical Taurus traits—tenacity and loyalty—shine brightly in serving those goals. You might become a defense lawyer, join Doctors without Borders, or find a career that allows you to fund good causes. A birth number of 5 connects beautifully with these goals, offering strength, faith, adaptability, and quick reflexes to rise to any occasion.

Your hobbies typically reflect charitable goals. Rather than go to the game on Sunday, you'll volunteer at a soup kitchen. This is relaxing and personally fulfilling even though others don't seem to completely share your enthusiasm or understand it fully. Yours is a truly kind heart, sympathetic and fiercely courageous. There's no room in your life for bias, but be careful that others don't abuse your good will.

You have an insatiable hunger for romance. Right next to the idealistic image of how the world "could" be, you house an image of true love (that's sometimes a bit hard to live up to). You balance those images with even-handedness so long as your lovers show sensitivity and devotion.

Gift idea: a pocket watch.

QUESTION?

How did Mother's Day begin?

In the late 1800s a woman named Anna Jarvis organized a group of mothers to help direct people's attention to the poor living conditions in her neighborhood. This was called "mothers work day." Fifteen years after that first effort, Julia Howe (writer of the *Battle Hymn of the Republic*) organized a mother's peace rally. These two events laid the groundwork for Anna Jarvis's daughter to start the campaign for a national mother's day upon the death of Anna in 1905. It was 1908 when Mother's Day was first observed by presidential proclamation. It was nationally recognized by Congress in 1914.

May 19

You certainly don't lack for personality, and you typically become a leader at a very young age. You have an eye for detail, and with a birth number of 6 you want to fix anything that detracts from the overall ambiance of a situation or place. With the Capricorn decanate, there's no question that you have the fortitude to finish any project you begin.

You are very resourceful and full of original thoughts. This can naturally lead you into careers in the arts or invention, so you can bring those inner visions into reality and share them. In fact, people find your ideas fascinating to the point where ongoing discussions might detract from actually accomplishing your goals. You enjoy lively conversation, but you really do have those tasks to finish. One way to marry your vision to your gift of gab would be with a teaching career focused on the arts or design.

Intimacy in relationships is very important to you, but it helps a lot if your potential partners are good looking. People should not mistake this for shallowness. Rather, it's the pesky birth number 6 seeking always after the most beautiful and refined things in life, which you will cherish completely once you find them!

Gift idea: a glamour-shot photo session.

May 20

Being born on the Taurus/Gemini cusp makes for an interesting mix of flavors. You're very adaptable, inventive, well balanced, mature, and relatively composed. Additionally, you are likely to achieve success relatively early in life, being able to juggle a variety of responsibilities and yet never lose sight of home, family, and friends. In fact, maintaining that symmetry between your personal and professional lives has been among your life's most important goals.

Within your own environment, you collect a lot of stuff—most of it quite expensive and elegant, with a flair for the spectacular. Many of these items are not lifelong possessions; they'll change with personal experience and reinvention. You can rely on your gift for reinvention in a pinch. Adapt and transform is the path of the most extraordinary people.

Externally you seem very smooth and confident, but that's not always matched within. You have distant periods of self-examination and insecurity that any partner needs to anticipate and prepare for, understanding it's only going to be a short time before their sweet lover returns.

Gift idea: a family photo album.

May 21

You enjoy the creativity and communication skills of Gemini with the even-tempered nature of Taurus. You lose interest in things quickly if they're not ingenious (a Gemini trait), but also recognize that sometimes you have to dig in and finish what you've started. Otherwise, you never earn the appreciation you so crave from others. Your birth number 8 wields a strong, earthly influence.

Eight also affects your personal interactions. You offer fidelity, constancy, and responsibility at work, home, and play. However, you might be a bit of a control freak, and you have enough influence and articulation to get your way. Nonetheless, you would make a good administrator or business leader.

Love might have a hard time catching up to you, since you are perpetually in motion. A lover should appeal to the side that yearns for a little TLC, approval, gratitude, and family to get you to slow down and take notice.

Gift idea: collectible coins.

Those born under the sign of Taurus love hobbies that allow for some type of acquisition. For example, if an athlete you will want to compete for metals or statues that show that achievement. If a gardener, that patch of lawn is typically the envy of the flower club, winning every competition for splendor. If a chef, you're at every cook-off, getting consistently high marks for presentation. Other hobbies enjoyed by Taurus are those that focus on the beautiful things in life (often the arts).

If you want someone to help you plan a budget or guide investments, seek out a Taurus. They'll rarely take risks with personal funds, let alone those of friends or lovers, and always have an eye on what's best for long-term value.

May 22

You're the kind of person who doesn't take no for an answer, who opens locked doors, and who goes out and finds opportunity. Waiting isn't in your program, which some people misinterpret as impatience. But really, you thrive on fresh experiences and just don't want to miss anything! Nine is another number that contributes to your personality, specifically with its idealism and insight. Whatever you can imagine, you can make into reality!

You probably love books, and consume them voraciously. Or you might be a perpetual student of life. Your quick, outside-the-box mind is always hungry for more of the "real thing." Situations or people with even a hint of disingenuousness won't be tolerated. Sincerity is the key to keeping your interest.

That is certainly true in relationships too. You maintain a healthy optimism about your personal interactions, but if someone loses your trust, it creates a nearly irreparable gap (and you don't forget quickly!).

Gift idea: a book club membership.

May 23

Understand the past; build the future. This is a phrase you live by. You have an amazing grasp of patterns and cycles, and you're naturally curious. This creates a good foundation for those who'd like to pursue careers in forensics or as a private investigator.

Your birth number of 1 can be rather demanding. You want to present a unique picture to the world, and thanks to your proactive concepts, you get attention for doing just that. Whatever you do, have fun with it! Otherwise your infectious zeal wanes pretty quickly.

With friends and lovers alike, you love to talk (and you have great oratory skills). The only problem is when you try to talk before thinking things through—the words come out in a kind of mental shorthand that confounds all but the most intimate of companions.

Gift idea: a Japanese calligraphy set and language tapes.

May 24

Like many Geminis, you have a tendency toward going to opposite extremes. Your emotions swing, your focus shifts, and your energy goes spewing in all directions. Thankfully, you have a birth number of 2 offering some semblance of balance. Now instead of being the world's arbitrator, however, you must become your own moderator, and rein in those polar opposites. At some juncture, these two minds must find a way to agree and work together, otherwise life may prove to be a series of possible successes that turn into unfortunate failures.

In your home, the contrast becomes even more obvious. Toys might sit alongside a perfect piece of art, or dirty clothing atop a pristine tablecloth. It's all a bit confusing, but it can also be enthralling. You're an interesting conversationalist, but like to spin a clever web of incomplete information and half truths.

As one might expect, your relationships can be tumultuous. One day you manipulate, the next you romance, and the day after that—who knows? Your best partner might be a Libra who can bring symmetry and some stability into your life.

Gift idea: an old fashioned-brass scale.

Interesting historical events occurring in May: Empire State Building opened (May 1, 1931); *Good Housekeeping* magazine appeared on newsstands (May 2, 1885); Academy of Motion Pictures founded (May 4, 1934); Theory of Relativity presented by Einstein (May 11, 1916); regular airmail service began in the United States (May 15, 1918); Amelia Earhart began her solo Atlantic flight (May 20, 1932); first images from Hubble Telescope received from space (May 21, 1990); Brooklyn Bridge opened for traffic (May 24, 1883); *Star Wars* movie first released (May 25, 1978); Columbus began his third voyage to the New World (May 30, 1498).

May 25

Between shrewd psychological insights and a little bit of psychic aptitude, you can always spot a lie. Despite a defined perceptive ability, you struggle with ongoing self-doubt, and that nagging uncertainty repeatedly undermines your creativity and progress. Thank your lucky stars for a birth number of 3! That optimistic energy is exactly the cure for what ails you: it helps motivate success. Once you overcome your personal demons, you will make an excellent counselor, spiritually or psychologically.

You probably have always wanted a personal space—an artist's loft, or any room that was entirely yours to define. This is where you process data, internalize it, transform it, and eventually use it as you go back out into the world. Without that downtime, you feel lost and overwhelmed, and that also holds true in your relationships. Your partner needs to understand that space is a friend and ally to longevity.

Gift idea: a flowering indoor plant.

May 26

You probably feel like you've heard "make up your mind!" over and over. People simply cannot keep up with your two sides, but you expect them to! This isn't fair to friends or family, and it's something you have to remember. Your birth number of 4 here might help some, giving you guidance on what's realistic. No matter what, you're not a conformist by any definition of the term. This can make certain jobs difficult, especially those that require you to conform. Consider career paths in computer programming, drama, or the creative arts.

You are very creative and typically talented, but you need constant reassurance about that talent, until around the age of forty. Sometimes you seem needy, and that can turn people off. Your inventiveness eventually finds a suitable outlet that's also financially rewarding. Your hot-and-cold behavior is also a test of others' trustworthiness; suspicion guides all your interactions.

Your relationships are often bumpy. One Twin's insecure, and houses lots of jealousy, possessiveness, and an unforgiving nature for real or perceived disloyalty. But the other Twin is loving, intense, romantic, a good parent, and sexually creative. A partner can unlock your best aspects with patient reassurance.

Gift idea: a digital camera.

May 27

You accomplish so much in one day that you seem like two people. You're a powerhouse, especially when it comes to grasping new ideas and digesting information! Better still, you have the stamina to finish anything you start, something rather unique among Geminis.

The downside is you can become impatient with individuals or situations that can't keep up with you. Alternatively, you may have a hair-trigger temper that goes off unexpectedly. In both cases the emotions pass as quickly as they come, but make for very uncomfortable moments. Your birth number of 5 may help here with its upbeat outlook. You would do well to work in physically demanding jobs that hold your attention (this helps burn that excess energy).

Then again, you're one heck of a lover! You can go all day and all night, with all manner of flirting, romance, and charm. With this in mind, seek out someone with a similarly passionate demeanor and love of physicality.

Gift idea: a lava lamp.

FACT

In May the earth awakens fully, hence the full moons of this month are known by the more upbeat names of Corn Planting Moon, Full Flower Moon, Hare Moon, Milk Moon (milking cows), and Joy Moon. In French, the month is Mai, in Latin it's Maius, and in Old English the Latin designation remains. According to Greek mythology, Maia was fittingly the daughter of Faunus, who ruled over nature and fertility and provided humankind with natural signs and omens.

May 28

You have a quick wit, clever communication skills, and an outgoing demeanor that endear you to friends, family, and strangers equally. People seem to automatically trust you, even with very intimate information. You also have a very convincing personality that loves being lavished with attention, and periodically your influence overwhelms weaker personalities. Having a birth number of 5 might offset that bigger-than-life intensity with idealism and sensitivity.

Your living space is typically very individualized. Rather than be trendy, you want personal comfort and whimsy. You're probably looking for a partner who's likewise unique, who will make you the center of the universe. But like a typical Gemini, you also want a fair amount of independence, which can be very confusing to a mate who has just been tending to your every wish!

In business affairs, you have a little luck working for you. Tap into that by working the stock market. For hobbies, you enjoy games like Trivial Pursuit or charades.

Gift idea: a Red Skelton DVD.

May 29

There are so many things you'd love to give time and energy to, but there aren't enough hours in a day to accomplish it all. While expending all that energy, you struggle to finish everything you start. Tie up loose ends and narrow your focus to achieve success and get those accolades you so desperately want.

You're likely to bend over backward trying to please others—a noble effort, but not terribly healthy. You should figure yourself out, and stay true to yourself rather than being a social chameleon. To achieve this goal, the birth number of 7 steps up to the plate with highly accurate instincts.

The desire to please spills over into relationships too. You'll steal fire from the sun for your love, even if you get burned. Consequently you should find a partner who offers the same amount of effort, and who makes it clear that it's the person (not the presents) that make this relationship special.

Gift idea: a sunstone.

May 30

You are a truly liberated soul, with a ravenous curiosity and thirst for adventure. Your gypsy spirit cannot sit still for very long, and you are often traveling abroad seeking out the next great personal quest.

One of your life's lessons is to slow down just a little bit. Smell the roses, and watch out for those pesky thorns! Impulse has always been part of your nature, and thanks to a little luck it often works out for you. But it also can land you in hot water! Your birth number of 4 can be a great helper here, as it stabilizes that tendency and inspires you toward something with greater security and longevity. Now that doesn't mean for a minute that your career needs to be dull—you thrive on excitement. You really need that element in your life to be happy and successful.

In love, you're a bit like a honeybee, winging from flower to flower. You will stay a while, love sweetly, then move on to the next destination. A lot of this has to do with your transitory nature—you don't settle down in one spot long enough to grow roots. Potential lovers should be ready to pack!

Gift idea: a portable karaoke machine.

Fun and Funky May Holidays & Celebrations: May 1: Mother Goose Day; May 2: International Space Day; May 4: National Candied Orange Peel Day; May 5: Oyster Day; May 8: No Socks Day; May 10: Clean Up Your Room Day; May 11: Eat What You Want Day; May 12: Limerick Day; May 14: Dance Like a Chicken Day; May 15: Hug Your Cat Day; May 16: Love a Tree Day; May 18: No Dirty Dishes Day; May 20: Good Neighbor Day; May 30: Water a Flower Day.

May 31

You are like a Taurus in your rather stubborn, staid approach to life. Humor is often lost on you, and you appear to be wound very tightly, metering each moment and thought with a focus that's not at all typical of a Gemini. Unfortunately the birth number of 9 accents your inner contemplation.

You need to come to terms with your heart. Emotionally, some part of you has shut down, but it need not stay closed forever. Don't fear losing control so much that you miss out on the tremendous amount you have to give to the right people. Just be selective in your circle of friends. One or two good companions will feed your spirit significantly.

Also, don't let this reserved nature deter love. You can't approach relationships with the same carefully measured outlook as you do everyday life. People's emotions just don't work in a logical way! Let loose once in a while; find your inner romantic and let that person out to play.

Gift idea: some really mushy chick flicks!

Taurus

Sign: Taurus
Date: April 21–May 21
Ruled by: Venus
Element: Earth
Lucky Color: Pink, pale green
Gemstone: Emerald
Keynote: Determination
Positive Traits: Patience, tenacity, dependability, consistency, great work ethic
Negative Traits: Habitual, may procrastinate, dislikes change, does not forgive betrayal
Famous Taureans include: Carol Burnett, Cher, Salvador Dali, Sigmund Freud, Golda Meir, Tchaikovsky.

To use the word "earthy" when describing Taurus is almost unnecessary. These people are incredibly grounded and centered. Luck has very little to do with the Taurean success. Rather it's hard work and diligence that pay off in this sign's life. This dependability and sense of company loyalty inspire trust and respect from everyone around the Bull. Where coworkers may fail or grow weary, the Bull keeps on going.

In relationships Taureans have huge hearts with lots of love to spare. There's a naturally warm, peaceful quality about them and the way they interact with others. Consequently the Bull's home tends to be socially oriented.

Relationships, and preserving those relationships, are of utmost importance. Unfortunately this can lead to being a little overwhelming with attentions and input. If the Bull thinks a friend or loved one is off base and losing stability, they're going to rush in and try to take over. Nonetheless, the Taurean sense of humor and good-natured intentions typically win out.

The Bull can seem unforgiving (and rarely forgives, let alone forgets, betrayal). Yet Taureans tend to be sullen and stubborn about minor points in love, especially those things that require change. That earth element sometimes ties the Bull down, to the point of seeming to be lazy. In an odd dichotomy, even when insisting on sitting still, the Taurean can be dreaming of much more wild adventures. They may never go there, but the love of good things (music, fine art, gourmet food) may drive them into amazing places never anticipated.

Chapter 8

June

In Roman times, June was the fourth month and contained only 29 days. This changed in 46 B.C.E. with the reform of the calendar. This month is especially welcome in northern climates, with spring ending between June 20 and 22, making way for warm summer weather. The month opens with the restless, active sign of Gemini, and closes with Cancer. In the Far East, the snake governs June, a creature of wisdom, humor, and charisma that has particular good fortune with money. Numerologically June adds up to 8, implying abundance.

June 1

You love the spotlight, and are happiest when the stage around you is busy and filled with admirers. You have a very fidgety spirit, and aren't likely to wait around if things aren't moving at your preferred pace. The birth number 7 could prove a great asset in slowing things down, by providing reason and foresight.

As with most Geminis, you're smart, typically in a highly refined area of knowledge. You can also explain this information effectively, thanks in part to the Libra decanate that gives versatility in communication. The only problem is that sometimes you become so verbally pointed as to come across as antagonistic, which is really not the case.

For relationship building, you have a rather naïve and youthful approach to friendship and love. Actually it's rather charming, and attracts a fair amount of wishful thinkers. Unfortunately, getting too close also scares you, so any long term partners require a lot of emotional fortitude and sensitivity.

Gift idea: a book of trivia.

June 2

You are very socially oriented. There's very little in life that provides a greater rush than being at a party with lots of activity. And if there's excitement and juicy gossip, all the better! You love to get the scoop on people, places, and situations, the only problem being that you don't always get accurate information from reliable sources.

You're probably pretty easygoing. Some people misinterpret this as superficiality, but that's really not the case. Your Libra decanate means you simply don't have a lot of raw emotional buttons and prefer objectivity—especially when it comes to a career. Combine that with your aptitude for data mining and you could make a great investigative reporter (so long as you really dig deep for those facts). Trust your birth number of 8 to help you with that discovery process by providing balanced perspectives and firm foundations.

When it's time for love, while the idea of love sounds good, flirting is a lot more fun and less work. It's likely you won't enter into a serious relationship until your mid thirties, if that early. After that point, home becomes a much stronger focus, where you seek peace, passion, and pleasant company.

Gift idea: a PDA.

FACT

The June birthstone is the pearl. Pearls begin as a piece of dirt or sand inside an oyster. This gets covered by layers of nacre inside the shell-fish and slowly forms a pearl. Most pearls we have today aren't naturally occurring. Rather, they've been cultured by purposefully inserting a small item into the shellfish. Throughout the world people have valued pearls and felt they had a variety of attributes. The gift of a pearl symbolized a person's purity and bravery. Carrying a pearl inspires love, prosperity, and good fortune along with wisdom and the ability to balance your karmic wheel.

June 3

You don't slow down for much of anything, unless it's an opportunity to share your ideas on a subject that's close to your heart. When you give yourself to a cause or an ethical subject, everyone listens (and usually agrees!). Your birth number 9 emphasizes that empowered optimism, and also offers very astute insights that other people completely miss. It may also cause some dissatisfaction, in that the solutions you see aren't necessarily easily obtainable.

You can sell fire in hell and ice on Pluto. You're very persuasive, and consequently make an effective leader. Typically this leads to success in any career path. In particular, public speaking, politics, or advertising are the types of positions in which you thrive.

Being so busy and popular creates some tension in love, especially when you get completely absorbed in personal interests instead of couple-oriented pastimes. Whatever partner comes into your life can't be selfish, overly needy, or jealous. The social arena is very important to you, and it won't disappear after making an emotional commitment.

Gift idea: comfortable walking shoes.

June 4

You are as responsible and dependable as any Taurus! You're far more focused than your Gemini fellows, in part because you have a real goal in mind for the future, and in part thanks to the influence of Libra in your chart. Once you set a goal, nothing is going to stop you because of your discipline and conviction. Your birth number of 1 certainly drives that yearning to stand out from the crowd.

For work, you will do very well in fields like advertising, where your winning personality sells the product or service as much as the ad campaign does. Alternatively, look to the arts where inventiveness, an eye for detail, and that Libra decanate's passion for beauty can express themselves fully.

As for personal issues, there's no question you want the warmth and security of a family. You'll seek out clever, independent thinkers who strive for actualization as both friends and lovers.

Gift idea: a family portrait.

June 5

You enjoy thinking about all manner of things thoroughly—be it a decision, a design, or a premise, it's all worth pondering. But you have too much zest to sit still with those thoughts. Once you've had time to process, it's time for action! Take care, however. Some people see this as officious. Try to express your enthusiasm in a way that doesn't come across as demanding.

At work, you prefer something that exercises mental muscles, but just theory isn't enough. As with personal musing, you won't be content until you can manifest those concepts in reality, or at least make progress in that direction. One warning: your independent nature means you might either rush what can't be rushed, or set out alone even when you know you need help.

That hurried nature comes out in relationships too. You fall in love very quickly, and expect your feelings to be returned. The wisdom and balance of the birth number 2 may come to the rescue here, helping to pace interactions.

Gift idea: a framed image of "The Thinker."

or friends could join you in seeing the world and experiencing its wonder! Adventure shared is adventure truly enjoyed.

Gift idea: roadmaps and travel guides.

ALERT!

Historical events in June: Edward White is the first American to take a space walk (June 3, 1965); Robert F. Kennedy is shot and wounded (June 5, 1968); Nero dies in Rome (June 9, 68 c.e.); patent issued for first U.S. gas-powered car (June 11, 1895); Benjamin Franklin proves lightning is electricity (June 15, 1752); President Lincoln signs legislation abolishing slavery in the territories (June 19, 1862); United States institutes National Minimum Wage law (June 24, 1938); Labor Day becomes a federal holiday (June 28, 1894); U.S. interstate highway system created (June 29, 1956).

June 9

You need to be sure that what you think and what you say match. Sometimes your words get garbled, emotions blur your meaning, and the outcome tends to be confusion at best, a huge misunderstanding at the worst. You'd do well to consider taking some breathing or meditation classes that improve your ability to order your thoughts into a coherent structure before trying intricate communications.

You might be confusing, but you're never mistaken for lazy. You have tons of get-up-and-go and the ability to overcome great odds. During leisure hours, you can often be found at dance clubs, beach ball games, and enjoying other physical activities. A birth number of 6 ensures that your high energy level continues professionally, especially if directed toward humanitarian pursuits or the arts. (But you should avoid anything that requires a lot of talking! You are one of the few Geminis who stumble in verbal communications.)

This issue with talking could hinder relationships. It's best to seek out a very insightful, intuitive partner who needs no words, but rather trusts that what they see is what they get. In this situation, you become a gentle, vulnerable, and highly passionate lover.

Gift idea: a journal.

June 10

You have a courageous, self-assured demeanor that inspires others. Your birth number 7 implies a perfectionist's nature—you expect the best from friends, coworkers, and lovers alike, and thankfully you have the charisma to motivate them!

You are a very dexterous Gemini. This aptitude could be used in fields from professional typing to massage therapy. Privately, you enjoy interesting fabrics for furniture and clothing alike.

When it comes to friendship, you have a variety of tastes, but also an unfortunate knack for landing in the middle of a crisis. You're attracted to over-the-top personalities who need to learn from your refinement. Every new friend or acquaintance becomes a project, and that habit is something to guard against when it comes to love. Your life mates want acceptance, not an ongoing training course.

Gift idea: a huge, warm, fuzzy blanket.

According to old wives' tales, a calm June puts farmers in tune, and a June that's damp and warm, does farmers no harm! To the Romans, June is the most fortunate month in which to get married (being named after Juno, a goddess who blessed marriages). Also, no matter what the calendar says, some believe summer hasn't truly arrived until the elderflowers bloom.

June 11

You put the word "happy" into "happy homemaker." This doesn't necessarily mean your home is always pristine. Rather, you focus on creating a loving, hospitable atmosphere. Anyone who visits you immediately feels at ease, comfortable, and well fed in body and spirit. You encourage people to let down their hair and really relax. As a result, your home and your kitchen are famous for great gatherings! Be careful not to give so much to others that you forget to refill your inner well. Also, don't take the smallest of suggestions as a criticism. You're prone to sensitivity, and just because someone mentions a spice preference doesn't mean you've totally failed!

You can really get people to open up, and careers in counseling or psychology should prove successful. That aptitude receives some great support from a birth number of 8, which provides diligence.

All that thoughtfulness spills naturally over into your relationships. You're giving, loving, and considerate to lovers and friends. An ever faithful companion, you only have to be careful that your kindness isn't abused.

Gift idea: a gourmet kitchen utensil.

June 12

Your disposition is typically happy: you'd much rather focus on potentials than problems any day. Better still, using wit as a coping mechanism, you engage life with an enthusiasm that's infectious. You don't need to say a word to inspire others—your life speaks for you! About the only thing that may hold you back periodically is the dissatisfaction you feel because of the profound birth number of 9. To counter this, try being realistic rather than overly idealistic.

You would be good at motivating others or working for an aid organization. For example, you'd do well as a personal fitness trainer or as a fundraiser for a charity. However, you have little patience for woe-is-me types. In fact, you'd be likely to tell such individuals to get off their duffs and make a positive change!

As for relationships, you make a wonderful friend and lover. In friendships, you stay fun-loving and compassionate, and with life mates there's no end to passionate, playful embraces.

Gift idea: a vibrant flowering plant that can enjoy the window ledge and be seen every day.

June 13

You have a birth number of 1 that's unique, spirited, and innovative. What's most important to you is the vision in your heart, and it's usually one that's very forward-thinking. Having an Aquarius decanate also means that your perspectives are incredibly inventive.

You can often be found staring into the stars and wishing that galactic travel were feasible, or looking within yourself to discern the deeper mysteries of life. In either case, you are likely to go one step further and seek out careers that could potentially bring those wishes into reality. It doesn't matter if something seems hard—as long as it's got promise for building a better tomorrow, you're there!

Your relationships tend not to be very physical; you'd much rather find a mentally compatible partner who understands you and your goals—you can spend your nights together talking about those dreams.

Gift idea: a bronze seafarer's eyeglass.

ALERT!

Those born under the sign of the Twins prefer "no fuss, no muss" clothing. You're not looking to keep up with fashion trends, and don't worry terribly much about what other people think of your attire. Typically, you prefer casual—something comfortable and functional for the occasion. No tight, constraining items for these Twins (the men who have to wear ties hate them!). As a teen, your mother was probably constantly nagging about picking up your clothing. As an adult, the organizational method is still gravity centered. Clean clothes make it to the floor long before the closet, and from there they mix and match at will. All in all your style is quirky, but charming and always cozy.

June 14

What people see of you is exactly what they get, and that is exactly what you expect from others too. You don't care for insincerity or pretense. You want people to be honest and forthright, or not to waste your time. Woe to those who try to pull a fast one on you! They cannot expect to be forgiven quickly, if ever.

Your personal space is likely filled to overflowing with lovingly accumulated movies, books, and music. You will never give away a book, and are a bit of a clutter bug. While you're not completely antisocial, you do enjoy private time and the comfort of your nest, especially since your rich imagination can take you anywhere! If you wanted to, you could easily apply that creativity to script writing, storytelling, and other written or spoken arts successfully.

When it comes to relationships, you have an underlying shyness to overcome. You aren't certain you can trust anyone enough to enter into a long-term relationship, and part of your free spirit would really rather avoid that whole messy commitment thing. Whoever you choose as friends also cannot constrain you, otherwise you retreat back to your den alone. To overcome this tendency, you would do well to turn to the birth number of 2, which encourages partnerships and a more social outlook.

Gift idea: a movie-club membership and popcorn.

June 15

You know your mind, have very specific goals, and know how to achieve what you want. If someone or something gets in your way, your quick wit and astute people skills typically remove that obstacle easily. A birth number of 3 certainly agrees with you! All that happiness, strong communication skills, and inner drive help you accomplish a lot without upsetting anyone, which is just as well. You deplore confrontation and avoid clashes like the plague.

You learn new skills and comprehend even difficult subjects with relative ease. That allows you to seek out nearly any career path you wish, but the birth number 3 implies that the job is probably going to focus on written or spoken communication. Additionally, you don't want an overly physical job—you're not fond of dirt and seek out orderliness professionally and personally.

That comes into play in relationships too. If something seems emotionally untidy, you are likely to avoid it. A clear-cut friendship is fine, but loving one person forever isn't really in your game plan.

Gift idea: a good pen.

June 16

You mix principles with logic, a craving for prosperity with a charitable spirit, and a love for fashion with a gypsy's eye! Needless to say, this can confuse acquaintances, and even you sometimes get lost in the fast-changing tide. This is particularly dominant in your younger years; later in life you begin to get control of your variable nature. Let your birth number of 4 lend a hand in this, with its solid, earthy energies.

You have an open mind but a guarded heart. Intellectually it's easy to reach you, but appealing to your emotions is risky at best, a turn-off at worst. People should present concepts and proposals to you in a forthright, well-reasoned manner if they want to be taken seriously. Likewise, you are more attracted to structured, mental jobs that offer stability to your changeable personality.

Lovers will discover in you a flirtatious, confident demeanor covering up a very vulnerable interior. It takes time and effort to get through that outer shell. You have probably been burned a lot, and while true love would make a great salve, your belief in such relationships has to be rebuilt.

Gift idea: a briefcase.

QUESTION?

What type of things do Geminis do for fun?
Being an Air sign, they always enjoy being outdoors. Bike riding in particular soothes the Twin's hunger for change (the scenery around them keeps changing). Alternatively, they will fly model planes or go hang gliding with a friend. Two other good pastimes for people born this month are scrapbooking and journaling. This provides an all-important creative outlet. And, if they're not writing and gluing, reading a good book will certainly fit the bill! Interestingly enough, these kinds of activities are also the times when Geminis discover the solutions to various problems—it helps them to process information and ideas.

June 17

Conservative and career-minded, it seems like you would be naturally successful. One thing hinders you: uncertainty. You have trouble choosing just one life path. Even once you make that leap, you might find it difficult to work under someone else. You're a closet rebel, who wants nothing more than to break free and do something crazy (something a birth number of 5 would sincerely appreciate). Yet you hold back, fearing misunderstanding and negative reactions from others.

Doing something creative could provide a blessed balance point in your life. Take your seemingly crazy ideas and roll them around. Then, give them some of that control and structure for which you're well known. Examples: write jingles for commercials or an eerie score for a thriller, or reform and refresh a protocol that's gotten outdated.

In relationships you combine slow, old-fashioned approaches to courting with a very devoted and nearly idyllic view of marriage. Your underlying misgivings about getting hurt certainly curtail any temptation to rush to the altar, but once married you are a very devoted and faithful companion.

Gift idea: a sketchbook or modeling clay.

June 18

You've got a quirky way of looking at life, and find a lot of people and situations highly amusing. Just be careful about the games you play, with whom and where. As much fun as it is to sit back and watch the show, the results and repercussions could be anything but amusing. Trust your birth number 6 to help you know where to draw the line. This number's charitable nature will keep you from doing something that's too over-the-top.

Your birth number also implies that you love exquisiteness, especially in people. This isn't superficial, however. No matter how silly you seem, you have another side that's incredibly sensitive and moved by even the simplest kind gestures, mushy movies, and intense art.

In love, you run somewhat hot and cold. Your personal pursuits take priority over the effort of working for a long-lasting relationship. Also, there aren't a lot of folk who can handle always being the brunt of your pranks. You should seek out someone who has a similar eye for loveliness, and turn that toward building a truly "beautiful" love.

Gift idea: cufflinks or earrings with definitive style.

June 19

With Cancer exerting a little influence, you have a strong drive to nest and relax, but only if you can do it with true Gemini flair! Combine this with a birth number of 7, and it's possible that you could become too reclusive, especially when despondent. Take care, as that would be very unhealthy.

Outside the home you may enjoy things like yoga, meditation, or palmistry—you turn inward, hoping to find a tranquil sanctuary for your restless spirit. The visionary nature of 7 definitely plays a role in this focus, and motivates deep thinking. All that internalization doesn't hold you back in the least. You want to put all that thought into action, and this might naturally manifest as a career in comparative religion, sociology, or philosophy.

As for personal interaction, eventually you will want to settle down and share that tenderly created nest with someone of like mind and soul. It may not be a traditional marriage, but it definitely will be an adoring spiritual partnership filled with sensitive lovemaking and long, deep talks about what life is and what it could be.

Gift idea: a garden pagoda.

June 20

Continuing into the Cancer-Gemini cusp, you blend Cancer's affectionate nature with the Gemini imagination. You have tremendous potential as a creative, sincere lover so long as your partner is entirely aboveboard. You are devoted to integrity and originality, and want your friends, business associates, and mates to have honor and some sort of creative aptitude (this keeps you from losing interest).

Your birth number is 8, symbolizing accomplishment, success, and firm foundations. This energy typically gets applied to your career, and, when mixed with the Gemini love of a good mystery, you might end up being a forensic scientist, an investigator, or a researcher. Just don't give in to your irresistible attraction to juicy gossip instead of hard facts. Instead, dig through the gossip to find tidbits of truth!

For long-term relationships you seek out a mature, respectful person who appreciates home, family, and a good surprise from time to time. Your home environment will be warm, whimsical, and welcoming, just like the sex!

Gift idea: a massage for two.

June 21

Like most people born on the cusp, you have the benefit of mixing the traits from two signs. Your Gemini half can communicate (in fact, the phrase "gift of gab" comes to mind). Self-expression is something that energizes you completely. Make sure you can recognize when you're out of your element knowledgewise. It's okay to let someone else have the floor from time to time. Meanwhile, the Moon rules your Cancer aspect, making those discussions very emotive and changeable.

The talkative aspect of your personality could work to your benefit if you apply it artistically, like by becoming a newscaster or actor. Unfortunately, the birth number of 9 does nothing to prevent mood swings. Nonetheless, your uncanny insights often make all that chaos worth enduring.

You ideally want a personal space filled with sensual experiences. Bright and airy spaces scented with incense, textural furniture, and colorful art are common. Like a Gemini, you are a collector, often of antiques or oddities. And like a true Cancer, you prefer large kitchens and a wood-burning stove.

In relationships, you feel things very strongly. As a result you tend to avoid sappy partners who only feed your lunar changeability. Thus, you should find someone with a healthy portion of common sense.

Gift idea: a mood ring.

FACT

Solstice, the longest day of the year, arrives on June 21 or 22 annually in the Northern hemisphere. Many ancient societies celebrated this moment with a variety of rituals. In Egypt, for example, the Temple honoring Amen-Ra has one spot in which the Solstice light reaches the interior brightly. In China, observances were held in the Forbidden City, designed to encourage Yin (feminine) energy. No matter the region or culture, however, fire was always a central element to today's festivities. Some groups, the Celts for example, drove cattle through the smoke from ritual fires to ensure the animal's health. Others lit fires to honor the sun and encourage ongoing fertility in the land and its people.

June 22

You have a good sense of humor, but it's more of a defense mechanism than anything else. Behind the smile and silliness you are a little uncertain and insecure. When you laugh, you can move past that barrier and act with sensitivity and ingenuity.

Today's birth number is 1, indicating that you initiate a lot of projects, but may not complete them. If you get the ball rolling on something, it's likely to keep moving on its own. This is especially true in innovative careers requiring unique vision.

Your friends find you very devoted and caring. On the down side, you constantly pinch pennies, making you appear selfish. This is not the case. That frugal nature originates in the same insecurity as the nervous laughter, so it's not just being cheap. Besides, if a really rainy day happens, the true friend inside comes out, with pocketbook in hand.

As for love, this Crab has huge trust issues. They don't trust themselves, so it's hard to believe in anyone else. If this Cancer can find a partner who builds self-esteem, however, the relationship has a fighting chance.

Gift idea: a night at the comedy club.

June 23

If your birthday falls on this date, you have a strong future vision, and thanks to a negotiating birth number of 2 you also have the aptitude to communicate that vision effectively to others. You have a lot of upbeat energy and a beautiful mind that seeks after a philosophical framework for daily living. This shouldn't be mistaken as building castles in the air, however. Whatever ideals this Crab chooses will have firm foundations in word and deed.

With the moon as a constant companion, you're likely to be moody. It's just the nature of the beast. The key here is to learn what's really coming from you, and what's coming from external sources. Don't sweat the small stuff, and realize that other people's expectations can never rule your heart (there's too much of a closet hippie inside of you!). Also, it's fine to care; it's wonderful to have compassion. But, don't take on burdens that aren't yours to bear in this life.

Friendship doesn't come easily to you. You're very choosy about those you bring close to the heart, and you will likely only have one or two truly trusted friends in life. With lovers, the emotional swings can stress the relationship. You want to settle down, but you often can't figure out where the path of true love lies. If you can learn to allow the rational self to speak when it comes to partnering, you'll be much more successful and happy.

Gift idea: a picnic lunch at the beach.

FACT

June has been designated as the official month for aphasia, dairy, safe driving, the U.S. flag, fresh fruits and vegetables, roses, safety, and gay and lesbian pride. Some of the more interesting festivals during the month include: June 1: Dare Day; June 5: World Environment Day; June 8: Best Friend's Day; June 11: Hug Holiday; June 13: National Juggling Day; June 18: National Splurge Day; June 24: Take Your Dog to Work Day; June 26: National Forgiveness Day; June 30: Meteor Day.

June 24

You care a great deal about relationships. While there's a lot of professional drive in the background, ultimately anything that gets in the way of solidarity among family and friends quickly gets dropped on the priority list. One key reason for this is that family and friends protect you—they stand between the world and your vulnerable nature. Please know, however, that the people in your life want to offer this safety. Your fidelity and kindness have earned that type of reciprocity.

You have a very soft shell, meaning your feelings get hurt easily. That's the moon's influence again, but it's not all negative. This Crab understands other people's hurts and feelings of overexposure intimately. Consequently, you would make an excellent counselor. That type of work also helps direct your attention away from your personal problems for a while.

Your birth number of 3 offers relief with all its optimism and levity. This is just the medicine you need to keep from constantly retreating into your shell. Mind you, it won't help much with decision making, but hey one out of two isn't bad!

Commitment doesn't come easily to this Cancer. It takes very special people to earn your trust, and you have very high ideals for what constitutes a solid friend or lover. Creative individuals with tender, compassionate natures who also enjoy nurturing might fit the bill.

Gift idea: a long wool coat.

June's flower is the rose. Tradition tells us that the color of a rose bears meaning. A red rose, of course, means love. Cardinal red represents desire, while fire red symbolizes passion. Yellow is for friendship, and white is for peace and devotion. Pink roses communicate a refined demeanor, purple says, "I am charmed by you," orange speaks of pride, and blue is the hue of impossible tasks.

June 25

Today is the birth date for great thinkers. This Gemini scuttles along life's path seeking elusive insights and knowledge, especially those things that seem to plague the world and dim future prospects. Exactly how this quest manifests itself is unique to the individual, but it wouldn't be surprising to find him or her researching cures for cancer or seeking the Holy Grail. And with a birth number of 4 guiding action, it's likely these individuals experience fair success in their goals.

Those born today love living water (water that's moving). Be it a stream, lake, or ocean, you find yourself constantly drawn back to the waves to refill and think. That tendency is common among Cancers, but for you it's a very important pausing point where you can integrate all that's happened and sort out those very important concepts that could literally change the world. With this in mind, this Crab's home often has an elaborate bath/shower setup fit for a king or queen! The rest of the house is cozy, for sure, but that room must have special flair!

In love, remember that the fires of passion cannot burn out of control. Too much flash and fanfare, and relationships could suffer burnout. In this, you would do well to trust your evolved reasoning skills for balance.

Gift idea: a shower organizer.

June 26

Persistent and reliable, everyone knows that you're someone they can call on for assistance. Like all Crabs, you're a very social being anyway, but that logical approach to any situation is what really sets you apart from the crowd. If a situation needs to be reigned in—you're the Cancer for the job. If circumstances require a game plan, you've got that too! There's no question your birth number of 5 is a great ally here, providing quick reactions, a variety of skills, and the ability to hit the floor running.

In our Crab's crib, we're likely to find blue and purple highlights everywhere. Additionally, sea green plays into the equation (frequently in choice of clothing). When there are guests, they immediately feel nestled in warm security. Today's Cancer works very hard at creating that ambiance, so make sure to compliment them on it!

This Crab is a diligent worker, who knows how to regulate cash flows. By midlife, you have garnered a solid bank account and respect from peers. In particular, positions in construction, planning, or the financial industry seem most promising.

And what about romance? Today's Cancer is steady as the day is long with a partner who appreciates consistency and dedication. You demand loyalty, but you return that gift with tremendous amounts of attention and devotion.

Gift idea: a security camera.

June 27

Individuals who share this birthday tend to be rough-shelled Crabs. You have a somewhat gruff demeanor that hides a heart as big as a house. A birth number of 6 accentuates that loving nature with both strong ideals and humanitarian goals. In short, your crotchety bearing is only a ruse that neatly weeds out individuals who would otherwise abuse your Cancerian generosity.

In work and life, it's likely you put everyone else's needs before your own. You can truly feel the pain of the world, and are ready to carry that burden alone if need be. Take care, however. To really change things for the better, you must focus on one or two attainable goals. Don't scatter your energy in too many places, or nothing will get done!

On the path to success, money isn't a huge factor. While you want to make the monthly bills, your job must have a strong ethical foundation. It's not uncommon to find you in positions like registered nurse, teacher's aid, and holistics as a result. Caregiving is definitely something that supplies you with a lot of satisfaction.

That nurturing sense spills over into relationships too. You want only the best for those you love, and will do everything possible to manifest just that. Note, however, that this Crab won't "do the work" for someone else. Instead, your way of living inspires positive thought and action in others.

Gift idea: a desktop fountain.

June 28

The phrase "ambitious adventurer" comes to mind. You've got a more engaged, outgoing personality than many people born under this sign, meaning you'll never be a wallflower, no matter the situation. Sitting on life's sidelines just isn't your game. You love trying new things, seeing new places, and meeting new people. And in very un-Crablike manner, if feeding that hunger for experience means not having a permanent residence, that's fine by you!

People who share this birthday have a birth number of 7. This number tempers the potential wildness in today's personology forecast by offering a little more head-heart balance, and the periodic need for alone time. You will always find a way to mark your territory (even if that mark is just the "Do Not Disturb" sign on your hotel-room door). It's during your hermit crab stages that you can be most creative, which manifests itself in moving around the furniture, painting a room, or coming up with new recipes!

Being on the move so much makes it hard to maintain long-term relationships, but it can be done. Our Crab has lots of allure. You simply need someone who enjoys activity as much as you do. Perhaps a gregarious Leo will be the perfect match.

Gift idea: new luggage organizers.

QUESTION?

What famous people were born in June?
Marilyn Monroe (6/1), Angelina Jolie (6/4), Bill Moyers (6/5), The Dalai Lama (6/6), Frank Lloyd Wright (6/8), Cole Porter (6/9), Johnny Depp (6/9), Jacques Cousteau (6/11), Harriet Beecher Stowe (6/14), Donald Trump (6/14), Paula Abdul (6/19), Errol Flynn (6/20), George Orwell (6/25), Helen Keller (6/27), Bob Keeshan/Captain Kangaroo (6/27), Pat Morita (6/28), Lena Horne (6/30).

June 29

Ah, dear Cancer, sometimes a rock is just a rock. While there is certainly more to life than meets the eye, stop looking for specters around every corner, and problems where none exist. Trust the more sensible nature of your birth number 8 in sorting out those things that really require your time and attention, and release the rest.

People celebrating birthdays today are all about achievement. You want to leap into the fray, driven by the winds of purposefulness (or at least the prevailing breeze of the moment). The key here is for our Crab to really trust those gut instincts in knowing when to act, and when to hold back. When that voice gets ignored, all manner of problems erupt, derailing any future movement until the mess is cleaned up.

Around the house, you are pretty much the poster child for Miss Manners. You're finicky about how your space gets maintained, and probably know exactly which fork goes where in a formal table setting. There's no plastic on your furniture, however (thank goodness). Manners are one thing, comfort is another! As with most people born under this sign, having that sense of ease at home is a primary requirement. Additionally, you enjoy sharing this space so long as friends and partners alike do their fair share of maintenance (leave your shoes at the door, please!).

Gift idea: a welcome mat.

June 30

Home is where the heart is. (As much as practicable, life is tied up completely with that piece of property both inside and out.) Happy to create and implement ongoing household and landscaping projects, you are perfectly content to putter around the house. In fact, many individuals who share this birthday would be pleased to be the "happy homemaker" if finances allowed. With the perfectionist nature of a birth number 9, there's no question that the results will be the envy of neighbors, friends, and family alike.

In business, if you must be outside the home you would enjoy positions that somehow help others with living spaces. Becoming a design consultant is one option, or perhaps trying your hand as a landscape artist. Or, for something a little less technical, you might work at a bed-and-bath-type shop, offering a keen eye to customers! In any of these settings, this Cancer tends to take the lead, using strong organizational skills to make everything work together smoothly.

In relationships, you have a great deal to offer, wanting to shower your mates and friends with plentiful love and attention . . . a partner who joins you in home and garden projects—doubly so!

Gift idea: quality gardening tools.

Gemini

Sign: Gemini
Date: May 22–June 21
Ruled by: Mercury
Element: Air
Lucky Color: Yellow, gold
Gemstone: Agate, garnet
Keynote: Conversational
Positive Traits: Curious, young-at-heart, creative, multitalented, unique
Negative Traits: Gypsy spirit, lack of follow through, easily distracted, highly emotional
Famous Geminis include: Jefferson Davis, Sir Arthur Conan Doyle, Bob Dylan, Ian Fleming, Errol Flynn, Peggy Lee, Judy Garland

Geminis have a yearning for learning. This ever-inquisitive mind is always hungry for more, and then wants to share what it's gathered. This makes the sign of the Twins one that ca.n be highly private (when learning) or highly communicative (when sharing). Consequently, many people in the Gemini's life will see him or her as somewhat eccentric, a perception supported by the pleasure Geminis find in toys—all kinds of toys! Geminis are somewhat like magpies astrologically: they want to collect something! Once that hobby starts taking shape it's likely to drive them to distraction until something else engages the Twins' time.

Speaking of time, it's rarely wasted on organizing and neatness. There are way too many other things to do. As a result, Geminis tend to get into everything but complete nothing, having spread themselves too thin. And, like the weather, both the heart and mind of this sign can change in a heartbeat. This can making loving a Gemini, let alone keeping up with him or her, difficult.

Relationships are important to the Twins, so long as they don't completely hinder other pursuits. Gemini does well to seek out highly intelligent and interesting people who can feed the Air element within with lots of diverse topics of conversation. This aptitude will be among the keynotes to successful long-term interactions with Gemini, as even when they infuriate you with changeability, their warmth, humor, charm, and ability to see the world through a child's eyes are always engaging.

Chapter 9

July

On the Roman calendar, July was the fifth month. Romans called it Quintilis, which translates as "fifth." Later, Julius Caesar gave the month 31 days, and the Roman Senate renamed it Julius in his honor. Astrologically, Cancer predominates during the first 22 days of this month. Unlike what we think of when we hear the word "crab," this sign is anything but short-tempered. In fact, they're quite group oriented. Toward the end of July, Leo comes into the picture—a sign full of good fortune and intense personality.

July 1

The men and women in this Cancer's life discover you have a knack for balancing out gender-oriented frameworks within which many of us still live. Women suddenly find their power and leadership aptitudes leaping out when you inspire them, and men similarly unearth a more feminine side, with great results. These people are born leaders, something a birth number of 8 supports completely. Unfortunately, you have trouble balancing out your own life. As with so many born under this sign, the moon's influence causes fast tempers and hurts, often when neither is warranted. Eight could come to the rescue in this too, being a stabilizing force.

If you share this birthday, you're a very determined individual who sees challenge as something that pushes your limits in positive ways. Having a quick mind and aggressive personality means that you rarely wallow in indecision when there's something positive to accomplish. Some may interpret fast action as being too hasty, but you know all too well what happens when you delay—the spark goes out!

Do watch out for that temper! For all the influence water brings to Cancer's personology forecast, there's a lot of fire here simmering under the surface, and sometimes you're afraid of boiling over. Again, look to the earthy nature of your birth number 8 so you can ground unnecessary anger and use that residual energy more effectively elsewhere.

Today's Cancer values a relationship that has a reasonable balance of support and freedom. While family and home are important to you, that's only one part of a bigger picture that includes a career path, hobbies, and a social life. If partners are too needy or shy, they're not going to last in a relationship with this Crab.

Gift idea: an amethyst to inspire greater self-control.

July 2

If you were born on this day, you definitely have two sides to your shell. One side offers compassion and amusing insights on life, some of which are so accurate as to be unnerving. The other side is very temperamental, losing patience or being overly sensitive at the slightest change. With the birth number of 9 added into this forecast, you spend a lot of time trying to figure out exactly what flips that switch in a never-ending quest for self-improvement.

Today's Cancer must ultimately realize that life itself is a mixed bag. Both aspects of your personality have value if applied effectively. For example, if you feel overexposed, retreat and regroup, especially in the safe space of home. Be it an apartment, trailer, or house, this is one area where you've consistently achieved balance. Light a candle, put on your favorite music, and sip some tea while thinking about what button got pushed and why. On the other hand, if you're seeing or sensing something that others miss, share that wit and wisdom. It's welcome and enjoyed! In fact, those perspectives serve you very well in positions like quality control management.

For friends, you like smart, clever, and actualized individuals with whom to share time and hobbies. In love, you have a laissez-faire outlook, knowing that eventually the right relationship will come along. There's no need to push relationships too quickly. Let feelings ripen and you'll get a partner who's very loving and responsive.

Gift idea: a home-cooked meal.

July 3

You have a lovely balance between pragmatics and humor, emotion and mindfulness. Thank a Scorpio decanate for calming the moon's influence to a dull roar, along with the birth number of 1 that convinces you that you have a fate to fulfill. Scorpio's influence may additionally turn that sense of purpose toward highly compassionate goals. This could lead to very successful leadership positions in philanthropic companies, or groups that somehow support the little guy whose voice isn't heard otherwise.

At home, your things are stylish and tasteful, but also very functional. There's no question you love the finer things in life, but you aren't afraid of the hard work it takes to get them. Additionally, there's a huge distinction between something useful and things that just collect dust. If an object has no real-life application, the money will likely go elsewhere (with the minor exception of wall art, which is highly meaningful and visually intense).

If you share this birthday, friendship comes fairly easily to you. People enjoy your generous and engaging personality. Love is something you take seriously, and don't give lightly. You'll probably experiment with a variety of living situations before you settle into a long-term commitment. After that, however, your promise is golden forever!

Gift idea: a full-length terrycloth bathrobe in blue, green, or white.

July 4

As one might expect of someone born on Independence Day, these people have brave hearts and very autonomous spirits. You love a good challenge and enjoy the company of good people who are also not afraid to draw lines in the sand and fight for what's noble and honorable. As a birth number 2 suggests, working with a group only improves the results. Among like-minded, motivated folk, there's very little that could ever hold you back.

The influence of the number 2 shows in your career path as well. You want a social and idealistically supportive atmosphere at work, and you do expect a lot from coworkers. Our Crab has to be careful not to get too bossy, even if the motivation is a good one. Sometimes you get so excited that words come out before you consider the impact. That natural intensity is yet another area in which birth number 2 can be depended upon to offer greater insight and symmetry. In any case, people who share this birthday often do very well in positions like theatrical agent or promoter.

In relationships, you can be depended on to always support your friends fiercely, especially when you perceive inequity or cruelty. This does not lead to enabling, however. That's the juncture at which this Cancer believes in tough love. With mates, you require a certain level of autonomy—clingy companions need not apply.

Gift idea: a flag.

July 5

You seem over the moon—by that, I mean that you've somehow managed to conquer the moon's influence on emotions. Where so many other Crabs are very up-and-down, you're steady, mentally firm, and innately clever. In some respects people think you're even too logical. It's as if you've put a tidy box around your heart. There was certainly a time in your life when you needed that safety zone, but at some point you'll need to come back out of your shell in order to answer love's song. Don't miss that refrain when you hear it, because of past experience. Live here, now!

In both work and life, you're on a quest to make others feel protected. So don't be surprised if you find yourself working in home security, on a police force, or as a domestic violence advocate. At home this sanctuary theme continues, stressed even more so by the birth number 3 that thrives by making people happy. Our Crab may not outwardly show it, but nothing pleases more than compliments on a good meal, or praise for the furniture arrangement.

As to relationships, this Cancer doesn't really "need" people (per se). Because you are still somewhat closed off emotionally, it's hard to break that loner cycle, which has now become comfortable and secure. Consequently you're more likely to spend time with acquaintances with whom a little superficiality is expected and doesn't insult.

Gift idea: a car alarm.

ALERT!

Independence Day is celebrated on July 4th in the United States as the day that the Continental Congress ratified the Declaration of Independence. At that time there were only about 2.5 million people living in the colonies. The United States isn't the only country to celebrate this type of observance in July, however. The French have Bastille Day on July 14, Canada Day is July 1, and Peru's Independence Day is July 28, just to name a few.

July 6

Those born on July 6 create a tribe, clan, or family for themselves, no matter where life takes them. You're wholly "into" people, and feel that those connections are nigh onto sacred (and you guard them accordingly). Those you welcome into your virtual longhouse are individuals of exceptional quality who you want to keep close forever. And with a birth number of 4, it wouldn't be surprising if you accomplished just that. There's little question that you'll have an open door and a warm bed to greet you in nearly every corner of the world.

The one danger with an inclusive and somewhat obsessive personality is that sometimes relationships don't work out, or prove unhealthy. Normally the birth number of 4 sends up a pragmatic warning sign before things get that far, but when that's ignored be prepared for a bumpy ride. You don't like giving up or letting go, meaning you might endure negativity for far longer than necessary in order to get closure. This means that romance could prove far more difficult for today's Cancer than other types of relationships. You have no problem giving love, it's intimacy that's the real issue.

Professionally you do very well in positions that require a good eye for quality personnel, or those that require getting a diversified group working together. In particular, careers in human resources seem very apt (so long as the Crab carefully separates professional and personal interactions).

Gift idea: a photo album (or CD).

QUESTION?

According to numerology, what number is July?
By the modern system of numerology, July adds up to a 5, making it an adventurous month, filled with pleasant interactions and offering us the opportunity to build new relationships. By the Cabalistic system, July adds up to 2. This number adds sensitivity and good communications into the equation, encouraging motivation and peace.

July 7

The whole truth and nothing but the truth—that's your motto. You cannot tolerate hidden agendas, sneaky approaches, or falsehood in any way, shape, or form. It's a rare person who will get a second chance with you too, so it's best to make your position clear from the get-go.

Be aware that it's very difficult for people to live up to that all-or-nothing ideal; our society is one that seemingly accepts all those little white lies. Being completely honest doesn't usually "win friends and influence people," especially when a lot of people don't want to see or hear that truth. And with a birth number of 5 constantly pushing the envelope of what's "ordinary," this whole honesty gig could prove to be a lifelong struggle that even you don't completely understand. The good news? The people who stick with you in life and become good friends are there because they appreciate your candor, and never have to second-guess your motivations.

In the work-a-day world, there are many paths on which "know thyself" becomes the motto for success. You can fare very well in a variety of fields, ranging from religion or the arts to entrepreneurial pursuits, simply because you know your own limits and strengths, and focus on the latter for upward movement and motivation.

Gift idea: an Om symbol (perhaps artistically depicted for the Crab's home).

July 8

Willful as a seven-year-old in the midst of a temper tantrum, today's Crab is wholly indomitable. You're not afraid to misbehave to get what you want, when you want it. You've got a defined plan, a tremendous amount of tenacity, and enough roguish tendencies to be able to fly under the wire when need be. It's important, however, that you consider the potential consequences of your actions. Skirting the boundaries of social acceptability can prove dangerous. Trust your birth number of 6 to be a moralistic guide to knowing where that invisible line lies.

Perseverance isn't the only attribute today's Cancerians hold in common. You're typically outgoing, creative, and adaptable. When plan A fails, there are always plans B and C ready in the wings. Eventually, your ability to prepare and organize leads to success in your chosen field. In particular, consider investigative reporting, skip tracing, and other related fields where the ability to work in gray areas improves the results.

While superficially you might come across as a hardened character, just the opposite is true emotionally. A lot of the external bravado is just a smoke screen and coping mechanism. Under the surface you have a somewhat frail heart that leads to an exaggerated need for solitude. Partners who manage to get past that thick-skinned persona are pleasantly surprised to find a very committed companion underneath.

Gift idea: a favorite cologne or perfume.

July's birthstone is the ruby. According to superstition, if a ruby becomes dull or cracks, it forewarns the owner of trouble ahead. Many ancient people associated the ruby with the power of love because of its vivid red hue. In durability, this gem is second only to diamonds. The stone probably originated in India, although it was found in other regions as well. In Sanskrit, ruby bears the name *ratnaraj*, meaning King of Gemstones.

July 9

Where other Cancers flip-flop emotionally, you have physical highs and lows. Think of this as a biorhythm to which you need to pay close attention. When your energy's up, it's potent. Direct that strength to those things that really motivate you and make you happy. When you feel your energy waning, turn your attention to personal needs, in particular your health. This helps you avoid burnout during the more manic swings.

On a personal level, you are incredibly insightful, something that a birth number 7 accentuates geometrically. Your gut hunches are nearly as good as other people's facts, and can be trusted in a pinch. This could well be applied to positions like stock broker, where working with a combination of historical knowledge and instinct creates financial rewards. You are also very astute with people, which could lead to a career in psychology or related fields.

In relationships, it's absolutely vital that you trust the instincts that you so readily use professionally or for other people's benefit. You are easily hurt, very passionate and intense in love, and those nearly psychic flashes often keep you from unhealthy situations where you could lose yourself completely.

Gift idea: a holistic first-aid kit.

July 10

Dear Cancer, seriously consider coming out of your shell just a little more. Yes, you're shy, but there's really no need to be! Your devotion to family and friends and ability to see the optimistic view of any situation are naturally endearing. Being a little more open will make a lot more options available to you. It doesn't mean you have to take the limelight, just step out of the shadows! From there, you can moderate your exposure as the comfort zone dictates.

Around your personal space, you like things comfy. There's not a lot of flash here, as it's people, not things, that the home celebrates. Consequently, you'll find many family photos and pieces of memorabilia dotting each room instead of art or knickknacks.

For careers, you do well in quiet professions where you can extend or retract your personality. Examples include massage therapist or dental assistant. You rarely move into leadership roles, even though your talents and diligence are both well worthy of recognition. A birth number 8 implies that today's Cancer is additionally very responsible, and constantly places high demands on personal performance. This, in turn, can negatively reinforce your tendency to withdraw, due to fear of potential ridicule.

Your shyness also makes it hard to initiate relationships. But inside you are a very giving, sensual being just waiting for the right person to give yourself to wholly. You are the most considerate friend and you remember everything!

Gift idea: a family portrait.

July 11

You are like a child to which every new experience is a wonder. The freshly sprouted flower, the ringing of lighthearted bells, a playful wind—it's the simple beauties that bring a smile to your face. Additionally you've got all that vital energy with which to spread carefree joy. The only drawback is that the world isn't always kind, gentle, or understanding. Cruelty is something you simply don't understand and it crushes your spirit. You have to find a way to safeguard your heart from that kind of damage.

Careers may prove difficult unless you can find a position that requires a lot of imagination. The internal landscape of today's Crab is rich with idealistic imagery. That imaginary world is a great escape, but it can also become a trap. It's so much easier to live in that space rather than the real world. The birth number 9 could encourage that tendency to retreat, especially when it seems like the dream is completely unobtainable. To counter that, positions that may provide an effective outlet include cartoonist, fiction author, and toy designer.

In love, you want to be the knight in shining armor or the damsel in distress. That fairy-tale ideal permeates interactions with friends, family, and potential life mates. In some ways that's charming, at least until the portrait doesn't hold up in day-to-day life. Any partner must understand this impractical romanticism and try to bring firmer foundations to the relationship for it to last.

Gift idea: a computerized art program (painting or drawing).

July 12

Luck seems to walk at your side like a constant companion. You've grown used to the essence of synchronicity in your daily reality, but never undervalue it. Many fortunate circumstances have actually come about as the result of your awareness and keen attention to detail. If you get lazy or sloppy, you'll lose that all-important edge. So don't rest too long on your laurels before getting back to the business at hand.

With a Pisces decanate playing its hand, you are bound to be creative, intuitive, and a good listener, but just as moody as is typical of this sign. A birth number of 1 additionally puts forth a dynamic character and stubborn independence, making for a very interesting and captivating package. While people sometimes find keeping up with this Crab's emotions frustrating, they also can't seem to disengage. All in all, this could be the ideal mix for directors, thespians, and actors.

In love, you become relatively mischievous, and enjoy a partner who can tell a sexy story or playact a fantasy. This role-playing offsets a craving for diversity, but it may in itself not be enough to dampen our Crab's hunger. So partners, don't depend on fidelity—or if you receive fidelity, be aware that the relationship may not be "happily ever after."

Gift idea: chocolate-covered strawberries and a lottery ticket.

ALERT!

Generally speaking, people who have Cancer the Crab as a birth sign love romance, their home, children, nature (especially water), and socializing. Like Taurus, they enjoy good food, some travel, and thoughtfulness (especially from family and friends). Conversely, Cancers do not like being bossed around, delays, unsolicited advice, an unsettled working environment, or individuals who rearrange or mess up their personal space.

Being ruled by water makes Cancer a very emotional sign that can wax and wane with the tides or the lunar sphere. That means these people can be incredibly perceptive one moment, and overly sensitive the next. Likewise, protectiveness can turn into being clingy, and their imaginations can run wild. That means the best partners for the Crab would be Pisces or Scorpio, both of whom understand intense emotions.

July 13

When people think of you, a slightly geeky image comes to mind. You've always been the slightly awkward kid with book smarts instead of street smarts. Growing up was sometimes lonely because your mind was ahead of your body (in many instances teachers became better friends than peers). Out in the "real" world it wasn't much easier. At least you never had to talk to your books! The good news was just around the corner, however—adulthood. This was the time when you came into your own professionally and personally, and all those bits of collected knowledge finally came in handy.

At work, life's lessons have created a tough but fair associate. Everyone around you knows you're fully capable, and they're very respectful of, and motivated by, that aptitude. Combine that with our Cancer's no-nonsense, down-to-earth communication skills (inspired by a birth number of 2) and you've got a person who's ideally suited to group leadership positions, negotiating, or instruction.

As a friend, you really understand what it's like to be on the outside looking in. As a result, you often surround yourself with brilliantly awkward individuals who haven't completely turned into butterflies yet. In truth, this is very nourishing for everyone involved. Love is a slightly trickier affair, in that there's still some lingering teenage angst that plays in the background of our Cancer's mind. It takes some TLC from a mentally and spiritually stimulating individual to overcome that barrier.

Gift idea: a solid wood bookshelf.

July 14

Today's Cancerian is very mysterious and indefinable. You're in a class of your own! You're very social and liked by nearly everyone you meet, something the charming nature of your birth number 3 certainly assists in. At the same time there's always a distance maintained, carefully and dutifully. You've got no intention of being tied up in other people's dramas or issues, or losing your sense of autonomy. This detachment can result in rather superficial friendships, which is something you may wish to change. Fair-weather friends aren't going to help much when it comes to crunch time.

You are relatively successful in your career path. Having a lot of social aptitude doesn't hurt. Blustery group dynamics never get under this Crab's shell. Additionally, you show a propensity for highly innovative communication skills, an upbeat demeanor, and astute business sense, all of which the birth number of 3 advocates. Put this all together and it creates a great foundation for instructional positions, politics, receptionist, and other jobs that require strong people skills.

Love can cause some internal conflicts for you. You value independence, but like all people born under this sign you have a deep desire for home and family. True romance may not bloom until you reach the age of forty, by which time the staunch liberal is ready to settle in and commit.

Gift idea: a bottle of rich, red wine or a basket of organic grape juices.

What famous people were born in July?
Princess Diana (7/1), Ann Landers (7/4), P. T. Barnum (7/5), Nelson Rockefeller (7/8), Yul Brynner (7/11), Julius Caesar (7/12), Henry David Thoreau (7/12), Patrick Stewart (7/13), Harrison Ford, (7/13), Rembrandt (7/15), Ginger Rogers (7/16), John Glenn (7/18), Diana Rigg (7/20), Ernest Hemingway (7/21), Robin Williams (7/21), Oscar De La Renta (7/22), Amelia Earhart (7/24), Alexandre Dumas (7/27), Peggy Fleming (7/27), Beatrix Potter (7/28), Peter Jennings (7/29), Henry Ford (7/30), Arnold Schwarzenegger (7/30), J.K. Rowling (7/31).

July 15

You're in love with love, and the spirit of that emotion colors every aspect of your life. It's very likely that you enjoy chick flicks, old romance novels (the gushier the better), taking long hand-in-hand walks, and sipping drinks by the ocean at sunset (complete with violin music in the background!). Your home is likewise quixotic, with touches of deep red, Victorian art, and furniture that screams: "snuggle here!"

Easygoing and very sweet with friends, today's Cancer is also a good spectator, in that they're very aware of the environment and people that surround them. This ability partners with the diligent nature of the birth number 4 to make careers in technology or the sciences something to which you could easily apply yourself. Additionally, these fields give you a much-needed break from feeling so much, so deeply, by engaging the logic centers of the mind.

Long-term relationships might prove disappointing, in that maintaining a heated, intense level of passion is nearly impossible. If our Cancer can remove the rose-colored glasses and recognize love and relationships as a process with ups, downs, and lulls, they'll make wonderful partners.

Gift idea: something utterly romantic (like a candlelit dinner with rose petals everywhere).

July 16

Those born today will always celebrate with a huge bash. You're the veritable party animal of Cancers, absolutely feeding off the energy of a crowd. The problem is that there's a strong tendency here to take things too far. You border on having fanatical traits that lead to compulsive behavior including gambling, drinking, or potentially joining a cult. Having a birth number of 5 isn't much help here in that it craves ongoing, fresh experiences. On the other hand, the restless nature of 5 may keep you from getting in too deeply so you can keep moving. Just be careful and watch for warning signs.

On the home front, today's Cancer has everything necessary to entertain. The bar, a karaoke machine, and party games take a place of honor alongside the kitchen. When there's a party here, it's over the top! And the stories afterward are likewise bigger than life. That tendency to exaggerate (tell fish stories) is one thing you need to work on so people don't perceive artistic license as fibbing.

Spiritually speaking, this Crab looks the world over for a soul mate. If you find someone who seems to fit the bill, there's a tendency to collapse into that relationship until it becomes unbalanced. What's more, while you love the idea of happily ever after, you also have a wandering eye that makes that scenario difficult.

Gift idea: silver cocktail stirrers and glass charms.

July 17

People celebrating their birthday today have a Taurus-like determination and fortitude. Your life plans focus on home, family, lifelong friends, and a successful career. For a water sign, you're very earthy, and everyone respects your pragmatic nature when it comes to finances or problem solving.

While at first this sounds rather dull, there's another side to this Crab. You love a good mystery! If there's a secret to unravel, you can bet today's Cancer will be there with a monocle, a notebook, and a list of clues on which to follow up. In fact, it wouldn't be surprising to see this person in an associated field like political reporting, or police investigation. About the only thing that may deter such goals is if the position holds danger. You wouldn't want to put family or self in harm's way.

July 17 works out to a 6 numerologically. This brings the energy of idealism, realness, and a passion for beauty into our Crab's personality, frequently manifesting in relationships. Friends feel confident of this person's honesty, and mates enjoy being adored for inner splendor rather than superficial qualities. However, be aware that sometimes our Cancer is fragile and may get cynical or clingy as a result. Just bear with it—this is a normal mood swing for this birth sign.

Gift idea: a handheld tape recorder (dictaphone).

July 18

Seize the day! That's your motto. You hit the floor running from the womb, and haven't slowed down much since. In everything you do, you give of yourself fully; in fact, probably a little too much so. People have gotten so used to your outstanding energy and performance that they neglect to say thanks—or worse, just expect that you'll handle everything yourself. Don't do it! You're only cheating yourself. Instead, pat yourself on the back and learn how to say no once in a while. Your birth number of 7 could be a good helpmate here. Let it balance out that overactive responsibility gene with some self-love and TLC.

Another issue in today's personology report is self-actualization. You are so busy with tasks that you're always "doing" and rarely "being." While this makes you highly successful at work, on a personal level there's no real sense of self, especially in the first half of life. This, of course, can hinder intimate relationships, because partners can't get to know you on a deep level (even though you are an amazing lover!) You need to take time out and discover who the real Cancer inside is! The counsel here is to appeal to the romantic nature of this individual as a way of getting them to open up and explore not simply Self, but the sacred We.

Gift idea: a long, gentle massage.

July 19

Mirror, mirror on the wall, I'm the sexiest Crab of all! Sound immodest? Not at all. You've worked very hard to create an attractive physical appearance, sometimes in unhealthy ways. Crash diets just to handle those two pounds of water weight is a tad extreme. Nonetheless, you've achieved your goal externally, now it's time to turn your attention inward; otherwise people will judge you as being shallow. What they don't know is that you maintain high expectations for yourself in all levels of life, thanks in part to number 8 exerting its comprehensive, goal-oriented nature.

At home, the high focus on body sculpting typically manifests in having a gym or workout space with good-quality equipment. Oh, and don't forget an entertainment center. Just walking on a treadmill is mind numbing!

Socially, you trust your hunches, often jumping into situations or projects without getting enough information. The same holds true with relationships, sometimes with disastrous results. Lovers see you as intimidatingly beautiful or handsome and nearly worship that image rather than seeing beyond the surface. You may fare best with a sensitive and insightful lover, such as a Pisces.

Gift idea: a basket of classic toiletries.

Cancers value comfort. The old pair of jeans that fit just right, the soft fuzzy sweater and slippers during the winter, and nearly anything else that's pet-able fills the Crab's closet. For women, it doesn't matter from what era the clothing comes, but the lines are usually soft (periodically bordering on what some consider frilly, especially for the bedroom). For men, a well-loved flannel shirt, with shorts, sunglasses, and practical sandals or loafers appeal far more than a suit. But if a suit must be chosen, you'd rather a tux! Beyond this, Cancers love adornment—especially items with green or blue stones, which are lucky colors.

July 20

You are naturally insightful, but you brush off those gut feelings as nothing special, then wonder why a relationship or situation goes awry. Once you really listen to that voice, you'll discover that a lot of problems and insecurities begin fading.

People love your caring nature and empathic aptitude, two things stressed by the birth number 9 and having a Pisces decanate. You have a natural tact, hate conflict, and just generally like to make people feel good. Nonetheless, the visionary nature of 9 leaves you feeling as if the weight of the world lies on your shoulders, and you want to save every last stray you come across. The problem is that you haven't fully figured out how to save yourself, let alone anyone else. Step back, fix your own back yard, then reach out to the rest of the world in careers like counseling or nursing. Alternatively, just make folks happy with party planning or hosting.

In relationships this Crab is a natural nurturer. Anyone who enjoys a relationship with you finds themselves wrapped in warmth and understanding, imagination and romance.

Gift idea: a kitten.

July 21

Quirky and adaptable sums up today's personology report rather succinctly, which a birth number of 1 finds marvelously perfect. You are a mover and shaker, and someone who leaves nothing in the hands of fate. You make your own destiny, and boy have you got a story to tell.

Like a chameleon, you move into situations or jobs, change your stripes, and make it work with uniqueness and flair! Being highly flexible, bold, and enthusiastic, there are few careers that won't suit this Crab. However, since you often struggle between emotion and logic, a steady position that encourages balance would be a good choice. Nonetheless, the birth number 1 implies today's Cancer is likely to do something more daring, like being a safari guide!

Love is an interesting matter for you. Your youthful outlook borders on being emotionally undeveloped for long-term serious relationships. However, that young energy and curiosity prove incredibly fun in bed.

Gift idea: rainbow-colored scarves or tie.

FACT

July's flower is the water lily. Writings from the Egyptians indicate that water lilies were an important element in folk remedies. This flower also took part in mourning rites and vision quests. Throughout the region, lilies symbolized the sun (Ra) and rebirth, and eventually became the flower representing Upper Egypt. William Culpeper (1653) consigned this flower to the rule of the moon, and in the language of flowers it symbolizes someone pure of heart.

July 22

People celebrating birthdays today are incredibly artistic and wish to immortalize a little of themselves for prosperity through some medium. The problem is which kind of art, and what aspect of self? For this Crab is a little shy, yet still ambitious. Your art is one way to open up in a safer forum. You struggle with framing concepts, but once that barrier is breached—what wonders come into being!

Having a birth number of 2 means that you enjoy working with others. In fact, having partnerships or small artistic groups might be the perfect way to find some structure for the ideas that whirl around your mind. Additionally, you really want to make it financially so you can buy all those lovely things your eyes feast upon. Use the Leo voice (reaching over from the cusp) to exert your charm and manifest that goal!

Relationships are a bit whimsical for you. You want both space and intimacy, and you love to flirt. This could lead to an unconventional situation to keep variety available.

Gift idea: a certificate for an art supply center or a trip to a gallery.

July 23

Happy birthday Leo! Wow, does this sign start off with a bang. Today's Lion is one hot pussycat—suave, smart, energetic, and highly successful at nearly everything they touch. A birth number of 3 adds even more spectacular energy to this with an upbeat demeanor and overall sense of happiness that nearly oozes out of you.

In daily life you're highly dependable and honorable. If you give your word, you mean it and will never go back on a promise willingly. Additionally, anything that you commit to doing gets done, and done well. Laziness and half-hearted efforts aren't even in your vocabulary.

People who share this birthday have the ability to take any situation and turn it around for the better. Lemons into lemonade—why stop there? Grow lemon trees, bake lemon pies, make lemon incense! This creative ability may lead to a profession in the media, but no matter the job, success is in the air!

To top off the package, our Leo is a great lover, and incredibly charismatic. But you tend to be a bit of a flirt, and enjoy a lot of variety. Long-term relationships may not be in the cards.

Gift idea: Cirque du Soleil tickets.

July 24

Individuals born today will never, ever fit any status quo. Being humdrum or commonplace isn't even a consideration. Danger is the name of the game for this Leo, the wilder the better. The only thing that might prevent accidents or social faux pas is the birth number of 4 that's more staid and focused on security.

If your birthday is today, you're not easily frightened. You roar in the face of adversity and challenges, and consequences—what consequences? They don't matter so much as the thrill of the moment. Why not apply all that adventurous spirit toward a suitable job like stunt double or acrobat? For hobbies, skydiving and bungie jumping of course!

And in love, your partner had better be able to keep up with you and want to try a new position every night (you keep a copy of the *Kama Sutra* in the night stand just in case!). Additionally, you gather individuals into your life who illustrate creativity and the social graces you sometimes lack, making for quite the odd couple. Even so, opposites attract, and once a spark ignites, a fire surely follows.

Gift idea: safety equipment or a book on manners.

ALERT!

National Salad Week (U.S.) is July 25–31. It's estimated that salad dressing has been part of human culture for about 5,000 years. The Chinese used soy sauce; Babylonians applied vinegar-and-oil blends; Romans enjoyed their greens with simple salt (at that time a sign of prosperity and honor—hence, "a man worth his salt"); and Egyptians added many different spices to their oil/vinegar mixes. It was not until about 1920, however, that salad dressings were marketed to the public. Today the most popular flavors are Ranch, Blue Cheese, Italian, French, Thousand Island, Caesar, Honey Dijon, Poppy Seed, and Vinaigrette.

July 25

You're as emotional as a Cancer, yet have the force of the Lion, and the dualistic nature of Gemini. No wonder people find you confusing—you can barely keep up with yourself. The key to resolving this is slowing down a bit, processing everything in your mind, then acting or talking. Allow the adaptive nature of your birth number 5 to offer assistance here, along with the strong Leo presence that requires that dignity always be a primary consideration.

Your friends admire your insight and loyalty. Nonetheless, you have a very restless soul and may not stay in one job or one place long enough to really nurture those friendships. Thankfully the Lion has an outgoing nature and loves to talk, so you can adapt to new surroundings and make new acquaintances quickly.

With friends and lovers alike, you want periodic private time and above all else to maintain independence. You will not stay with overly jealous or needy partners, and seek something more spiritual in your intimate connections.

Gift idea: travel vouchers.

July 26

You still have a lot of Cancerian energy, so you're going to feel everything very strongly. Don't start to roar about something until you've had time to think it through. And, don't let the Leo side of you bite on a morsel of gossip without having solid information with which to make a critical decision. You probably have very good friends who seem to understand your emotional nature. You will satisfy your wanderlust in the future, and you have a knack with numbers that will help you save for your next great adventure.

Your birth number of 6 indicates that you love beauty, and may focus a little too much on superficial appearance instead of substance. With friends and lovers alike, you will want periodic private time, and above all else to maintain your independence. If that doesn't happen, you may become grumpy or a little haughty. You generally will not stay with overly jealous or needy partners, and look for something more spiritual in your intimate relationships.

Gift idea: a subscription to *National Geographic*.

July 27

Oh, my, how you love to hear yourself roar! Today's personology forecast indicates that you love a good discussion or debate, and that you don't sit still very well. All too often the activity in your life causes a fair amount of anxiety, which you hate, but it's like a vicious cycle—you just have to be busy or you're not content, and then that schedule makes you unhappy. Here your birth number of 7 might offer a haven. Consider a spiritual or philosophical approach to living that affords a less demanding pace.

People who share this birthday want to be appreciated for their work. You need that verbal stroking, even though your idealistic nature knows it's a little silly to be so needy. What's more, like yesterday's Leo there's a little too much attention given to outward appearances. Why not put that knack to work and become a hairstylist or makeup artist?

In relationships, you collect a full pride of admirers, but typically don't stay with any one of them for very long. To maintain a relationship, this Lion's partner will have to be very clever, and very energetic.

Gift idea: a decorative mirror and hairbrush set.

Important dates in July history: Amelia Earhart is lost in the Pacific (July 2, 1937); the Bikini is first modeled in France (July 5, 1946); Pasteur uses the anti-rabies vaccine on a boy successfully (July 5, 1885); the Bahamas are granted independence (July 10, 1973); the French Revolution begins (July 14, 1789); Oklahoma City starts using parking meters (July 16, 1935); Disneyland opens in California (July 17, 1955); Rome begins to burn in the Great Fire (July 19, 64 c.e.); Neil Armstrong walks on the moon. (July 20, 1969); the Postal Service is established (July 26, 1775); Bugs Bunny debuts (July 27, 1940); color motion pictures are shown (July 30, 1928).

July 28

You look simply amazing! You radiate with all the golden sun energy of Leo, bearing a huge aura, yet you remain neatly aloof. To be honest, you never liked that much attention because it robs you of privacy. Like it or not, however, people are attracted to you like moths to a flame, and that energy is also what produces the most success in your life—so embrace it and find a way to make it work for you.

Today's birth number is 8, reflecting a strong work ethic and the desire to achieve financial stability through your profession. Most who share this quality achieve those goals, thanks to having self-confidence, control, the Lion's bravery, and tenacity. Truthfully there's little you couldn't do successfully, but all that charisma might be well applied in a dramatic field.

In love this Lion is really a pussycat in disguise. You crave the love of someone who sees your true self, not just outer appearances. Nonetheless, you must take care that the sometimes bossy, demanding nature of Leo doesn't screw up a good thing.

Gift idea: a new purse, wallet, or hip pouch.

July 29

Helper, healer, visionary—your birth number 9 takes all these aptitudes and adds in a psychic, prophetic flair just to keep things interesting. When you listen to other people, you really hear what they're saying, and take it to heart. When you talk, it's not idle chit-chat, but a real conversation. If you ask, "How are you?" you want the whole picture, not just a socially acceptable response.

This well-rounded, tactful nature makes today's Leo an ideal candidate for jobs like early childhood education specialist and psychological evaluator. Alternatively, you might use your ability to fairly sum up individuals in a job placement agency. And don't mistake that calm demeanor for weakness! There's an aggressive Cat here, one who will apply appropriate amounts of pressure to get the best possible outcome.

With friends and family, you are wholly devoted. You are a one-man-woman, or one-woman-man, period. Family and its structure are incredibly important, and our Lion wants an entire litter of kids to lavish with attention.

Gift idea: a dream diary.

July 30

Lady Luck runs with this Lion throughout life. You have been fortunate at the oddest of times. Frequently this occurs with money, which you spend on lavish things for your lair. You figure, enjoy the money while it's here. Worrying about tomorrow only spoils the fun. "Live in the moment, and don't get tied down" sums up your philosophy of life very tidily. It's also the perfect philosophy to "marry" to the ever-independent, self-expressive birth number 1.

Individuals celebrating with you today love to travel and explore, and may find themselves attracted to jobs that focus on either or both. Additionally, like many born under Leo, you are a good communicator with lots of brainpower, which could lead to reporting or publicity. Whatever the job, it's nearly guaranteed to be exciting and bring in a hefty paycheck.

Being on the move and a little self-absorbed make you hard to get to know. You're certainly not in a hurry to firm up a commitment (that would tie you down!). And you're also not afraid of what might be considered unconventional relationships, which provide more options and more chances for excitement.

Gift idea: a lightweight racing bike.

FACT

Toward the end of July, Hopi rituals that commemorate supernatural beings (the Kachina) culminate, having begun in February. It's said that if these ceremonies are enacted by people of pure heart the Kachina will bless the tribe with nourishing rains for the crops. The final dance of this festival begins at sunrise and acts as an elaborate farewell to the spirits as they return to their realm at sunset.

July 31

This Lion is sticking its nose into everything! You are the archetype of an information gatherer, but in the process your entire sense of space and time disappear. You're always late for dinner, if you even remember that it was cooking! Oh, true, you find a lot of good data, and once it's in your paws you can apply it effectively. But with Leo as your birth sign, and a birth number of 2, you can only live like a hermit for so long. You need adoration and attention, and when you appear long enough to receive it don't forget—this is a good launching pad for your ideas.

The problem-solving nature of 2 couples with this Lion's diligence and sense of purpose. You really want to make all those dreams a reality, and if you get some worldly status for it, that's ideal! While the achievement itself is more important than anything else, Leo still likes to shine and be in the spot light.

In love, today's Leo is far more sensitive than one might expect. There are some very tender spots along this Cat's belly that, if poked, leave you sulking for days or weeks. Ego stroking is necessary for any successful partner to the Lion, along with faithfulness.

Gift idea: an old-fashioned globe.

Sign: Cancer

Date: June 22–July 22

Ruled by: Moon

Element: Water

Lucky Color: White, silver, pale yellow

Gemstone: Moonstone

Keynote: Sensitivity

Positive Traits: Empathic, service-oriented, protective, social, hard working

Negative Traits: Low self-esteem, possessive

Famous Cancers include: Princess Diana, Rembrandt, Bill Cosby, Caesar, Olivia De Havilland, Phyllis Diller, Ernest Hemingway

The moon exerts considerable influence on Cancerians. Even as it waxes and wanes, so too does the heart of the Crab. One moment this person can be laughing, the next crying. The strength of these emotions often takes other people along for the roller-coaster ride, so wear a seat belt!

Cancerians are somewhat conventional. While new things might be of interest, comfort and long-term functionality hold favor. the Crab will take the old, fits-just-right couch over a new leather sofa any day. Additionally, a Cancer's home is their castle—they love to fuss over this space, and bring other people into it to similarly nurture those relationships.

Cancers are good humanitarians. They truly care about others, often showing compassion and charity in the most unexpected and delightful ways. This is when the Crab is fully out of its shell, and shining as a bright, warm spirit. The only problem is that once begun, the nurturing can turn into smothering. When Cancerians realize what they've done (or when they get hurt), they retreat to the shell, gathering all the tokens they love along with them, and wait for the storm to blow over.

In long-term relationships Cancerians must take care to balance their heart and head. Insecurity is a huge factor for the Crab, which can easily turn into the green-eyed monster. Once a Cancer overcomes that tendency, they become very dedicated, empathic mates and friends.

Chapter 10

August

August was originally the sixth month on the Roman Calendar. It was named simply Sextilis (six). Later, the name of the month was changed to honor Augustus Caesar. Leo rules the first part of the month, when the sun is shining at its brightest. Leo is a flashy sign, enjoying the good life and being lucky. Following that we have Virgos, who are very introspective, inquisitive, and humorous. In the Far East, August is ruled by the goat, which is like Virgo in charm but like Leo in its love of beauty.

August 1

Standing out from the pride and being the apple of another's eye is what this Leo is all about. You love attention, showing off, and listening to the adoring words of "fans." This seemingly egotistical nature is off-putting to some, but if people take time and get to know you they'll be pleasantly surprised. There's a very inventive, able go-getter in there just waiting for someone to tap that potential.

Speaking of creativity, people who share this birthday often do well in the arts because of a unique perspective on the world. You can take any situation and translate it into comedy, tragedy, or whatever suits your fancy. Your birth number of 9 is a great asset here, in that it has strong visionary potential. There's not much that can get past you, and if you apply these capabilities you're a very good leader in the making! Alternatively, why not try your hand at fashion design and put that trend-setting aptitude to work.

Love is very fickle creature to this Cat. You like playing with your prey for a short time, then moving on to another pretty, shining face. You aren't one to settle down, at least not in a conventional sense of the term, so marriage may not be in the picture.

Gift idea: a subscription to a fashion magazine.

August 2

Like an intuitive cat, you are overly aware of everything, sometimes to the point of experiencing sensory overload. At those times, you need to retreat to a den, lick your wounds, and de-stress. Some people may not understand this, and see you as antisocial. That's certainly not the case. It's just that the public has to come in small doses.

Your birth number is 1, which drives incredible individuality. You want to do something and make a difference in the world, but you aren't wholly sure where to begin. Your sensitivity would indicate that your energy might best be directed to a more solitary field like research. Books and computers don't leave you completely drained at the end of the day—people do.

Relationships can prove difficult simply because our Cat knows when anyone tells a fib. You want an honest, stable relationship, and most folks aren't truthful 100 percent of the time. Once you discover a salt-of-the-earth person, the love flows freely and thoughtfully.

Gift idea: a psychic self-defense book.

August 3

Taking "no" for an answer is not in this pussycat's playbook. Like many born under Leo, there's a lot of pride here, and a firm resolve too. When there's an unsettled issue, it's not something that can wait. You push brashly ahead and want to get things settled as soon as possible, feeling that all that negativity or disorder simply delays progress.

Those who share this birthday have a lot of power at their disposal. Use it carefully. A birth number of 2 can come to the rescue here, encouraging cooperation, better people skills, and greater patience. Actually, if you apply the people-oriented nature of 2 in conjunction with those decision-making abilities, you'd make an excellent negotiator or moderator. Politics is also a good potential career path.

As to friendship and romance, the egotistical Leo can be a little over-shadowing. You want lavish adulation, and when there's not enough you get grumpy and as hard to handle as a wet cat. So long as partners understand that regular stroking is a requirement, they can tame the Lion effectively.

Gift idea: a bundle of sunflowers.

QUESTION?

What occasion does Lammas commemorate?
Throughout much of Europe, August 1 was once a time to celebrate the earth's bounty. This was when the harvest began, and farmers would save the first sheaf of corn and bring it for blessing. Loaves of bread were also made from this crop, some of which would be sprinkled at the corner of their land to bring good luck. Thus Lammas is sometimes also known as the "loaf mass." According to folkways, this is an excellent time to prognosticate about future partners. Alternatively, some young couples would dedicate themselves to a trial marriage for the duration of the festival to see if their relationship would work out.

August 4

The terms "avant-garde" and "adamant" sum up today's personology forecast very neatly. You are a bit of an oddball, and completely content to be so. Somewhat like a hippy born to the wrong era, you typically prefer the company of trees to people, but are pragmatic enough to realize that you have to interact with the real world. That doesn't make interaction easy. Most folks find you a little demanding and impetuous. To tame that, look to the joyful nature of your birth number 3. Happiness is contagious and will smooth over those rough spots nicely.

Career paths for this Leo run the gambit. You have a lot of notions rattling around in your mind, but can't seem to adequately express or activate them. This means you have to overcome your social awkwardness in order to really succeed in business. However, if you find one or two strong, intuitive people who can grasp those ideas and put them into a functional construct, the partnership could be stunning.

Being pretty much a loner, friendships and love are an accidental occurrence in this Lion's life. You may wake up one day and find that it's there, like magic. This is a wonderful bit of luck, as you would never go seeking that kind of closeness.

Gift idea: a carving of a bird in flight.

August 5

Uniquely unassuming for a Leo, you actually have a huge aura and very strong bearing that attract people to you in droves. It's even more attractive that you don't seem to be aware of the interesting energy you project. Where some Leos roar and prance for attention, you get it by just walking into a room and have no clue as to why. Sometimes all this attention makes you uneasy. You need to become more comfortable in your skin, and use this natural magnetic personality for good purposes.

People who celebrate their birthday today have a birth number of 4. This provides stability and an excellent capacity for handling money, which is a good thing, because prosperity comes to you. Mind you, an overactive work ethic helps in that a lot. Getting you to relax isn't an easy task. You have to take away the phone, fax, email, cell, etc., then go to a place where there's no work-oriented distractions.

As one might guess, it's not hard to find people interested in romancing this Leo. The problem is that you're not interested in someone whose perceptions cloud seeing the real Lion within. You're also a little timid, and need a charismatic partner who is also forward and real.

Gift idea: a day in a hot tub.

ALERT!

> The symbol, or glyph, associated with the sign of Leo looks, at first glance, like a lion's tail or mane. Some experts, however, believe that it represents the two halves of the heart, the area of the body associated with this sign. A third possibility is that it's an emblem of the Sun, the stellar body that governs Leo. Finally, in the Vedas, the image symbolizes inventiveness, life-giving power, and a new beginning.

August 6

Wit and wisdom are this Lion's guides in life. No matter how bleak things get, you see something positive and find a way to ease tension by bringing a little levity to bear. People adore you for this great equalizing gift, and return repeatedly for more advice and trusted insights. Needless to say, having an ongoing line of needy people isn't easy, and may drive even the most kindhearted kitty to lash out periodically with claws. This is doubly true for people who refuse to help themselves. While today's birth number of 6 calls in a humanitarian sensibility, that doesn't mean enabling!

Being upbeat suits you, and it also suits your career. The quest for peace and beauty permeates your reality. Whether you become a renowned negotiator or painter doesn't matter—what matters is that the results bring a smile, and somehow leave the world a better place. Any business would be lucky to have such a warm, insightful person on staff.

That accommodating nature spills over into your friendships and love life frequently. It's okay to want to help others, but don't overdo it or you'll start feeling resentful. Remember that the relationship game is supposed to be fifty-fifty. If you keep it in balance, all is right with the world.

Gift idea: a statue of Bast in her cat form.

August 7

Today's Leo often acts before thinking things through completely. You have a compulsive craving for fresh experiences, adventure, and input that easily distracts you from daily tasks. At least one lesson for this Lion is to slow down just a bit, let ideas cook, and pause before going into the fray (at least long enough to ascertain potential hazards).

A birth number of 6 does little to help obsessive tendencies but for the fact that it offers a little good fortune, even when dealings aren't overly wise.

Those who are celebrating birthdays today have fantastic imaginations. You can see things clearly in your internal landscape. Just be careful that you don't get too caught up in those daydreams. Rather, apply that creativity to a career path, like writing great romance novels. This type of work provides a perfect outlet for your vision, and it can be highly profitable.

Turning your attention to relationships, there's going to be lots of them. You love variety, and exploring each aspect of Self as it mixes and mingles with others. Additionally, your fantasies can lead to very unrealistic images of what constitutes a "good" relationship. Find a multifaceted partner (perhaps a Gemini) who can fulfill some of those whims.

Gift idea: a huge box of crayons (as many colors as possible—don't forget metallics!).

August 8

Where yesterday's forecast described a fly-by-the-seat-of-your-pants Leo, you are just the opposite. Serious, steady, and steadfast, people know that they can depend upon you even when it's not convenient. You've worked very hard to develop trust among a variety of friends and coworkers. Employers see you as loyal, responsible, and very task-oriented. Just remember to let your hair down from time to time.

A birth number of 7 represents an aptitude for balancing head and heart (this Leo's head usually wins). For careers, you can certainly manage or tackle any tasks that require a logical approach. Being somewhat of a perfectionist, fault-finding from others sometimes meets with Lion-like resistance, however. But if your associates hang in there, eventually they'll see that your sense of honor will allow you to listen more openly. Additionally, the influence of a Sagittarius decanate affords a pragmatism that helps you internalize advice, even when your picky nature might otherwise want to resist.

In a relationship you are a devoted partner who will do everything to watch over your family with due diligence. No person or situation will dare threaten this Cat's den! And if anyone turns out to be that foolhardy, they'd best be prepared to put their head in the Lion's mouth!

Gift idea: a letter opener.

August 9

Today's Leo is all wildcat. There's no taming or restraining you. As a child, it seemed as if you were solar powered, up with the sun and still completely charged late at night. The youthful exuberance lead to more than just bruised knees—likely several broken bones and bloody noses. As an adult that energy continues, expressed in a very outgoing, social, and curious nature. Life is like a flourishing banquet of which our Cat doesn't want to miss one little bite.

Having a birth number of 8 steadies today's outlook a bit. Whereas you might otherwise be reckless and dangerously excessive, the motivation to achieve stability tones that down. That doesn't mean you don't enjoy being the class clown. In true Leo style, you love lots of attention, but will try to limit that showmanship to times and spaces that don't affect your security. This may lead to feeling as if you're struggling with yourself—the part that yearns for freedom, and the other, more responsible and respectable half. Take heart; eventually you'll find a peaceful middle ground. Additionally, the Sagittarius decanate has already mastered the balance between inspiration and common sense, which keeps things optimistic.

Relationships run hot and heavy for our Leo. You love a good, long chase and teasing banter. Play hard to get and this pussycat's passion goes from a slow purr to a full-out rumble!

Gift idea: a basket of gourmet goodies.

FACT

Peridot is a form of olivine, a lovely green stone that's the birth gem for August. It's been a part of human history as far back as ancient Egypt. Some ancients, like the Romans, called it the evening emerald because of its rich color similarities. At first, it's likely most peridot came from near the Red Sea where it formed from volcanic activity. Aptly, Hawaiians liken the stone to the Volcano goddess Pele's tears. Superstition claims that anyone who wears one of these stones will receive the power to persuade people.

August 10

You have a lot of psychic aptitude, and the sense that you want to be remembered for something special in life. In younger years, that awareness kept you strong in the face of bullies, and as an adult it continues to drive you forward with hope in your heart.

Your day will come, but it requires a leap of faith. Like the Fool card of the Tarot, you never quite know what opportunities lie around the corner, but you do know you need to go there and at least try. As you do, remember that part of the Fool's allure and wisdom comes from innocent faith—in this case, trust yourself to be a guru and guide.

Having a birth number of 9 helps build that self-trust. Those hunches are almost always spot-on, so stop thinking that feeling down deep is just indigestion! Additionally, a Sagittarius decanate encourages taking that renewed conviction and exploring its various applications within and without.

As for friendship and love, you are sweet, gentle, encouraging, and confident. You give of yourself wholly to whatever relationship you're in, and don't worry about the tomorrows. Love is precious, and it's meant to be experienced fully.

Gift idea: a jazz CD.

August 11

For individuals born on the 11th, life is truly what you choose to make of it. In fact, the law of like-causing-like manifests for you daily. When you're sad, it seems as if everyone around you suddenly has a bout of depressing matters. When you're happy, the world is your oyster and everyone around you experiences all manner of good things. That's because you're a natural facilitator and projector, which is a wonderful gift but also a heavy responsibility. Be aware of it, and use it for the greatest possible good.

In business, your friendly nature bodes well for the future. Working with a local group or community brings personal fulfillment and joy. There's typical Leo willpower here upon which to draw, meaning those special projects are going to shine with success. Additionally, the Sagittarian decanate gives you lots of cleverness, which in turn inspires the admiration Leos so appreciate.

All that courageous zeal doesn't seem to help with romance, however. Today's Lions are bashful and a little unsure. As a result, you may try to compensate for confidence issues with nervous laughter or odd body language. The best partner here is one who's creative, self-aware, and loyal.

Gift idea: a business-card holder.

August 12

Happy and actualized, you certainly know how to take any situation and put a positive spin on it. In fact, as a career you might well consider political damage control and related fields. Literally, there's nothing you can't make sound better with a little clever tweaking (and in many cases that fixes the problem!). And the Sagittarian influence in your chart ensures a plentiful supply of charm, so everyone listening or reading can't help but be engaged.

People sharing this birthday live moment to moment. Tomorrow manages to come all by itself, and thanks to a relatively wide streak of good fortune, that approach works perfectly well professionally too. You need an employment environment that grants personal expression, and if possible permit you to make your own schedule. Telecommuting would suit this Lion just fine. That way you could be in the den, enjoying the rather fanciful environment that surrounds you. Don't be surprised if you find glitter on our Leo's ceiling just for a starry effect.

Interpersonal communication is very playful and flirtatious. Like a kitten, you pounce and run, wanting a good pursuit. Once you find someone who enjoys that good-natured teasing, you'll settle into a very giving, loving relationship.

Gift idea: a fully stocked gift-wrapping kit.

In a classical Tarot deck, the card of Strength portrays a woman holding a lion's mouth without fear. Alternative depictions show a woman riding a lion. Originally this card was aptly called Fortitude and symbolized the need for balance—knowing when to act, and when to stay put; when to go into the Lion's den, and when to retreat. In short, this challenges the Leo arrogance and love of the limelight with some sense.

August 13

You are the handyperson of all Leos. If it's broken, you can fix it with bubble gum and duct tape. If it's lost, you'll find it, and if it doesn't exist yet—you'll make it! Thanks to having a Scorpio decanate, you're very disciplined and logical. Learning and intricate thinking have always come relatively easy to you, but not without an awareness of how valuable those things would be in your life.

Lions sharing this birthday often go into scientific fields because of their passion for invention and discovery. Alternatively, you might find helping with hands-on exhibits at the children's science museum appealing (the playful nature of a birth number 3 makes sure that our Cat doesn't take things too seriously, which otherwise would be a danger). The ambitions that resonate with 3 make a very good partner to this goal-minded creature.

The one place where logic falls down is in the area of love. Now you become a little quirky. You seek out odd people as friends, typically ones with brilliant minds and lousy social skills. This provides a comfort zone where personal insecurity takes a back seat to the conversation. In mates, stability is important, as is an upbeat spirit.

Gift idea: a set of microscope sample slides.

August 14

Those born today have the patience and commitment of Gandhi. While you choose your causes carefully, once you've put your paw into the mix, it's not budging until something positive happens. If that means moving mountains, so be it! And, if you use your words wisely, even rocks will listen to you. Better still, you're a very nurturing influence—as you talk to new people, they open up and blossom like flowers in the sun.

With your penchant for communication, you could become an excellent speech therapist or public-speaking instructor. Even though there's humanitarian tendencies here, they're controlled somewhat by the birth number 4 that requires more than just wishful thinking to commit a lifetime to any cause (or career for that matter). And with an Arian influence coming to bear, any emotional extreme likewise gets restrained. There's no flashy or fast moves in this Cat's repertoire, but rather well-thought-out tactics.

One problem you experience is analyzing personal relationships to death. Unfortunately people can't be reduced to calculations. While you know how to handle words, there's a time for silence too. You need to allow your partner a private space within—one that's not probed with ongoing verbal inquiries.

Gift idea: a tape recorder.

August 15

What's up, pussycat? You, of course! Like any Leo, the limelight is your friend, and you absolutely love adulation. Thankfully your personality is strong enough and your aura large enough to bring the attention that soothes your spirit and nourishes that ever-lingering sense of self-doubt (not that anyone would ever see that part of you!). Additionally, the upbeat nature of the birth number 5 sends out good vibes. Since people enjoy being around an upbeat person, you rarely have to worry about being alone unless you so choose.

Those moments are few and far-between (typically occurring on bad mane days).

In the business world, we can often find this Lion in fashion design, running a trendy clothing or jewelry shop, or in the theater. Any of these choices is perfectly apt, and our Leo has the stamina and enthusiasm to really make a go of it! Whatever the job, it must be something you love and a position in which you remain center stage. And with an Arian decanate you will accomplish exactly what you intend, using a seemingly unending well of energy to make it so.

As for love? Well, the idea is fanciful and fun, but sometimes those rose-colored glasses get in the way of substance. You love the idea of romance, but you don't always want to invest the time and attention for something deeper. Also, you tend to wear facades, transforming your external self to please whomever you're with, so serious partners must do a little digging to find the real person inside.

Gift idea: an iPod.

ALERT!

Poppy is the birth flower for the month of August. Historically speaking, we find references to these flowers as early as 3,000 years ago in Egypt. In Ancient Greece the poppy represented fertility, vitality, and power (the seeds were mixed with honey and wine and given to Olympic athletes). Romans brought poppies to England, and said that the god of sleep controlled this plant's spirit.

August 16

You've got undeniable magnetism and know how to use it to get your way. Unfortunately, sometimes that game face becomes manipulative because you crave notice and admiration even if you haven't really earned it yet (a downfall with which many born to this sign struggle). Lean on your birth number of 6's moralistic idealism to land firmly on your feet, and keep that gregarious attention-seeking cat restrained to the right times and places.

Not surprisingly you will make your mark no matter the career path you choose. This is not a Lion who sits idly on life's sidelines like a wallflower, or who constantly mourns after "greener pastures." Rather, you'll bite into the slice of life you've been given with ferocity, motivated partially by 6's very zealous nature. Again, however, this cat has to watch for uppity attitudes—the King of the Jungle's dominance and haughtiness can become huge barriers both situationally and personally.

Friendship and sex are often tools for you, and you frequently seek out people who can somehow help you improve your status and security, and who assuage that ever-hungry ego. The best way for partners to get through that cloud of pretense is by being aloof. Let the Cat wait and wonder. Eventually their curiosity and hunger get the best of them!

Gift idea: a hand-carved box.

August 17

If you're actually celebrating your birthday today, it's probably because it fell on a weekend. Otherwise, there would be no time for socializing. You'd be at your job plugging away no matter what holiday or celebration was afoot. Being a workaholic serves you well financially, but it doesn't allow for the birth number of 7 to bring heart matters into the picture. You'd do well to listen to 7's advice—give yourself a break regularly, pat yourself on the back, and go enjoy the company of family and friends. The work will still be there tomorrow!

Wanting to be successful brings out a very diligent and strong characteristic in today's Leo. You will take on tasks happily, and are an apt multitasker even if it means self-neglect. Those close to you have to watch for signs of burnout and gently guide you toward periodic retreats to avoid a complete meltdown. Know too that you need a good cry now and again. It's like releasing steam from a boiling pot—better that than a messy explosion. Allow yourself the healthy expression of emotions whenever possible.

As might be expected, there's very little free time in your life for dating, let alone in-depth relationships. If partners can distract you long enough from work to consider love, they should take pride in that accomplishment and not let up! The reward will be a very devoted mate for life.

Gift idea: a high-quality mechanical pencil.

QUESTION?

What famous people were born in August?

Francis Scott Key (8/1), Peter O'Toole (8/2), Martha Stewart (8/3), Neil Armstrong (8/5), Alfred, Lord Tennyson (8/6), Esther Williams (8/8), Alex Haley (8/11), George Hamilton (8/12), Alfred Hitchcock (8/13), Danielle Steel (8/14), Kathie Lee Gifford (8/16), Madonna (8/16), Robert Redford (8/18), Patrick Swayze (8/18), Orville Wright (8/19), Gene Roddenberry (8/19), Gandhi (8/20), Kenny Rogers (8/21), King Louis XVI (8/23), Leonard Bernstein (8/25), Sean Connery (8/25), Mother Teresa (8/27), Scott Hamilton (8/28), Jean-Claude Killy (8/30), Richard Gere (8/31).

August 18

Today's Leo is set for battle—claws out, eyes open, and muscles poised to move on a moment's notice. There's such a fierce and nearly unshakable spirit here that finding yourself in danger rarely surprises you. If you don't find peril, peril often finds you. Having a birth number of 8 only emphasizes that cycle in your life with the characteristics of persistence and protectiveness. However, before you rush in, stop for a moment and consider what it is that you really want to fight for. Perhaps this isn't your battle after all.

Aries is today's decanate, which ups the stakes even more. This Cat is brave and edgy. It would not be unusual for you to choose a military career, but you'll constantly strive after leadership roles (being subservient isn't in your drill plans). The soldier-of-fortune image fits, and it gives you an opportunity to travel (something that fulfills the yen for unbridled adventure and risk taking). Other possible career paths include racecar driver, stunt double, and trapeze artist.

Pushing the limits doesn't end with physical endeavors. You also want escapades of the heart and body, and while you may stay for a while with creative, vibrant individuals, you can be easily lead astray by life, or by another energetic person whose bedside manners awaken curiosity.

Gift idea: an antique sword or dagger.

August 19

Like a cat lounging happily in a purrfect sun puddle, this Leo isn't rushing into anything. Besides, you have so much allure that people and situations often come to you without your having to really raise so much as a paw. It's not that you're lazy, or that you don't appreciate the attention It's just that you want to savor the moment, and rushing doesn't allow for that. Additionally, that slower pace gives you time to contemplate life's mysteries more fully, something your birth number of 9 appreciates. Just be careful not to get so mired in what-could-be that you completely miss important matters right here, right now.

A birth number of 9 implies that you might consider a career in the travel industry, but nothing overly rushed (being a flight attendant, for example, isn't going to appeal whatsoever). Perhaps acting as a high-class tour agent would suit (that also appeals to the natural Leo ego and enjoyment of finer things). Considering the Aries decanate, you'll provide people with calm reassurance when they would otherwise feel out of their element, so being a fashion advisor or career counselor might work too.

When it comes to love, would that it also came easily. Romantic moments are more interesting than the hard work a long-term relationship requires. Additionally, your decisions in love haven't historically been the best, so you shy away from too much commitment.

Gift idea: a certificate to a tanning salon.

August 20

The kingly nature of the Lion comes through today's Leo very strongly. You're not arrogant, but your poise and demeanor speak volumes. When you want to, you can lead with confidence and competence. Your voice and bearing pack a wallop, but inside you're really a gentle soul and even a little insecure. That actually makes a good balance and keeps the normally arrogant Leo demeanor from taking over (not to mention your birth number of 1 that wants to be noticed!).

The influence of number 1 expresses itself in today's personology by giving you strong ideals that act as an anchor to all of life's storms. You don't compromise on important things, and challenges to your moral structure get met with a righteously indignant roar. On the other hand, you love people, and are admired by many. There's no question you could easily administer a group effectively, gaining loyalty through your direct, no-nonsense truthfulness and honest efforts.

That approach is exactly the same in relationships. Today's Leo wants very much to be a good wife or husband, and a good friend. Sometimes you try a little too hard, but those efforts are so sincere that no one seems to mind.

Gift idea: a bright birthstone ring.

August 21

Kismet walks with these Cats, but only so far. It won't help much when you recklessly put yourself into risky situations just for fun. Wanting to be the biggest, toughest Lion in the den manifests in a roguish rebel personality that people find either irresistible or completely unnerving. Truth be told, you like to keep people off balance. Nonetheless, your birth number of 2 suggests an aptitude for communicating to a wide variety of individuals, so for the most part people will smile at your wild endeavors and want to be around to see the outcomes.

Your life lesson is to slow down and be more cautious. More than once you get your tail caught in doors and under chairs, having an odd aptitude for being in the right place at exactly the wrong time (and all too often choosing that timing). Thankfully, you usually have rescuers—people who hover at the edges of the action because they know the inevitable is coming. As for jobs, as anticipated, you're daring—think lion tamer, trick horse riding, and matador!

This Leo's sex life is very entertaining and inspiring. There's a very playful kitten here who enjoys experimenting and will gleefully try new things with a good, fun-loving partner. That youthful outlook may mean you avoid commitment until later in life, when you're ready for more leisure, as well as to give up the crowd's adoration for the love of one good person.

Gift idea: a special "lucky" coin minted in your birth year.

FACT

Several very interesting events took place in August, including: the first modern Olympics were held in Berlin (1936); the first Gulf War began (1990); Flag Day was established (1949); the U.S. Department of Energy was created (1977); Hiroshima was bombed (1945); President Nixon resigned (1974); the U.S. withdrew from Vietnam (1972); The Berlin Wall was erected (1961); copyright laws were established (1856); the phonograph was patented (1906); the National Park Service was established (1916); Cleopatra committed suicide (30 B.C.E.).

August 22

Leos born today seem blissfully unaware of Virgo's impending influence. You're absolutely brilliant, but not overly dependable when it comes to finishing a task. Oh, the intention is honestly there—but if something distracts your focus, you become as changeable as a Gemini, with communication skills to match! Orderliness and the other rather fastidious Virgo traits are nowhere to be found, which is just as well since those things drive this Cat crazy.

If you share this birthday, be aware that sometimes you speak too quickly and hurt people's feelings. Your clever wit may be able to smooth over those rough moments, but that's likely what got you into trouble in the first place. Awkward social relations are normal for you—this comes from spending more time with your nose in books than socializing. That effort serves you well in intellectually oriented careers, or ones where you can apply that great vocabulary, but in other settings you feel a little uncomfortable. When that happens, lean on your happy-go-lucky birth number of 3, smile sweetly, pretend you meant to do that, and try again.

Friendships and romance may be likewise uncomfortable for you. People don't completely understand the way you think. Additionally, with an Aries decanate, you love to wander the jungle unhindered and unrestrained (even when it might not be a great idea). Any partners need to allow the Lion a lot of independence if they hope for any type of longevity.

Gift idea: a giant crossword-puzzle book.

August 23

Happy birthday Virgo! Virgo's emerging energies make an impression with lingering bits of Leo, specifically in the way these individuals balance their work and home life. While you are very diligent and focused at work, the pressures and worries of that job neatly stop after crossing the threshold come the end of the day. Likewise in your personal space, you stay alert, informed, and involved. If single, you're wholly aware of every mechanical situation in the building. If coupled, you listen intently to a mate's day, and respond with useful insights. If a parent, you're on the school board and involved in PTA.

Those celebrating birthdays today have an appreciation for the arts. You may indulge in one personally for relaxation, and encourage others to explore the wonders that culture provides. This is also part of that "rounding out" and balancing act common to today's personology profile. The words "all things in moderation; all things in their space" probably leave your lips fairly regularly. It's a very admirable quality, and one that your birth number of 4 supports in spirit and action.

With all this in mind, it's easy to see why you do very well with friendships and long-term relationships. Your easygoing, attentive manner endears you to many. In turn, you enjoy the stability of lifelong, cooperative interactions.

Gift idea: aromatherapy candles.

August 24

Those born today start out the Virgin's sign with typical attentiveness. In this case, you are a people watcher. This isn't idle gazing, however. You're watching for opportunities to bring a smile or offer some type of assistance. Either that, or you're going to provide advice on how to put a chaotic life back in order (another very strong Virgo trait). Just pause to think before offering such advice assertively—as good as your aptitude for structure is, not everyone is ready to acknowledge their shortcomings.

Today's birth number is 5, meaning you love to learn new things, and often try to take on too much information or responsibility through hands-on endeavors. One of your life lessons is learning not to overextend yourself. Giving and doing make you feel great . . . great, that is, until you're completely washed out emotionally, physically, or spiritually. All that kindness and compassion needs to be turned inward somewhat regularly or you crash and burn pretty hard.

In love, this Virgo is uncompromising. It must be the right, best person forever or nothing at all. That means you may marry late in life, preferring to wait until that Prince or Princess Charming arrives on the scene to make everything perfect.

Gift idea: a camera.

ALERT!

August is known as Family Fun Month, Peach Month, and National Picnic Month. The second week of August is National Smile Week. Beyond that, here are a few more festive celebrations: August 2: National Ice Cream Sandwich Day; August 5: Sisters Day; August 6: Forgiveness Day; August 9: Book Lovers Day; August 15: Relaxation Day; August 16: National Tell a Joke Day; August 17: National Thrift Shop Day; August 21: Hawaii Day; August 25: Kiss and Make Up Day; August 31: National Trail Mix Day.

August 25

You see life as a great opportunity to stretch, learn, and grow beyond what society or circumstances have placed before you. As a result, this Virgo sometimes gets into awkward situations, even dangerous ones, with the goal being "just experience it!" Worse, you have enough charisma to take tagalongs into potentially iffy conditions quite unwittingly. A birth number of 6 implies these situations may have very wonderful ideals behind them, but that doesn't make the effort any less risky. So the real question for this Virgin should be: is the risk worth the reward?

If you're celebrating a birthday today, yours is a life of synchronicity, and you've learned to run with those odd twists and turns of fate. However, let the more orderly nature of your birth sign bring your brashness back under control and give you the ability to adapt to all that uncertainty, using wisdom and discrimination as effective guides.

You easily find love and lots of admirers. For some people this would lead to being rather superficial and facile in relationships—but not with you. Although very real and personable once you choose a partner, it might be hard to stay faithful with all those wishful thinkers about. The chance for unfaithfulness increases with jealous or overly controlling individuals (and in fact this partnering could prove disastrous for both parties).

Gift idea: a freshwater aquarium.

August 26

In typical Virgo manner, you absolutely love organization and structure. A good, well-conceived routine is a complete joy. People can set their clocks by your daily rituals. Mind you, those who live in the same space may find the lack of flexibility a little annoying, so learn to give a bit. Just as much as you need that routine, other folks have different ones that provide comfort too. In this, if you want a peaceful home, agree to disagree. Your birth number 7 can offer assistance here, blending logic with emotion and wisdom.

Speaking of home, when anyone visits your space they'll find it pristine, yet you demurely apologize for the "mess." This Virgo will not tolerate clutter or disorganization. To help ease the tension this may cause, it's good for you to have one spot that you can detail to your heart's content. Within that space, you can express all that fastidiousness, neatly distracting from the messes of others.

Similarly, others must realize you are just as detailed in your professional life—having it all mapped out and scheduled long in advance. That's one of the greatest challenges for those sharing this birthday—learning increased flexibility to meet unanticipated situations. When the road has a pothole, or there's a detour, you become disoriented and depressed, sensing failure when it's not your fault—it's just life!

Relationships fare better, however, thanks to the amount of energy our Virgo gives to them. Like all else in your life, no detail is overlooked when it comes to a loved one, and no important dates forgotten.

Gift idea: a wooden filing cabinet.

August 27

You're somewhat of a pessimist about life in general, seeing gray clouds hovering on the horizon. You're not content to leave things in that gloomy state, however—you want to fix everything right here, right now! That can lead to working in various charitable positions, but even such noble efforts never quite satisfy. Having a birth number of 8 means that you'll always try to fulfill the goals and expectations of others, but within yourself it never seems like enough. Holding high expectations is one thing, but it's okay to pat yourself on the back for a job well done too!

Today's Virgo needs to stop looking for trouble. There's more than enough of it in life without cultivating that negativity. Sadly, an imperfect world is part of what bugs this entire birth sign, which is happiest when things go exactly as planned. The calculating nature of the birth number 8 isn't helping matters much, so just try to cultivate a little more positivity in your life, as best you can.

As a friend or partner, you're relatively shy. A lot of that withholding comes from a certainty of getting hurt. Loved ones are going to have to jump through a few hoops before that wanes. However, if they show you that their intentions are honorable, you'll reward them with unbridled passion.

Gift idea: a sun lamp.

ESSENTIAL

The number for August is 8. This implies a month that's filled with social occasions, opportunities to enjoy nature, and some nice rewards coming from your hard work. If you've been facing a tough situation, hang in there—this is a time for change!

August 28

This is a Virgo perpetually on the move! You know who you are, and you know what you want out of life. Unlike those individuals who depend on others for a sense of accomplishment, you use your sign's organizational skills to set and meet personal goals regularly. Then you neatly pat yourself on the back. Before this sounds a tad self-centered, have no fear. You care about other people deeply, and use your personal confidence as a means of inspiration and transformation.

You are incredibly pragmatic, with the ability to look at any situation and figure out good options. A birth number of 9 supports this aptitude with keen insights and the ability to activate potentials. Consequently, positions in fields like promotion or acting as an agent suit you very nicely. Another alternative might be career counseling.

The discontentment of birth number 9 may hold our Virgo back in love. You wisely know life isn't like a greeting card, and you fear bad outcomes. Nonetheless, the idealistic perfection of that greeting card is exactly what you'd wish for, so having the attentions of a highly romantic partner is the best bet.

Gift idea: a Rockwell print.

August 29

Virgins celebrating their birthday today have strong entrepreneurial spirits. You're a hard worker intent on succeeding in whatever career path you choose (the sciences, accounting, and teaching are three good options). In the process, there's definitely a financial incentive that motivates you so you can enjoy the best things in life. Now, these choices aren't without typical Virgo reasoning—if you need a coffee pot, for example, it's going to be a high-end gourmet-quality machine that will last for years. "Buy once, buy right" is your motto.

All that spending might make people think there's nothing left to spare, but not so. You've got a head for numbers and can stretch a penny into dollars. You also know all the time and energy it's taken to accumulate that nest egg, and have no intention of letting it slip away. The dynamic, goal-oriented, and original energies of a birth number 1 certainly support this overall mindset. Additionally, this aptitude could lead to a job as a professional shopper, an accountant, or a financial advisor.

As for relationships, you have an engaging personality. It's not that hard to develop a respectful friendship, but love is a little more work (something this Virgo isn't afraid of). Overall you make a very attentive and diligent mate.

Gift idea: gourmet coffee.

FACT

The full moon of August was often called a Sturgeon Moon, after a common fish in the Great Lakes that was caught at this time of year. Other names include Red Moon, Corn Moon, and Grain Moon. Speaking of names, when the Romans decided this month should be named for Augustus, they didn't stop there! They gave the month 31 days so that it held equal weight to Julius's (July). Heaven forbid that Augustus seem in any way substandard! But that left a problem in the calendar. So February was reduced to 28 days but for leap year.

August 30

Like a cat, you always seem to land feet first, and after that you just keep moving! You've got a quick mind, great reflexes, and the agility of a gymnast all bundled into one very attractive package. Even with all that, however, you find yourself somewhat dissatisfied with life because you need ongoing opportunities to apply those diversified interests and abilities. Having a birth number of 2 will lend an assist in this, offering you the opportunity to mediate among them. You don't have to be "doing" 24-7. Sometimes it's good to just sit, socialize, and be!

You have a restless spirit, and this translates into a home or apartment that's more cluttered than characteristic of this sign. Tossing off clothing, changing for the next gig, and running out the door is par for the course here. So neat freaks be forewarned, living with this Virgin might try your patience a little bit. On the other hand, you have amazing mental organization skills.

You'll rarely (if ever) be late, and you remember every special occasion for friends, family, and business acquaintances.

The high-paced nature of your life can make love a little hard to catch up with. Nonetheless, you are very tender and expressive with lovers, and could make a great partner for the right person.

Gift idea: a wipe-off planning calendar.

August 31

Purpose is the name of the game for today's Virgo. You want the most competent approach to everything in your life—be it work, a hobby, or love. Time is something you treasure, so developing diversified aptitudes is one way of saving man-hours and accomplishing a lot more. Disorder is something that's intolerable, however. When the framework you've carefully constructed gets disrupted or falls apart, it puts you in a truly inconsolable, foul mood.

You use a very practical approach to daily tasks, and consequently do very well in office and highly professional settings. You could lead, but are typically inclined to be part of the process rather than the head of the pack. Having the positive, joyful energy of a birth number 3 makes you an excellent team player, with perseverance and a positive outlook to inspire many.

That dependable and cheerful nature influences relationships positively. You are honest and kind toward those you love, and give affection freely. Most likely you will settle down to a happy long-term marriage or commitment filled with tenderness.

Gift idea: a portable spot-cleaner kit.

Leo

Sign: Leo
Date: July 23–August 22
Ruled by: Sun
Element: Fire
Lucky Color: Gold, vibrant yellow
Gemstone: Gold topaz, ruby
Keynote: Leadership
Positive Traits: Friendly, giving, energetic, secure
Negative Traits: Temperamental, loud, haughty
Famous Leos include: Neil Armstrong, Lucille Ball, Bill "Count" Basie, Helena Blavatsky, Alexandre Dumas, Cecil B. De Mille, Amelia Earhart

In a pride of lions there's always one who wants to be head of the pack. That's true for most born under this sign. At work, at home, and in social settings, Leos make excellent leaders and facilitators.

Being ruled by the sun, Leo wants to shine with talent, passion, a regal air, and uniqueness. At times this larger-than-life persona can come across as superficial or arrogant. While both can be a Leo shortcoming, normally the lion really dislikes haughtiness—in other words, it's all for show.

Every part of a Leo's home expresses the self in some way. In particular, mirrors seem to be a common theme not so much to be arrogant, but to make sure the lion's mane is always well kept. People born under this sign generally abhor messes, and that same attitude translates into every corner of the living space.

The roaring lion has strong dramatic tendencies. You want center stage and seek out the spotlight. Conversely, the Lion can purr with charm, nobility, and incredible charity. This odd mix brings out confidence in your associates, and you choose those people mindfully, seeking a loyal and idealistic nature.

Relationships with a Leo are romantic and full of fire. The drawback for such a personality is the temptation to give in to ego, never admitting a wrong. Nonetheless, as partners they share compliments and appreciation equally. If you want to tame this kitty, remember to return those strokes with healthy portions of love.

Chapter 11

September

September gets its name from the Latin designation for the number seven, *septem*. In Japan it's considered the month of the long moon, because of the moon's visibility in the night sky. The Swiss consider it a harvest month, and among Jewish people it's a month filled with holidays, including Rosh Hashanah, the Day of Atonement (Yom Kippur), and the Feast of Tabernacles. Until September 22nd, the month is ruled by Virgo, the virgin or maiden. The end of the month belongs to the ever-adaptable Libra.

September 1

You're a Virgin with high expectations of yourself and everyone you know. This means being a bit hypercritical and easily disheartened when anyone doesn't measure up to a perceived potential. That tendency often leads you to doing everything yourself, feeling you'd rather just get it done right than be frustrated yet again. Unfortunately, not everything in life can be controlled, and if you spread yourself too thin you're going to be very disappointed in the outcomes, something that your birth number of 1 won't tolerate. You know you want to succeed, but sometimes you have to accept bronze or silver instead of always coveting gold.

As a career path, you have a rather odd caregiver tendency, but not with people so much as situations. You have no patience for messes. And since you can't sit still easily, you will take matters in hand and begin to re-order that situation. Most often people appreciate the help, but sometimes it takes you into places where you really have no business being. One way to avoid that is to direct personal energy toward careers that fulfill Virgo's need to stay on the go, such as a tour guide.

When it comes to relationships, friendship is okay, but love certainly isn't at the top of the list in priorities. Really, you are too busy to develop anything serious. On the rare occasion when someone manages to get your attention, that partner must be incredibly loyal, devoted, and understanding.

Gift idea: a surprise day of leisure (as far away from the job as possible).

September 2

People celebrating birthdays today have a knack with words in both written and verbal form. The only problem is that you sometimes wield them as weapons, being blunt. You have little patience for pussy-footing around when it comes to getting a point across, but remember that words can wound very deeply. Open the door for your birth number 2 in these moments so it can balance that fast tongue with harmonious intention. You already know when you tend to put your foot in your mouth, so just slow down and think first.

Your career may not be in full force until you're in your late thirties. Mostly this happens because self-motivation isn't your forte. You hate processing change, and would prefer to avoid it even though it's inevitable. On the other hand, today's personology report indicates you've got a knack for fashion, and might consider your aptitude with clothing as a bridge between what you fear, and what you know and love. Design the latest trends!

As for relationships? Well, this Virgo is a little demanding in love and not overly physical. You want a very attentive partner who's responsive to emotional needs, yet at the same time you hate being out of the driver's seat. When things aren't going as desired, you glower, making it hard to make up. Perhaps a mutable Gemini is the answer here.

Gift idea: a designer scarf.

Ruled by Earth, many Virgos greatly enjoy gardening and landscaping. If you don't have a yard, your house is likely filled with all manner of designer orchids or impeccable window boxes. And if you can grow something edible, even better. Try some basil in the kitchen to inspire love in the home. Other hobbies that appeal to Virgo sensibilities include macramé, decoupage, sewing, and cooking. Virgins also like to collect things, like crystal and mineral samples. Virgos enjoy practical hobbies, like restoring antique furniture. In any case, no matter the activity, the Virgin's tools are well cared for and immaculately organized.

September 3

Where many born under Virgo have highly critical personalities, people celebrating birthdays today break that mold. Life has taught you that adaptation is the name of the game, and you are great at it, perhaps a little too good. If you aren't careful you could begin to lose your identity to a group or situational mind.

As one would expect with a birth number 3, you're a very upbeat person. You manage to maintain your emotions with practiced control—except when someone threatens those you love or a cherished project. Then all hell breaks loose and everyone with an iota of wisdom gets the heck out of your way! Rather than automatically go into warrior mode, however, you'd do well to use your words. You've got the ability, and may even have pursued a career in writing or speaking, so why not use it?

With family and friends, you are very faithful and protective. Love isn't quite so simple, however. You have a dream of what true love should be, and it's a rare person who can measure up. Additionally, you aren't overly monogamous by nature, meaning any partners have to be truly liberated souls.

Gift idea: handmade writing paper.

FACT

Historical Events in September: WWII Begins in Poland (September 1, 1939); Viking II lands on Mars (September 3, 1976); George Eastman patents film camera (September 4, 1888); McKinley shot at the Pan-American exposition (September 6, 1901); Elvis first appears on Ed Sullivan Show (September 9, 1956); Lassie debuts on TV (September 12, 1954); first edition of *New York Times* published (September 17, 1851); Sandra Day O'Connor appointed to Supreme Court (September 21, 1981); Neptune discovered (September 23, 1846); *West Side Story* first appears on Broadway (September 26, 1957); Nuremberg Trial finds twenty-two Nazis guilty of war crimes (September 30, 1946).

September 4

Network, network, network—that's your motto. There is very little you can't accomplish by contacting a few well-chosen businesses or people, and you've got enough drive to see through any goal to completion. Your birth number of 4 stresses that work ethic, but may also put too much emphasis on monetary gain. There's little question you have a king's tastes, but what does the budget tell you? Be careful to remain realistic here, and value the people in your life as much as all those trinkets you've been collecting.

It's not surprising that today's Virgo excels in the career arena. You know how to work a room or a whole company! It's suggested that you look into careers that apply all that connectivity—and think outside the box here.

That talent applies to everything from creating search engines to being an information gatherer or investigator. No matter the job, it's important that your excessive nature not get the best of you.

And what about love? Just as sure as you want beautiful things, you also want a nearly pristine partner to show off like art. Consequently, you often end up with rather superficial relationships when what you really crave is substance. Once committed, this Virgo can be lead astray by her ever-wandering eye for beauty.

Gift idea: a crystal vase.

September 5

People born on September 5 are very imaginative. You have a rich inner life that often helps you develop great solutions for other people's problems, or ideas for their business endeavors. Unfortunately that creative aptitude seems to stop with you! And while that's frustrating, it's okay in that you can make a career as a business consultant, counselor, or anything where you can crunch ideas and let others manifest them.

As an individual, you are a "starter." You've got great enthusiasm for the start of a project, but get distracted around the midpoint and leave tons of loose ends (very unusual for this birth sign). Having a birth number of 5 constantly distracting you with that next project or idea doesn't help. That's why today's personology report steers you toward being an icebreaker— introducing concepts for more tenacious people to choose from and then complete.

What's odd is that relationships seem to be just the opposite. You stay in even unhealthy and mind-numbing situations because you've given your word. This happens because you have a happily-ever-after fantasy that you hope to fulfill, but sadly you often pick the wrong companion for making that happen.

Gift idea: a day planner to help stay on track.

September 6

Being a Virgo, you like order. Unfortunately, life seems to have something else in mind—a whole lot of unplanned, odd twists and turns of fate. Urgh! While you've learned it's just the way your life goes, that doesn't mean you've ever gotten comfortable with such changeableness. The idealism of your birth number 6 helps you adjust a little, but it also yearns for beauty—and as a Virgo, beauty equals planning and order. Needless to say there are some days you're just plain pissed off about this dichotomy, but eventually your sense of humor helps you past the hump.

People sharing this birthday have an interesting aptitude for counseling. First you need to take care of personal and family problems, since others' issues distract you completely. Your challenge is to become your own guru and guide so you can better fulfill the goal of helping others (something the humanitarian tone of 6 really stresses).

When it comes to romance, love hasn't always been kind to our Virgin. There are more than a couple of scars lingering in this heart, and those experiences have left you uncertain about choosing mates. Any potential partner needs to be very real, loving, and supportive.

Gift idea: some CDs with the sounds of nature for relaxation.

September 7

Today's Virgo has a nasty habit of spending way too much time mulling things over. While it's typical of the investigative birth number 7, and most people born under this sign do plan and ponder, you've got to periodically come out of that shell to deal with real life. Yes, it's hard because you're empathic, and part of that mental retreat is a protective instinct. And some people find it charming that you're so mysterious, but that still means you're not being wholly open with those who matter the most. Try building some psychic shields so that your sensitive self can be more expressive.

You tend to carry around a lot of stress because you don't like having your routines and procedures disrupted. This sets you into a rather grumpy and overly critical mood that doesn't wane quickly. With this temperament in mind, it might be wise to consider solo careers in areas like research (a field that the birth number 7 also supports). Even with a rather disagreeable personality, this is still Virgo, which means plentiful mental and organizational aptitude.

With friends and lovers alike, that picky nature continues and often causes problems. Those who care about you need to understand that those harsh words are really projection—you feel insignificant compared to those you love, but rather than see that personal fault, you lash out. Nonetheless, because of a Capricorn decanate, you can be reasoned with. When loved ones are patient and precise, everything will work out.

Gift idea: micro tools.

September 8

This Virgo is wholly grounded in reality. You have a somewhat suspicious nature, and rarely take any situation or person at face value. Yet in an odd dichotomy, you have little interest in anything spiritual or mystical—here and now is what matters, not something unproven. That rather concrete perspective is strengthened by the birth number of 8, which puts both feet on terra firma and keeps them there.

Personally and professionally, you are a what-you-see-is-what-you-get individual. No one ever has to question the meaning behind your words or actions. You've made everything abundantly clear from the get-go. Actually, this makes friends, family, and coworkers all the more respectful and could earmark someone who's a natural born leader. Having a Capricorn decanate improves that aptitude by providing this Virgo with a strong work ethic, enthusiasm, and precision.

In love, this Virgin isn't very spontaneous. You prefer to pace relationships and keep emotional growth neatly under control. Of course, relationships rarely prove to be that steady or regulated, which makes our Virgo rather nervous. It would be best to avoid signs like Gemini which are all about ongoing change.

Gift idea: a pocket watch.

ALERT!

Being detailed oriented, it's not surprising to discover that Virgos are very picky about their clothing. Many prefer timeless cuts that stay crisp and travel well. Elegance is preferred over drama, and gentle, practical colors win out over shocking hues (especially earth tones). You will rarely (if ever) find these people wearing torn pants or stained shirts, even when cleaning. In fact, if you peek in the closet or the drawers, you're likely to find even socks neatly matched and pressed for success!

September 9

You are no shrinking violet by any means. There's a raging storm inside you, one that needs regular venting to keep from boiling over. Part of the fighting spirit comes from the birth number 9's influence. Ideals and the desire to create a better future are well and good, but there are some things that can't be fixed by fighting. This lesson is very hard for you, as you've got lots of courage and fortitude, but a short fuse.

Try to channel that brave spirit in positive ways. Look to careers that push you physically, like being a karate instructor or physical education coach. That will help burn off a little of that tough scrappiness, and also improve your sleep patterns, which often get interrupted when you're convinced trouble's afoot. Speaking of which, stop seeing specters around every corner. Not everything is a battle waiting to happen, and there are some things from which you should just walk away.

Another option that might help today's Virgo is sex—lots of it! This Virgin is already a hot, zealous lover, so why not make the most of it? Find a partner who's creative and energetic in bed to help release some of that pent-up energy.

Gift idea: a punching bag.

September 10

What happens when you combine a birth number of 1 with the finicky nature of Virgo? You get an incredibly goal-oriented individual who's insistent, uncompromising, and highly independent. You scoff at the notion that "no man is an island." Truth be told, you'd rather stand alone than with incompetent companions just to appease some social expectation. Additionally, today's Virgin has no patience for the users of the world. Woe to one who tries to ride your coattails.

You find yourself drawn to sports and physical activity. You want to "win" at something (that pesky birth number 1 again) and have the stamina to develop strongly in your chosen arena, be it sport fishing (which also gives you private time) or mountain climbing. Bear in mind, however, that Virgos like brain food too, so that competitive nature might express itself in things like champion chess.

While this personology report might imply otherwise, relationships turn out okay for you. Once a person manages to get into your heart, a change happens. Partners discover you have the ability to build self-esteem in others and respond very appreciatively. Partners just need to remember to remain somewhat aloof and give you plenty of independence to ensure the relationship's longevity.

Gift idea: a trip to a lake.

September 11

You tend to be a bit of a loner, especially early in life. Part of that comes from trying to figure out various matters that seem to have no viable answers. That philosophical, introspective nature begins to wane around thirty, which is when the birth number of 2 takes over and provides more social instincts. Once you come out of your shell it's time to share all those wonderful ideas you've been coming up with over the years. Trust yourself! These could be really BIG if manifested effectively.

Because of your inquisitive nature, you are good at research-oriented jobs. That Capricorn decanate offers methodical approaches and focus perfectly suited to scientific endeavors. And when it's time to reveal discoveries, the charm of the birth number 2 comes through in communication skills, getting people to listen and building enthusiasm.

You take your time with developing friendships and prefer one or two lifelong friends to dozens of so-so associates. In love, however, you aren't the least Virginal. You have a huge appetite for sex and sensual variety, and need a creative partner to help you explore fully.

Gift idea: a scrapbooking kit.

QUESTION?

What observances take place in September?
September is National Apple Month, an observance started by the U.S. Apple Association. September also hosts a variety of other month-long observances, including Baby Safety Month, National Chicken Month, Classical Music Month, National Coupon Month, National Honey Month, International Self-Awareness Month, and Tiger Month.

September 12

You're a very diligent worker, and you seem to have taken the Virgo concept of structure and applied it to every corner of your life. Part of this comes from desperately wanting security, which you think comes from meticulous attention to detail (and often you're right!). But don't completely forego a social life. Really, not every project has to be done three days ahead of schedule. In fact, if you take a breather it will allow everyone else to catch up to you.

Individuals sharing this birthday sometimes feel underappreciated for their efforts. It's a hard pill to swallow for you to realize that the extra work you've taken on dutifully has become the "norm" in other people's eyes. To offset this, consider keeping a progress log that illustrates successes and accomplishments to bosses, supervisors, and coworkers (especially come raise and bonus time). You make your "luck" through never-ending efforts and deserve a pat on the back.

Having a birth number of 3 is your saving grace in relationships. Where you've got very framed expectations and the typical desire to control common in this sign, the happiness inherent in 3 overshadows that with significant others. Partnering with this Virgo is a very surprising and expressive interaction.

Gift idea: ballroom dance classes.

September 13

You've taken all that Virgo specificity and applied it visually. You can walk into a room and see the smallest item out of place, or look at blueprints and quickly isolate problems. This is a fantastic ability that serves you well in careers requiring an eye for detail, be it as a lab assistant, prototype designer, or structural engineer. So stop thinking so little of yourself. It's okay to be proud of those accomplishments!

Those born today have a Taurus decanate, which certainly explains the ability to think outside the box as well as all that personal determination. This couples very nicely with the practical, focused nature of birth number 4. Additionally, Virgos love the structured energies 4 offers. Overall, you're not likely to find a more orderly, methodical person, respected by many and to whom animals gravitate like a fresh dish of food. Sometimes, however, you spread yourself too thin, finding it hard to say no. If you can loosen up periodically, it would alleviate a lot of stress.

Speaking of liberation, in relationships you like a highly spirited and independent mate. While birth number 4 wants security, you feel that at least part of the true security in a relationship comes with trust and with each person's being an individual in his or her own right.

Gift idea: a parakeet.

September 14

Ah, now we come to the quintessential Virgo perfectionist. As the saying goes, "the devil's in the details," and that's a motto by which you likely approach your personal and professional lives. There's no room for sloppiness or oversights, especially in highly technical matters. This makes you a great efficiency manager or inspector, because you won't overlook safety protocol. However, your coworkers might see you as bossy or unyielding. In this setting, that's just fine, as your responsibilities require that kind of dedication. Just remember to take off that hat with friends and family at home.

Having a birth number of 5 allows today's Virgo to develop a variety of skills and multitask with ease. You may also find yourself attracted to helping with situations where there's a perceived injustice. Nonetheless, come private time, you often choose to go it alone, getting caught up in detailed thoughts and mentally reordering the coming days.

That detached and somewhat standoffish demeanor may make relationship building difficult. It's not that you don't want companions, but you tend to hold them to the same standards as yourself, which are very high and very hard for anyone to meet. Any long-term partners need to be very diligent and sticklers for details.

Gift idea: drawer or closet organizers.

According to superstition, people who wear September's birthstone (the sapphire) are ensured of wisdom, protection, and clear mindedness. It's also supposed to attract love and joy to the bearer, only breaking if there's impending danger. Traditionally sapphire is given as a gift for the 5th, 23rd, and 45th wedding anniversaries. The stone is second only to diamonds in hardness. Star sapphires are actually rutilated, which gives them the appearance of having six or twelve rays emerging from the center of a cabochon. The most popular color for sapphire is blue, but it does occur naturally in other hues, including one type of stone that appears as different colors in different light.

September 15

You are a heart-and-home Virgo who truly enjoys having a pristine living space. But that doesn't mean plastic covering the furniture. Rather, your home is a reflection of good taste, artistic sensibility, and order. You truly feel that all else in life runs more smoothly when personal living spaces provide comfort, function, and structure against the world's chaos. Within this region, our Virgo loves to have company, nitpicking over their needs and desires, and of course showing off the latest edition to the home's décor! All of this detail makes the birth number 6 very, very happy indeed. Taking pleasure in beauty is what this number is all about.

Those sharing this birthday put just as much effort into their jobs. You take pride in being a good worker and giving your best daily. Better still, your natural charm and inventiveness get those efforts noticed. It probably won't take long before you're well on your way to raises or promotions no matter what career path you've chosen. However, because you have an eye for potentials, you might consider career counseling or job placement as options.

Come the end of the day, you want to return home to a genuine, loving, and stable partner (not to mention a peaceful family). Arguing at the dinner table is a huge faux pas no matter who you are!

Gift idea: a tea-rose bush complete with windowsill planter.

September 16

The instinctive, curious nature of a birth number 7 really comes out in you. There is little that you'll allow to stand between you and getting to the truth of a situation, or the real person beneath a visage. If you're a parent, your children think you completely psychic because they can't fib to save their lives. Very little gets by you, and that observant nature serves you well when it comes to finding opportunities or measuring up circumstances. Additionally, that somewhat spiritual edge allows you to see a bigger picture than most people. Thinking globally is definitely part of your philosophy.

Taurus is the decanate in today's personology report, bringing to bear all the determination, communication, and love that the sign offers. The ability to get across very difficult ideas in particular helps today's Virgo. You would make an excellent teacher in any setting. Alternatively a PR or speechwriter position, particularly in politics, is likewise an apt choice of career paths. In any case, you have plenty of energy and enough inspiration to motivate lasting changes.

Taurus definitely expresses itself again in your relationships. All the faces of love are important to you—be it the love of art, a pet, a career, or a partner. The expression of those feelings is also vital. You need an open partner who honestly articulates feelings and who listens equally well.

Gift idea: an anti-gravity space pen.

September 17

You express the Taurus decanate differently. You exhibit the willful, determined, and persistent nature of the Bull combined with all that Virgo organization. Just be careful. Sometimes you press forward not realizing you're running roughshod over others with all that comprehensive vigor—something that generates resentment from coworkers. If you're part of a team, you need to work cooperatively—something that your birth number of 8 can help with. Let it guide you in understanding the people with whom you interact so you can better apply all that energy.

Anything that requires detail and follow-through is perfect for you. Careers in research, design, and most technical/scientific fields are ideal. Additionally, you have a good knack for money, so you're likely to be very stable financially and able to help others get the budget under control. In return, if the person born on this date is your friend or mate—do them a favor. Teach them how to relax a little. The blending of energies here sometimes makes for a much too serious person who forgets that play and laughter are both healthy releases.

As for love, you want the happily-ever-after scenario, complete with kids and a white picket fence. Only one issue stands in the way, and that's an over-exaggerated sense of responsibility toward work. Once you learn to balance a personal and professional life, you make a genuine, passionate partner.

Gift idea: a day of pampering at a salon.

QUESTION?

What is the flower for September, and what does it represent?
September's flower is the morning glory. In the Victorian language of flowers it represents life's transience, but in bridal bouquets it symbolizes affection. They grow naturally throughout the United States, Brazil, and the West Indies. The flowers typically open just before sunrise, and come evening they close again. There are over 1200 species of this flower. The common morning glory can climb as high as ten feet to nearly cover buildings and fences throughout the months of June to October. They come in a variety of colors, including pink, red, white, purple, and variegated.

September 18

Those celebrating a birthday today have a very private side. While your charm and charisma make you the center of attention, there are many times you wish you could just hit the "off" switch and get some peace. You need periodic retreats from the hustle and bustle because you see and feel too much (thanks to the birth number 9 whispering all those truths in your ear). On the other hand, the humanitarian nature of your birth number makes it hard to say no. The best advice here is to remember that saying "yes" to your sacred Self sometimes means saying "no" to someone else, and in your case, it's very important for mental well-being.

In the professional realm, you could obtain mundane success, but often find yourself attracted to loftier goals. You may turn to religion and spirituality, or perhaps charitable causes. While the Virgo sensibility still requires making enough to cover bills, the idea of being rich when others are so needy is disdainful, as is any type of wastefulness on people's part. Would that such a person ran the government budget!

In relationships, the Taurus decanate stands out, demanding harmony and cooperation. You don't manage well in chaos, and shouting probably sends you right up the wall. Your partner needs a soft, sensitive voice and diplomatic skills to help manage the home.

Gift idea: create a special private space in the home just for them!

September 19

Today's Virgo has that certain "something"—it's alluring, curious, mysterious, and yet wholly indefinable. People seem to take to you like peanut butter to jelly, yet you're not wholly self-assured. You see all this admiration and can't figure out what all the fuss is about. That's part of your lesson in this life: seeing your own potential as clearly as do others. With that enthralling aura, there's much you could do—be it entertaining the masses or inspiring them to greater things.

Today's birth number is 1, meaning that ideals and morals guide your actions and reactions. You want to do something substantive that will remain in the memories of fellow workers, family, or associates for a very long time.

Today's personology report implies that you have the smarts to manage that, but not necessarily the patience or confidence. If you can develop those two attributes, watch out! The future is bright, indeed.

The lack of security manifests at the beginning stages of relationships too. You often look to others for assurance (be it in the bedroom or boardroom, you want a support structure). Know, however, that once this Virgo feels truly loved, that neediness begins to disappear and a very hot lover emerges.

Gift idea: an antique mirror.

FACT

Late September brings cooler air and turning leaves to our attention. Among earlier civilizations, this was when the fall equinox was celebrated, being the date on which day and night are equal in length. This was often the final harvest for the year, during which people would make offerings to the land and the divine in hopes that winter would be mild, and the following growing season abundant. Other rituals included symbolic practices meant to keep the sun strong, such as in Egypt, where an observance called Staffs of the Sun was enacted to support the solar disk in its travels. Because of the increasing darkness, some cultures began various festivals for the dead on or around this date, as in Japan, where ancestors are honored on this day.

September 20

The best word to describe today's Virgin is "selfless". You live to help others, and are constantly on the lookout for the opportunity to do so. Being very enduring and productive by nature, you're willing to wait for the time to be right or act quickly as situations require. Having a Taurus decanate doesn't hurt here, as it adds personal charisma. When you speak, people really listen, and when you lead, they'll usually follow dutifully. And thanks to your birth number of 2, you'll never abuse that trust.

Being a typical Virgo means there's a lot of attention given to details, in this case hygiene. The greatest torture for you is being stranded at an airport without a shower or freshly pressed clothing. This seems odd when contrasted with your humanitarian nature, but in your mind presentation counts for a lot, and those first impressions could make or break negotiations easily. It's a tactic that works, so why fight it?

Being a caregiver means that you sometimes find it hard to receive. That can make it difficult for potential partners to initiate a relationship, but stick to it! Those who serve need service and support, and eventually you'll learn to accept that energy with gratefulness and devotion in return.

Gift idea: a portable iron and some fabric freshener.

September 21

This is the point in the month when Libra begins to exert just a little influence. Unlike many Virgos, you're not tied to caution and structure. Instead, you appreciate innovative ideas and methods that can open the path to genius. In particular, your focus is drawn to concepts that can shape the future, even if only for a moment. This keeps you completely aware of societal trends, but by no means marries you to them. If you like a prevalent style (for example), fine—but if not, you're not afraid to make your own mark.

A birth number of 3 makes for a well-rounded personality that can laugh at life's odd twists and turns. You rarely get depressed, and even when things get tough it seems like serendipity favors you. In the end, you land on your feet as agilely as a cat (without a hair out of place). About the only things that seems to set you on edge are individuals who obsess over trivial issues that won't even matter in five minutes, let alone five days.

Turning to relationships, you need a fair amount of autonomy with friends and lovers both. You feel that relationships are a dance—moving close to and away from each other as life and circumstances dictate. You always have an awareness of each other, and a trust, but not a ball-and-chain that restricts growth and experience.

Gift idea: a night out dancing.

September 22

Those born on the Virgo/Libra cusp tend to be susceptible to sensual influences. Loud noises, coarse textures, intense flavors, etc.—all these things can positively or negatively affect your demeanor rather quickly. Be aware of that, and try to provide yourself with at least one room that supplies you with completely positive, restful input. Beyond this, you've got Virgo smarts and a Libra's people skills. Not a bad match with the Taurus decanate providing wisdom, reasoning aptitude, and expressiveness.

Today is associated with two birth numbers, 4 and 22, which work marvelously together. Twenty-two implies that you can manifest your hopes and dreams, and if spiritually inspired could be a truly enlightened soul. Four provides the pragmatic balance point for 22, emphasizing foundation building and diligence. In short, these individuals are very centered, earthy, and capable, which typically results in financial security and the respect of coworkers and employers alike).

Privately the Libra in you wants commitment, while the Virgin asserts independence. This can confuse friends and mates equally until they come to understand that natural cycle in your life. Those who learn to release and embrace as needed will be appreciated and adored.

Gift idea: a cuddly lap warmer.

September 23

Happy Birthday Libra! You have a gentle, sociable spirit that's common to people born under this sign. Being around others gives you a lot of energy, and it's not hard to find individuals with whom to share time. They come to you! That happy, warm, and very real personality is contagious. Hang on to that treasure, knowing that your demeanor blesses many even without your actively trying.

About the only thing your scale can't measure is petty arguing. When others bicker over silly things in front of you, they better be prepared to either get a stern correction or watch your clouds turn dark and foreboding. Your ideals find that behavior abhorrent and frustrating. That outlook is seconded by the birth number 5 that far prefers working on an opportunity over wasting time arguing about how many angels dance on the head of a pin. With this in mind, you might consider jobs where you can avoid office politics and group dynamics that are ripe with such trite influences.

Knowing that people find you attractive makes you cautious. You definitely want to enjoy closeness, but first you need to be sure someone's on the level and really see what's inside. Past that point, you become a very romantic partner.

Gift idea: a portable CD player (for musical distraction when arguments ensue).

ALERT!

In many cultures the full moon of September is called the Harvest Moon, as this is the time when farmers are collecting the fruits of their labors. One thing people don't know is that every third year, the harvest moon occurs in October (astronomically, it's the full moon closest to the autumnal equinox). Other cultures had different names for this moon, including Nut Moon (Cherokee), Singing Moon (Celtic), Calves Grow Hair Moon (Sioux), and Barley Moon (Medieval England).

September 24

You are everything positive a Libra was born to be—inventive, artful, charismatic, outgoing, fair, strong, and sensitive. And while that packaging would make some people egotistical, you feel no need to lord your positive attributes over others; rather, living them is your goal. The phrase "walking your talk" definitely applies in your life—you don't say it unless you mean it, and plan to be a role model afterward. Bravo!

People sharing this birthday usually have a buoyant perspective. You can see splendor and potential in the oddest things, something that the birth number of 6 adores! However, you might turn into a gloomy Gus when confronted by people who choose willful ignorance and hatred over more positive emotions and ambitions. Normally, that angst disappears around the age of twenty-five, but it may return periodically to nag your sense of right and wrong. With this in mind, it wouldn't hurt to seek out situations that resonate with beauty, such as working in an art gallery.

In relationships, keeping the peace is a central concern, but because you are even-handed to begin with, that's usually not too difficult. When dating, you keep a safe but interested distance until trust develops. In romance, potential mates should be prepared for a very entertaining partner.

Gift idea: a bouquet of wildflowers.

September 25

If you were born on this day, you have all the potential to be a shining star in whatever field you choose. Being highly captivating and magnetic is only half the picture. You're also an incredibly creative individual who's not afraid to work to accomplish whatever you want in life. In fact, you take pride in those honest efforts, believing fully that it's not just the destination that matters but also how one goes about getting there. You want to look back without regrets and idealistic misgivings.

Libras celebrating today have rainbow personalities—you sparkle with character and loads of talent. By the age of thirty-five, most have made a huge impact in some career or in the lives of others. Periodically prone to whimsy and adventure, not every single Libra escapade accomplishes something "big" (except for personal pleasure). Nonetheless, as a Libra you know how to bring things back into balance and ultimately determine your success by ongoing greatness.

About the only arena in which you fall down is love. Having such a big aura attracts a lot of admirers, and it's hard to pick and choose among them. This often lands you in dubious relationships. Plus, you have a strong sense of autonomy, not wanting to be overly tied down.

Gift idea: a desktop fountain.

September 26

If people didn't know better they'd swear you were a Taurus, because of your determination, or a Virgo, because you're so exasperatingly fastidious. It's a pretty potent combination, but one that's also highly competitive and demanding of your time and energy. Having a birth number of 8 only accentuates all this with its responsible, goal-driven nature. Take care here, as there's a tendency to lose yourself to a project or a situation in the haze of having to "do it all."

In professional life, you thrive on deadlines. It wouldn't be surprising to see you immersed in investigative journalism, for example. Stress is like candy—it provides a sweet motivation to get the job done. As one might guess, however, you can easily burn out, having taken on too much, too soon. Learning when to pull back and when to completely stand aside is one of your hardest lessons.

In relationships, you seem to lose all sense of balance. You seek a traditional love, but don't make real time for that relationship. While there's no question you're attractive to many people (having a great eye for style and overall good manners), it will take a very determined and clever mate to sneak onto your dance card and stay there. But once that's accomplished, you give your whole heart and complete loyalty.

Gift idea: no-iron clothing for the Libra on-the-go.

FACT

Famous September birthdays include: Dr. Phil (9/1), Charlie Sheen (9/3), Raquel Welch (9/5), Michael Keaton (9/5), Jeff Foxworthy (9/6), Adam Sandler (9/9), Hugh Grant (9/9), Kristy McNichol (9/11), Ben Savage (9/13), Tommy Lee Jones (9/15), B.B. King (9/16), David Copperfield (9/16), John Ritter (9/17), Frankie Avalon (9/18), Sophia Loren (9/20), Bill Murray (9/21), Ray Charles (9/23), Barbara Walters (9/25), Mark Hamill (9/25), Christopher Reeve (9/25), Olivia Newton John (9/26), Gwyneth Paltrow (9/28), Ed Sullivan (9/28), Fran Drescher (9/30).

September 27

The words "hungry for life" seem almost insufficient to describe anyone born today. People see you as being very centered and focused, but inside you're an incredible ball of ambition. Once you've sorted through the possibilities and set your sights on a goal, everyone had better move out of the way. There's no stopping you until you feel you've completed what you set out to do (and there are very few individuals who can maintain the pace you set). Just be careful to take that first introspective step of really looking at all the options. Otherwise you can run headlong into a brick wall. Your birth number of 9 is your best ally here—allowing you to determine what is true, and what is simply pretty packaging.

Professionally you exhibit a never-ending quest for perfection (nearly Virgo-like in its orderliness). You have no desire to be second best, and strive for that idealistic image painted by birth number 9 in body, mind, and spirit. That may naturally lead to some type of martial art (this combines the three aspects of human nature) as a hobby or a career. No matter the choice of jobs, the more complex the task given, the happier you become. You adore a good challenge, especially one that forces you into more self-improvement (something you can easily measure).

Love is a secondary consideration for today's Libra. Sometimes it's easier to go it alone when you're still very much the center of your universe. That doesn't mean you completely forego intimacy, but rather when it happens it's often a spontaneous moment of passion, or a chance to try out something new. Consequently, any long-term partners have to be very self-sufficient.

Gift idea: classical music.

September 28

Just as the scales depict, there are two distinct sides to you—the one you show to the world at large, and the one known to people in your innermost circle. Oh, certainly the two have much in common. Both exhibit a keen sense of protocol, kindness, and likeability. However, the secret self is also far more impulsive and direct than many born under this sign. You frequently struggle with that brashness, knowing full well that swift words and ill-considered actions have landed you in trouble repeatedly in the past.

In daily life it's not hard for you to find admirers. However, leadership isn't high on your list of goals. While a birth number of 1 might wish otherwise, you realize that kind of position is just too tempting to the foolhardy spark within. Oddly, that self-awareness is provided by your number 1 as well (the "I am"), and it's often a saving grace careerwise. Just about the

Virgo

Sign: Virgo

Date: August 23–September 22

Ruled by: Mercury

Element: Earth

Lucky Color: Midnight blue

Gemstone: Sapphire

Keynote: Detail-oriented

Positive Traits: Organized, proficient, giving, aware, gentle

Negative Traits: Victim mentality, overly critical, high anxiety/stress tendencies

Famous Virgos include: Dr. Phil, Sid Caesar, Queen Elizabeth I, Greta Garbo, Arthur Godfrey, Sophia Loren, Twiggy

Virgos are all about precision. At home, orderliness shines (even in the deepest recesses of the refrigerator). At work, discipline, self-regulation, and perfectionist outlooks prevail. While some people in the Virgo's life find this need for structure stifling, it's the way in which a Virgo creates a sense of security. The only problem here is that Virgos frequently get tied up in the details and lose the ability to think globally. This, in turn, can lead to being overly submissive or feeling underappreciated (often rightly so).

Virgos love conversation, and are often quite adept at it. There's one drawback though. What other people say, Virgos take absolutely literally—no shading, no nuance. Needless to say, this results in a variety of heated moments over the littlest thing. Add that to the high expectations Virgos hold for everyone, and it's hard for anyone, including even another Virgo, to measure up.

In terms of the Virgo outlook, this sign does not suffer fools easily (especially willful ones). Virgos expect people to be active participants in life and personal success. When someone falls short, a Virgo will provide useful ideas and insights to get things back into a practical, efficient order. Once on a task, just get out of the Virgo's way! In relationships, Virgos offer dependability and true devotion to those who can help them stop thinking for a while and start feeling.

Chapter 12
October

If you'd lived in ancient Rome, October would have been the eighth month of the year (but it still had 31 days). It gets its name from this ancient placement—*oct* meaning eight. October begins in the birth sign of Libra, the Scales, which belonged to the Roman goddess of justice. Romans believed that the city of Rome was founded when the moon was in this sign, symbolizing the balance it would bring to the civilized world. The month ends in the sign of Scorpio, the Scorpion.

October 1

Today's Libra has the attention-seeking motivations worthy of a Leo. Thankfully you've got loads of aptitude and charisma, so much of the notice you get comes without any real effort on your part. Additionally, a birth number of 2 means you've got this very natural way with people, one that seems almost unassuming. You probably find yourself entertaining frequently, often with guests arriving unexpectedly. And since your home is always tidy and stocked, you can make an easy go of a fun evening!

Careerwise, there's plenty of work ethic and ambition here. The only problem is determining whether those efforts should be cooperative (as the birth number 2 would wish) or independent (as is a Libra trait). Perhaps there's a way to put these together by becoming a media representative or spokesperson, both positions where there's other talent to draw upon, but where you have a solitary space.

Friendships and love are two areas where today's Libra struggles a bit. There's the green-eyed monster afoot just underneath the surface of that amazingly engaging smile. If you don't get adequate attention, you begin to wonder if someone else is in the picture. Additionally, in true Libra form, you're emotionally needy in other ways. The best bet is a very giving and sensitive partner who puts all those misgivings to rest.

Gift idea: sunglasses.

ALERT!

The birthstone for October is the opal. The concept that opals are bad luck is a relatively modern one. Romans regularly carried them to improve good fortune and as a protective or love-inspiring talisman. Many other peoples believed in the stone's magical qualities including the Greeks, who saw it as a prophetic gem, and Far Easterners, who believed beliefs that it was a "hope" stone. An Aboriginal myth says the opal was born from a rainbow that fell out of the sky; when it shattered the opal pieces remained. The word "opal" originates from various multiple roots. *Opallios* is Greek for "changing color," and *upala* is Sanskrit for "precious gem."

October 2

You have a very gentle soul, and you spend a lot of time thinking introspectively, often trying to figure out a way to make peace in various situations. You don't handle anger well, nor can you tolerate superficial people for very long. Rather yours is a quest for true depth and meaning in life. You'd probably be more maudlin but for the birth number 3's joy in your back pocket—in fact, you can be downright mischievous periodically (much to the surprise of most who know you).

In business and life, you tend to leap into situations enthusiastically if they seem worthwhile. You have a knack for looking at people and circumstances with a truly unique eye—one focused on solutions. These aren't extreme or fast fixes, but rather ones intended to last. Consequently, legal work, or other positions where a fair and balanced outlook is required, makes perfect sense.

What doesn't make sense is your love life. You seem to undermine yourself a lot, typically worrying over problems that don't even exist, or sweating the small stuff. This is really a shame, as you have a vivid personality and plenty of passion. If you can learn to stop looking for issues and focus on potential, you'll make a fine mate.

Gift idea: a light-up yo-yo.

October 3

You are the style maven of the Libra birth sign. You just know how to dress, and you've got a flair for helping other people look their best too. In fact, you might consider a career as a personal stylist or in fashion design, as it's the ideal showcase for your gift. The real beauty here is not simply that detail-oriented eye but the fact that you make everything seem perfectly natural for yourself or anyone you help.

Having the birth number of 4 definitely drives a hankering for money and success. One caution: don't become mired in the superficiality of prestige and prosperity. It's very tempting to people who share this birthday to look at only externals as the guiding force in decision making. Remember to unwrap that nifty package and find out what's underneath the surface; otherwise, what you don't know will come back to bite you.

In friendship, you prefer the company of knowledgeable but somewhat ordinary-looking friends so you can stay center stage. In lovers, you demand perfection—no bad hair days, ever! This, of course, isn't reasonable, but it is a tendency you'll grow out of in time thanks to the birth number 4's more reasonable, grounded influences, although not before a few really good potential mates run away.

Gift idea: a beauty treatment.

October 4

You've got a backbone strong as rock. If you believe in something, you will stand up for that ideal or person with unwavering certainty, and have a powerful enough personality to see any situation through to a resolution. And thanks to having an Aquarian decanate, your unique insights and inventiveness really make a mark on individuals and corporations equally, frequently leading to a strong financial bottom line.

With a birth number of 5, you are naturally curious and always trying to figure out new connections. That means that you may not settle into one career path immediately, and in fact may choose to change horses several times in your adult life. That won't matter in terms of success, as your determination and ability to learn quickly serve you well in any profession. In particular, jobs in history and research seem ideal.

In the relationship roundup, you stand by your convictions and will not tolerate wishy-washy companions, let alone people intent on revisionism. A lot of people are naturally attracted to your strength, but only a few ever get really close. Once in love you are completely devoted to your partner.

Gift idea: floating candles.

October 5

You have Libra's social tendencies, but express them through giving to others. You're very much a caregiver and "fix it" person, and likely have bandages in your purse or briefcase even now just in case! Everything in your life has been focused on social or global improvement, and what's truly unique is that you begin with Self. You know that the first step to making the world a better place is cleaning up your own backyard!

The birth number of 6 certainly supports that humanitarian calling. It also sings sweetly with the song of your soul that wants tomorrow to be a more beautiful, better day. The only downside is that your Aquarian decanate sometimes gets snitty and hypercritical; because you care so deeply, it's hard not to emote or become exasperated. The world is a very needy place, and one person has but two hands. Breathe and know you're doing the best you can, especially if using the written word to get a point across. There's tons of potential here for leading and motivating that way.

Whatever your relationships, you'll often be taken on the road. You love to travel but want someone you love to be there for all the excitement and wonder of it. You adore sharing life's small and great things, and sharing also holds your interest in the relationship, as long as partners don't mind sharing you with your causes.

Gift idea: a portable first-aid kit.

October 6

Hearts, flowers, violins, chocolate, long moonlit walks—you are a terminal romantic with all the schmaltz. Everything quixotic seems imprinted in your spirit, and your spirit yearns for that complete picture with a soul mate. To that end, you tend to be very accommodating of others, so long as they stay on the up and up with you. You like bringing people together in the hopes that not only you, but others, can find that perfect union. Hey, have you considered starting a dating service? It would be remarkably successful because you seem to know who fits with whom.

Libras sharing this birthday are the epitome of lovers, not fighters. You won't last long in positions that require confrontation and assertiveness. Rather you'll turn your hands and eyes to things that inspire joy and beauty, perhaps by becoming a florist or pastry chef! Similarly, socially you prefer pleasantries and will avoid head butting if possible. Harsh words and actions just don't fly in this Libra's reality.

As one might expect of this romantic, love is a huge thing. You see relationships as a soulful interaction that must have all the key elements—

attraction, passion, communication, understanding—to succeed. Wishy-washy partners need not apply.

Gift idea: silk sheets.

October's birth flower is calendula. Calendula is in the same family of flowers as marigolds. Historically it was one of the plants used for healing and in cooking (typically to season soups or as a coloring for cheese and butter). In particular it aids digestion. Calendula bears the folk names of husbandman's dial and summer's bride. In the Victorian language of flowers it represents grace. In Egypt (where it originated) and in many other regions it was associated with solar energies, because the flower turns and follows the sun in its daily journey. The Catholic Church called the flower Mary's Gold (marigold), and used whole marigold flowers or petals to adorn statues of Mary.

October 7

Those celebrating birthdays today need to find some firmer foundations. You're as dreamy as Pisces and easily distracted. While that rich imagination keeps you engaged in woolgathering, the world is whizzing by unnoticed. Remember to check in with reality on a regular basis before you miss something really important. Thankfully, you've got the grounding of a birth number 8 to assist you in that goal. Let those energies center you and bring focus when you'd otherwise drift away.

Eight also proves helpful to career goals. Without that influence it would be hard for today's Libra to succeed, simply because you're a procrastinator. However, if you find a way to use your creativity and vision (as in writing children's fiction), there's the chance for greatness—your inner landscape is incredibly wealthy with unique imagery that can easily inspire others when expressed in an effective medium.

What about love? Well, normally you have an overly romantic view of what constitutes a serious relationship. Of course, this is an ideal to which no one quite measures up. However, if the practical number of 8 is allowed to balance out those dreams, potential mates will find a tender lover in you.

Gift idea: glittery bubble bath.

October 8

Details, details, details. This Libra's life is wholly focused on jots and tittles, crossing T's and dotting I's. As such you would do well to consider legal careers or positions like compliance officer, where that strict nature will not only provide an income, but inspire respect from peers and employers alike.

Having a birth number of 9 may confuse matters a little bit. Nine isn't as focused on the construct as on transformation and results, not all of which can be neatly planned out. Mind you, you do have a very loving heart, and some of that organization hides it as a self-protection instinct. So, in the end you will exhibit some flexibility, but others would do well not to try to push that envelope too much!

In friendship and love, you have no room for liars. When you suspect a lie, you become moody and withdrawn until you can sort things out. You also tend to stay somewhat guarded even with trusted individuals, making it hard to get to know you fully. Partners need to be patient and have a strict code of honor to make a go of this relationship.

Gift idea: a wallet with security chain.

October 9

Unlike most born under Libra, you tend to be relatively hermetic. While you'll come out of seclusion to attend to various social and professional responsibilities, you prefer books, computers, music, and arts to other people. In particular, you excel at analysis and make a great data jockey. Alternatively, a research-oriented field would be apt.

Then we take to heart the birth number of 1, which brings a whole other dimension into the fray. When you'd rather retreat, 1 wants external recognition and approval. When you'd be perfectly content to work steadily on a telecommuting project, 1 cries out to be more showy. The way this resolves itself is usually by putting the best effort possible into your projects so at the end of the day whoever receives them says, "Wow," and cannot help but be impressed.

People sharing this birthday have a strong spiritual side that normally manifests in relationships. To be intimate, you must feel that unique connection with another person, and you'll happily wait on love until you find that spark. Once in love, you need to be needed, so an ideal partner will let you give freely.

Gift idea: a Tibetan mandala.

QUESTION?

What kind of hobbies do Libras enjoy?
Libra likes crafty, "hands on" endeavors. Some might sew all manner of quilts, others try decoupage, and still others tinker with grapevine wreaths or gourmet cooking. Additionally, Libra is an air-oriented sign, so anything that gets this person out into the open typically attracts. Think camping on windy mountains, bonfire dancing on a breezy beach, or even making and flying custom kites. Being a social creature, however, Libras often want to share these experiences with friends, so join in the fun!

October 10

Rather stoic for a Libra, you take life very seriously. You probably have friends and family constantly suggesting that you "lighten up." What they don't realize is that you're not gloomy, just staid, especially about important matters. Having a birth number 2 means that "important" usually has something to do with another's needs and problems. It wouldn't be surprising if you were attracted to the fields of health or psychology as a result. No matter what, that very calm demeanor also means that you'll catch subtleties that others miss completely, an aptitude that gives you a valuable edge.

Socially you may be a little awkward because of your very cerebral nature. Following a conversation isn't always easy for companions of this Scale. There's no question of your sincerity, however. That's obvious in the manner you present ideas, even if they're too intellectual to follow sometimes. Part of the challenge for you is finding ways to tone down or tune out the mind and simply relax a little.

The same holds true in relationships. While you're a very devoted lover, it's hard for mates to feel truly close. It's also hard for you to release and accept affection, as you get too caught in your head to enjoy physicality.

Gift idea: a ship-in-a-bottle kit.

October 11

An incredibly good "giver" who is not so great at receiving, today's Libra is very kind-hearted and charitable. You literally give until it hurts, which of course isn't always healthy, but it's simply your way. You see so much pain in the world that taking even an ounce of it on yourself seems better than doing nothing at all. And you're right: if you're to change the world, do it one moment and one person at a time. Your birth number of 3 gives you the perfect way in which to do this—through a smile, a hug, or even a little humor to break up the trauma.

Socially you'd much rather keep to a small group of highly dedicated individuals than expend energy on fly-by-night acquaintances. This works out very well for you, since those well-chosen friends also help rein you in when you might otherwise burn out or jump into a potentially hazardous situation.

And the spirit of love? It sings so loudly in your soul that anyone with ears can hear it. You have a lot of emotion, and lavish it on mates. Partners must remember that you have needs too (and are also giving out a lot of energy to other people).

Gift idea: a reflexology kit.

October 12

You don't sit still for very long. There's a whole lot of world out there, and you want to see and experience every last bit of it. The idea of settling down is completely foreign to you. More than likely you always have one bag packed and ready to go for the next adventure opportunity. Thankfully your birth number of 4 keeps you from anything too risky, and also helps you find a way to make money while on exploits. Your Aquarian decanate also pitches in here, revealing opportunity clearly when it knocks.

Those sharing this birthday have inviting personalities and the ability to adapt very well to nearly any situation. It seems no matter where you travel, you find an open door and a helping hand waiting. Mind you, you don't take this gift lightly and never abuse hospitality. You are a guest who people are happy to see arrive, and they know you'll always leave right on cue. That knack with people could easily lead to careers in the media, as a travel guide, or even as an international interpreter.

The harried nature of your life leaves very little wiggle room for developing a long-term romance. While you certainly would enjoy a partner, it's a rare person who can keep up. Perhaps a high-energy Gemini would fit the bill.

Gift idea: a sturdy backpack.

October 13

Today's Libra is a force to be reckoned with. You're incredibly strong in body, mind, and spirit, and you've learned over time how to manage all that brute force effectively. Don't be surprised if you find yourself naturally attracted to fields where you can use some of your power "hands on," such as martial arts, police work, or as a wrestler or a bodyguard. These are all very natural expressions of your aptitude, and ones that mix perfectly with the sensitive Aquarian who knows when the boxing gloves need to come off, and a softer touch applied.

In private or professional life, you can stick to tasks like peanut butter. This sometimes leads to being too absorbed, but that focus usually has a very good reason and often safeguards persons or situations very effectively. In an odd twist, it may be the very curious and independent nature of a birth number of 1 that keeps you from drowning in responsibility.

In relationships, your power and intensity can frighten people off, or at least keep them at a safe distance. Yet you really want a well-grounded relationship in which you don't always have to wear the "sturdy" hat. Like a wonderful surprise package, you long for a mate who will take a chance and see what's inside!

Gift idea: a gym membership.

FACT

Important historical events in October: Henry Ford introduces the model T (October 1, 1908); the Berlin Wall comes down (October 2, 1990); the World Series is broadcast by radio for the first time (October 5, 1921); film ratings are adopted by the Motion Picture Association (October 7, 1968); public welcomed to the Washington Monument (October 9, 1888); Pan American World Airways opens for global passenger travel (October 10, 1959); Kathy Sullivan is the first woman to walk in space (October 11, 1984); Department of Education signed into creation by President Carter (October 17, 1978); end of the Hundred Year War (October 19, 1453); the first electric light invented by Edison (October 20, 1879); women protest for the right to vote in New York City (October 23, 1915); Stock market crashes (October 29, 1929); Indira Gandhi assassinated (October 31, 1984).

October 14

Where yesterday's Libra was rather in-your-face, this one is just the opposite. You're not a real social go-getter, which is odd for this birth sign. There's a sweet bashfulness about you, and you rarely take the initiative in any activity. In part, you fear being misunderstood. You've always been rather intelligent, but find that getting ideas from your head to your words isn't easy. One thing that may help you is journaling. Put your ideas down in writing so you have a medium through which to sort and clarify them, then share the ordered concepts with others. You've got a lot to give, and owe it to yourself to open up a bit.

Having a birth number of 6 implies that you spend a lot of time and effort making your personal space absolutely stunning. Being somewhat of a loner allows for uniquely private expressions of self all around each room.

When others visit it's a perfect chance for them to see you in a whole new light. Friends, look closely at the decorations and ask questions!

Because you aren't overly self-confident, it takes you a while to warm up to potential friends, and even longer to trust in love. Even so, you make a very delightful partner with great sensitivity for the right individual (typically someone who gets past the walls and builds that assurance).

Gift idea: a blank book.

The average Libra loves a well-kept house. Cleanliness is necessary, along with a smattering of live plants and some charming antiques. No matter what, Libras will not buy just because they need something. They'll wait and find the right item to fill that need so that guests ooh and aah over the choice. For clothing, comfort is important, but so are decorative highlights—one piece of good jewelry, a sharp pair of shoes, or a unique belt to bring everything together. Natural fabrics feel better than manufactured items—cotton and silk are high on the list. As for furniture, there's no hurry. Several hours of perusing thrift shops always yield a treasure or two.

October 15

People celebrating a birthday today tip their hats and scales to the spirit of love and romance, wholly and completely. Your entire life has been a quest to understand every facet of this elusive emotion and to experience it fully. While most think of love as only hearts and flowers, you know it's much more. In your reality this feeling is so much greater than that—it's the passion felt toward a favorite hobby, the gentle warmth you get from a child's smile, and the unconditional trust of your dog. This outlook provides balance where otherwise you'd get out of tilt with impractical expectations.

Having a birth number of 7 is a great ally in maintaining some level-headedness in the emotional department. Seven encourages cooperation and communication between the reasoning centers and the heart, allowing you to keep one foot closer to earth. In turn, you have the capacity for well-rounded relationships. In fact, having you as a partner is pretty amazing. It seems as if you never weary of giving emotionally or physically to the ones you love. However, others shouldn't fall into the trap of taking that for granted. You need to receive too, and it's something you're not great at doing. Work on that to keep your relationships healthy over the years.

Gift idea: a candlelit, romantic meal with music and lots of finger food to feed each other.

October 16

Life's road has been filled with potholes for this Libra. It seems like nothing ever goes smoothly, no matter how much you plan or prepare. In your youth this was far more difficult to cope with than it is as an adult. Now you just get up, brush off, and start again with a unique acceptance and fortitude. This whirlwind reality may have brought you to a nontraditional religious path that provides comfort and inspiration in the storm. Don't be surprised if you feel moved to share that inspiration with others in some manner—such as singing in a choir, or lecturing at a special event.

Socially, you have a small circle of acquaintances, many of whom have similar life experiences and outlooks. You probably enjoy book clubs, intimate coffee houses, and yoga classes as perfect spaces for spending time together. Professionally, you are a very good worker. Driven forward by the demanding birth number 8, you want those firm, earthly foundations and a good income. This birth number is actually a very good balance for your spiritual pursuits.

On a more private level, you have some wounds that haven't healed completely. You're going to be very tentative in relationships, so potential mates shouldn't push for too much too soon. Additionally, you're going to be looking for substance and a soulful connection, both of which take time to develop.

Gift idea: a cappuccino machine.

October 17

Fortitude is the name of your game. As a child you probably memorized *The Little Engine That Could*, and took the message completely to heart. You truly feel life is what you make of it, and that to succeed in anything you have to be willing to commit 150 percent to learning, improving, and perfecting that skill. Friends, family, and employers equally admire you for that tenacity, with one minor exception: Sometimes you don't know when to quit. Having a birth number of 9 implies that you tend to be a bit dissatisfied with even the best effort, so learn to cut yourself (and others) some slack.

Professionally, this birth number may lead you toward humanitarian and global-minded positions, ranging from being a diplomat to trying to find a cure for cancer.

The decanate of Gemini provides you with the ability to make decisions quickly and an aptitude for resolving issues. Whatever the task, you are best suited to jobs that follow a set routine, as you don't like disorder or disruption.

Personally, you are a dichotomy. Some days you want company and intimacy, and other days you need to get away from it all, in part because of the stress you place on yourself. If you can find a Gemini who is in sync with this changing tide, it could prove a very affectionate relationship.

Gift idea: a locket or tie tack.

October 18

Sensible and stable: these are the two words that come to mind when thinking of this Libra. People trust you as a salt-of-the-earth type of individual whose honesty and good efforts easily inspire respect. Even with this adulation, there's a part of you that's insecure and fearful about the future. Fortunately, your birth number 1 will help overcome those misgivings by providing a better understanding of your importance and place in the big picture.

This birth number coupled with the ever-adaptable Gemini decanate makes a pretty strong force professionally. If you have a strong interest in a subject, you will succeed at working in that field. If you're zealous about the subject, you'll become a leader or teacher in that area. In particular, justice seems to appeal, as does any more communication-full position (the air element's influence coming into play here). However, Gemini's influence may also mean that you change career paths several times throughout your life, and quite happily so.

In love, you enjoy a hard-to-get lover who, at the end of the chase, collapses into cuddling and pillow talk. A little excitement, a little tenderness—that's the ideal blend for successful long-term relationships.

Gift idea: sturdy work shoes or boots.

ALERT!

The constellation of Libra is unique in the Zodiac, as it's the only one that's an inanimate object. In Roman tradition, it marked and maintained a space between Scorpio and Virgo. In the Tarot, Libra is associated with the card of Justice. Here a blindfolded woman holds a pair of scales. This association with justice isn't surprising. Over 4,000 years ago Babylonians connected the scales with judgment of the dead; in this region the constellation was called Zabanitu. Meanwhile, Egyptians consigned the constellation to Anubis, a god who with Maat measured souls against a feather. Greeks still connected that part of the sky with Scorpio, seeing the stars in Libra as the scorpion's claws. In India, people called these stars Tula (the balance), but instead of being feminine as with the Tarot, this image is of a man holding the scales. Finally, in ancient China, people associated this region of the sky with longevity.

October 19

Negativity is very unhealthy for you. If you're around pessimistic people, it will drag your energy and emotions down as surely as a hefty anchor. Worse, it deters productivity and progress in your life, much of which is focused on supporting a personal or group ideal. With this in mind, surround yourself whenever possible with individuals who have an upbeat outlook, and create a home environment with lots of light and color to maintain a more positive perspective. You might also want to carry a piece of jet to collect any negative energy and direct it away.

Personally, you are very appealing to others. Having a birth number of 2 gives you a very cooperative spirit, warmth, creativity, and the ability to navigate delicate circumstances effectively. Unfortunately, this means that business acquaintances often look to you to fix situations that won't be healthy for them, making things frequently awkward. There isn't an easy fix here, other than trying to build a harder outer shell to filter out the worst influences.

In relationships, you have the ability to see others' true selves. If you choose to be with someone, it's because inside and out that person is attractive. Mates never have to question your interest in them and they find you make a fun-loving and liberating partner.

Gift idea: a colorful bud vase.

October 20

People celebrating birthdays today are very youthful at heart. This doesn't mean that you're naive or immature. Rather, there's a playful, whimsical side to you—one that the happy-go-lucky birth number of 3 really accentuates. You love simple things, from gathering daisies and playing board games to just lounging in the sun with friends and good music. While there's a more serious side to you (one seen at work), in your own space and on your own time there's usually a smile on your face and a song on your lips.

In work, this personology report indicates that careers emphasizing self-expression suit you well. Consider being a drama coach, a day-care provider, or something similar where all that kindness and caring can come out unhindered. No matter what, being in a gloomy, stodgy, or boring atmosphere simply won't do. The higher and brighter the environmental energies, the happier you become and the better you perform.

Privately you make a very nurturing and compassionate partner and friend. You seek out other people who have positive, lighthearted approaches to life's classroom with whom to share your time and wonderful experiences. Just be aware, friends and mates, that like any Libra, this individual can have rather dramatic changes in mood. But hang tight, those downswings pass quickly.

Gift idea: a boom box.

October 21

Today's Libra has a motto: Let's get it done! However, others shouldn't think this attitude means you're rushed or overly focused on work. Instead, you know that if you get all that "stuff" off your desk, then there's more time for leisure and pleasure. And you also know that if you do it right the first time, everyone's happier. Your birth number of 4 cooperates exceedingly well with this pragmatic, organized approach to life with its foundation-oriented energies.

When you're not working, there's a bit of an adventurer in you. Since Libra is an air-oriented sign, you might enjoy hiking high, breezy mountain trails, camping at the seaside, or hang gliding as a way of gearing down and getting solo time (something you need periodically). These moments are when you collect your most interesting and creative thoughts and process information from daily life most effectively. Other possible pleasures include cultural cooking and organic gardening.

People sharing this birthday have friends everywhere, and a port in every storm. Love isn't quite that cut-and-dried, however. You need a partner who can balance work and fun, and who also wants to get out and explore all the wonders the world has to offer. If you find this person, the overall relationship will be exciting and caring, with enough freedom to make both people happy.

Gift idea: a pair of bicycles.

October birthdays include: Julie Andrews (10/1), Jimmy Carter (10/1), Groucho Marx (10/2), Sting (10/2), Charlton Heston (10/4), Ann Rice (10/4), Jesse Jackson (10/8), Chevy Chase (10/8), John Lennon (10/9), Scott Bakula (10/9), Helen Hayes (10/10), Martina Navratilova (10/10), Susan Anton (10/12), Marie Osmond (10/13), Nancy Kerrigan (10/13), Penny Marshall (10/15), Emeril Lagasse (10/15), Noah Webster (10/16), George C. Scott (10/18), Jean Claude Van Damme (10/18), Carrie Fisher (10/21), Johnny Carson (10/22), Hillary Rodham Clinton (10/24), Emily Post (10/26), John Cleese (10/26), Bruce Jenner (10/28), Julia Roberts (10/28), Winona Ryder (10/29), Dan Rather (10/31), Jane Pauley (10/31).

October 22

Today's birth number is 5, meaning this Libra learns through sensual experiences. Not being overly spiritual, you connect with ideas and information that you can taste, touch, smell, see, and hear. Usually one sense (smell) is stronger than the others and provides you with amazing inspirations and gut feelings that typically prove incredibly accurate. Pay attention to those! It doesn't matter if no one else comprehends why you're doing what you're doing—your inner voice doesn't whisper, it screams.

Many Libras sharing this birthday feel a bit out of their element. You have a strong perspective that's proactive and focused on what's best for the long haul, seeing what others often do not. Needless to say, that can leave you frustrated by constantly having to explain, and even then not being understood. In this the birth number 5 helps, offering greater adaptability and coping mechanisms.

Living by instinct is something that will eventually help in the romance department. No matter how nice the package seems to be, you are going to open and investigate it pretty thoroughly before making any type of commitment. Additionally, having a Gemini decanate gives today's Libra a great ability to communicate with friends, family, and lovers alike.

Gift idea: a cell phone.

October 23

Happy birthday Scorpio! Being on the cusp means that you've got the highly confident and mysterious demeanor of the Scorpion, and the irrepressible social charisma of a Libra. This naturally attracts people to you—you're a bit of a curiosity, and you like it that way. It gives you time to get perspective and sort through the signals you're getting from those higher senses that you've grown to trust.

In business today's Scorpio is clever, prudent, and persistent. Challenges don't daunt your resolve; if anything, a good challenge inspires greater brilliance. Once you're engaged and committed, you've got the devotion and ambition to see things through. Consequently, you often find yourself in a leadership position, even unwittingly. You would thrive in a career in social services or alternative medicine. These types of people-oriented positions appeal to today's birth number of 6, which governs humanitarian sensibilities. Alternatively, 6's love of beauty could combine with the Scorpion's huge aura for a viable career in performing arts.

In relationships, you are typically flirtatious, as are many born under this sign. Nonetheless, there's a very emotional being here, one who uses the flirting game to determine who's really serious and can't be easily deterred. Additionally, this back and forth hones communications and gives you time to scope out the overall vibes present.

Gift idea: a dowsing kit.

October 24

Today's Scorpio is very discerning. You seek out very specific people and situations—those that you find interesting, intriguing, curious, or enchanting. Without that kind of spark, there's no reason to invest any time or energy. Additionally, you like being noticed—there's a little bit of Leo-like regalness in you, and you probably spend a good deal of time honing your appearance. There's nothing wrong with that so long as it doesn't become a full-time, superficial diversion.

For a life's path, you are likely attracted to adventure and anything that holds a mystery. Fields like archaeology and cryptography that combine both elements really appeal. This Scorpio can work well with others, but will want the opportunity to shine at some juncture in any task. So long as the Scorpion doesn't pull out that nasty stinger to get attention, things will be fine—especially since a birth number of 7 ensures that this person sees openings and puts together solutions faster than most, inspiring more admiration than jealousy.

As with many Scorpios you have very strong emotions and regularly need some alone time. This need struggles with that craving for attention, but it's very important for decompressing. So long as you have that balance, your social and private lives will be very active and fun.

Gift idea: a full-length mirror.

October 25

People who share the birth sign of Scorpio are ruled by the element of water. They're highly emotional, and those emotions wax and wane like tides, in a very specific cycle. If you're born today, you're very familiar with that shift, especially one that's caused by head-heart conflicts. Your mind is very astute, and you've got an incredible creative flair, but it's hard for you to move beyond inspiration and planning into manifestation. Of course, then you're left making excuses for missed deadlines. Just know that this process is part of your life's lesson—translating ideas into viable action.

You are strongly influenced by the water element in your career too. You may feel attracted to creating the world's greatest soup, or oceanography! Having a birth number of 8 indicates a strong desire to succeed and create long-term fiscal security, but there needs to be an inventive element to the position to attract you and keep you productive over several years.

Potential mates, be forewarned that there is a darker side to this individual that may rear its ugly head in close relationships. If the Scorpion feels they've been mislead or wronged, even if that perception is inaccurate, they will lash out with that stinger and leave wounds in the wake of the outburst. The best way to avoid this is through ongoing communication and clarification.

Gift idea: tropical fish.

QUESTION?

What are some of the names of October's full moon?
The most common is the Harvest Moon. This is the full moon that takes place close to the autumn equinox. Alternative names include Hunter's Moon (it gives more light for hunting by night) and Blood Moon (to prepare meats for the long winter). There's the Full Barley Moon (as a reminder to harvest the barley), and Full Travel Moon (it was safer for wayfarers to move during the night). The Apache call it Corn Taking Moon, among the Cree it's Moon When Birds Fly South, the Shawnee used Wilted Moon, and the Hopi call it Month of the Long Hair.

October 26

Externally you seem very collected and certain, but others should not be fooled. You are still a Scorpion, and beneath the hard features and direct words beats a fierce and free heart that's incredibly passionate and motivated. Combine this with a visionary, compassionate birth number of 9 and you find an interesting mix that would do well in the public eye. At first glance, and even second ones, it's hard to find much to complain about here.

There's more to you than meets the eye, however. In particular, life has handed you a liberal amount of harsh lessons, some of which haven't even begun to heal. While you've become very good at hiding those sore spots, pushing key buttons neatly brings the whole house of cards crashing down. This isn't pretty, and it takes a while for you to recover your balance.

In love, those born today tend to hold back a little. You see intimacy as something that can potentially control you, which is simply not acceptable. It takes time and patience for lovers to get you out of your head and into your heart. At that point, however, ah . . . what wonders await!

Gift idea: a leather briefcase.

October 27

You love anything with an air of ambiguity because you want to venture forward and figure things out. Additionally, you have a lot of courage and backbone, which means you may try to unravel very dangerous mysteries without worrying much about personal welfare. Thankfully, Scorpios have that stinger, which provides nearly guardian angel–like defenses at just the right moment. No matter how hot the water gets, you seem to come out with only minor damage.

If you share this birthday your birth number is 1, meaning you really want to make an impact on reality. That also drives some of your adventures. Thankfully, it also motivates a clever and insightful tact. In short, you will stop and think things through before acting, which typically gives you just the right approach. Use this ability along with your birth number's dynamic nature in business to turn the tide your way!

You can also apply those talents to your personal life. By being thoughtful and insightful you can offer partners a nearly psychic responsiveness that really heats things up in bed. You do, however, require a dedicated and loyal partner in order to freely enjoy that type of amazing intimacy.

Gift idea: a detective's kit.

FACT

October has been named Breast Cancer Awareness Month, International Drum Month, and Seafood Month. The first week in October is designated Customer Service Week, and the second is Fire Prevention Week. Other interesting events in October include: Festival of the Moon, in China (10/1); World Teacher's Day (10/5); National Angel Food Cake Day (10/10); Farmer's Day (10/12); World Egg Day (10/13); Dictionary Day (10/16); National Nut Day (10/22); World Pasta Day (10/25); National Candy Corn Day (10/30).

October 28

Independent and idealistic, you can be successful at anything to which you apply yourself fully. There can be no half-ways here, no wobbling. You want everything done completely, and have a nearly electrical nature and energy to make sure that's exactly what happens. Some people find your intensity a little pushy, but once they see the results, they usually reevaluate those feelings. Be prepared—many will want you to lead, and having a cooperative, networking birth number of 2 means you're completely ready and able for just such tasks.

Financially speaking, people sharing this birthday seem to be relatively successful. Some of it comes from hard work, some from good fortune. We're not talking huge riches here, but certainly enough to be comfortable. Socially, this works out nicely, because you enjoy going out and mingling with like-minded people. Having a little extra cash allows for that freedom and all-important interaction that spark your very soul.

In love you are like a professional hunter. You carefully consider each potential target, run through various scenarios mentally, and then set your sights on the goal. From here, little will stop you unless you're firmly and vehemently told no. If you're considering a relationship with this person, get past that initial anxious stage and you'll discover a wholly devoted partner.

Gift idea: a lightning ball.

October 29

You have an aura as big as Texas, a sweet personality, youthful energy, and a buoyant perspective. Even so, there's a teeny bit of mulish stubbornness tucked just beneath the surface. This is actually a good thing. Without that determination you'd be very susceptible to mental wandering, especially in the face of problems or pressures. Truth is, emotionally you don't handle conflict well, and that rich imagination gives you a place to "be" when you don't want to get involved. However, there are some things you can't and shouldn't avoid.

Today's birth number is 3, which seems an ideal companion to your kind-hearted nature. Three's expressiveness and humor create an enchanting package. About the only downside here is that sometimes you become overly expressive, laughing too loudly (or at inappropriate moments), jumping into conversations at the wrong time, and being overly dramatic. This tendency is strongest during your teens as an expression of insecurity, and can be tempered with years and confidence-building techniques.

Friendship comes easily to you, but it can be somewhat unstable—you prefer playfulness over more serious discussions. That tendency can taint love as well until you find a partner who can keep you entertained completely (perhaps an ever-changing Gemini?).

Gift idea: a hula hoop.

October 30

Ever-dependable birth number 4, did you even remember it was your birthday? You're so busy doing that sometimes you forget to pause, breathe, and truly BE. Nonetheless, being focused on achievement and persistent in your goals has been a personally and financially fulfilling endeavor in your life.

You have seen with your own eyes and hands what old-fashioned elbow grease produces, and it's called success.

Now some people would rest on those laurels—but not this Scorpio. You like to take what you've learned and help others succeed too. With good communication skills and the ability to explain complex things simply, you would make an excellent teacher or mentor. Alternatively, if you apply yourself more physically than mentally, becoming a diet coach or personal trainer proves very enjoyable. In either case, your interactions certainly make you skillful socially, and friends aren't difficult to find.

Love proves to be another matter, however. You like to play hard to get even though what you most crave is a long, dependable, sensuous affair. That means this Scorpio's partner needs to know when to tease and when to please. Additionally, know that this individual typically keeps fairly close reins on emotional expression except when they feel wholly comfortable or out of the public eye.

Gift idea: a wipe-off monthly agenda board (and lots of markers).

FACT

Halloween began in Celtic tradition and came to the United States in the late 1800s with immigrants. The festival marked the end of summer and the beginning of darker days. Many people felt that the veil between the living and dead was thinner at this time of year, and that ghosts could come visit the living. Originally, turnips were carved with frightening faces to keep away unwanted spirits. Additionally, the Druids enacted a variety of divinations to predict the future, while the rest of the population wore costumes and tried to tell each other's fortunes.

Halloween is considered a fire festival because custom dictated dousing the hearth fire before the holiday began and relighting it at the end, thereby giving strength to the sun for its long winter journey. When the Romans exerted influence in Celtic regions, some of the Roman festivals found their way into Halloween celebrations. In particular dunking for apples is believed to have originated in the Roman festival for Pomona, the goddess of fruit trees, whose symbol was the apple.

October 31

Being born on Halloween creates some very interesting energies. You're sensitive to spirits and have a knack for discerning possible futures, which means that people sometimes find you a little odd, if not incredibly disconcerting, with all that perceptiveness. Thankfully you've still got a strong logical side to keep you grounded, and a healthy dose of skepticism to avoid over-spiritualizing the mundane. This is a really good balance point, especially considering a birth number 5 that would love for you to become a professional ghost hunter or spiritualist!

If you don't seek adventure with the residents of the afterlife, you may be drawn to mental explorations in technical or research sciences where you can get that rewarding "ah ha!" and share your excitement with other brilliant minds. Whatever the choice, you need to hear approving words and have your ego stroked regularly. Most of this has to do with lingering memories of failed situations for which you've never truly forgiven yourself. The sad part is that typically you weren't the problem at all—rather, you simply took the guilt upon yourself.

With the guilt factor in mind, it's not surprising that you find it hard to open up and receive. One side of you doesn't feel wholly worthy of love, and the other side is much too busy to worry about it. If you learn to trust your instincts more, you are, however, capable of being a very intuitive, proactive lover.

Gift idea: silver dowsing rods.

Libra

Sign: Libra
Date: September 23–October 22
Ruled by: Venus
Element: Air
Lucky Color: Purple
Gemstone: Opal, emerald
Keynote: Symmetry
Positive Traits: Team player, balanced vision, diplomatic, charismatic
Negative Traits: Self-absorbed, non-confrontational, fickle in love
Famous Libras include: Julie Andrews, Johnny Carson, Jimmy Carter, Mahatma Gandhi, Rita Hayworth, Charlton Heston, Groucho Marx, Barbara Walters

Libras are known for a gentle, delicate nature that seems to draw people in naturally. They have a love for beauty, fairness, and harmony, but have trouble maintaining the latter on a regular basis. In part this is due to the peace-keeping attribute of this sign. While Libra tries diligently to be diplomatic and restore order, the effort is not always well received.

In work and play, Libra measures everything, seeking ever after stability. Things too far outside the box, too risky, make this sign very uncomfortable. Fast decision making is not an attribute of the Scales, but once a choice is made they'll stand by it with ferocity.

At home the Libra loves elegance. Most born under this sign have an eye for placement, appreciate good art, and exhibit an uncanny knack for hospitality. Everyone in the home and those who visit can anticipate an eye-filling and tasty experience.

In relationships Libras seek ever to please, even if it means giving up personal desires. Friends, loved ones, and acquaintances alike find Libras open, welcoming, and approachable, being good listeners and genuine with words. But when the scale swings, suddenly Libras disconnect—they don't want to worry anyone, and in turn keep too much inside. Additionally, Libras hold on to the past easily, meaning this sign needs a partner who can help him or her maintain that delicate balance between learning a lesson and letting go.

Chapter 13

November

On the Roman calendar November was the ninth month (*novem*, meaning nine), and its number of days settled at 30 during Augustus's reign. Anglo-Saxons called it the wind month, which is certainly evident by the play of falling leaves in the cool air. In Finland it was called the month of the dead (perhaps alluding to the dying vegetation or the darker skies). November begins in the sassy sign of Scorpio. From approximately the 24th onward, the month shifts into the influence of Sagittarius.

November 1

You are incredibly edgy, energetic, and extreme, but not on the outside! To anyone who knows you, you appear the epitome of control and focus. Additionally, you've proven time and time again that you've got great logical aptitude and know how to apply it for positive results. This ability is something people admire, never knowing about all the heat that bubbles just beneath the surface. Take care, as you can become very scheming and battle-driven when that finally boils over, which has to happen periodically—it's like the vent to a volcano. Otherwise you'll get depressed and start shutting people out.

Today's birth number of 3 inserts an upbeat demeanor into this equation. The expressiveness and drive to succeed of number 3 work out well for you. Rather than be maudlin and bland about rationalizations, you can present optimistic ideas in clever and witty ways. This could easily lead to being attracted to careers in advertising, PR, and other positions that grapple with the public mind.

In relationships, today's Scorpio wants romance, but it has to be more than hearts and flowers. There's got to be fireworks and pizzazz—something that feeds your hidden intensity with regular wowing. Additionally, you often cling even to bad situations simply for the comfort and security they offer, so partners should be ready to offer guidance in these matters.

Gift idea: a mariachi band beneath the window!

November 2

You're incredibly insightful, nearly to the point of seeming psychic. You're also very objective, and while those two parts of you sometimes struggle, overall they make a great combination, especially if you choose a career in medicine, healing, psychology, or as a behavior specialist. People trust you and come to you quite naturally without any goading, meaning you're likely to handle some tough cases personally or professionally. Have no fear; you're perfectly capable of so doing.

Today's birth number is 4, which puts a firm, resolute foundation under everything you do. The ideas you present will never be flippant or half-baked—that would be dishonorable and unprofessional. Additionally, you truly appreciate social courtesies and hospitality, and treat nearly every situation with that kind of thoughtfulness. About the only thing that brings out the Scorpion's sting is people who are purposefully and willfully cruel, especially to those who have no real means of self-defense.

In relationships, you surround yourself with philosophical individuals as friends, and inspirational people as lovers. Bland personalities need not apply. Your partners should also remember that you don't always open up easily, trying to remain circumspect even with your heart.

Gift idea: an aromatherapy kit.

ALERT!

November is American Diabetes Month, Aviation History Month, Family Stories Month, Epilepsy Awareness Month, National Adoption Month, National AIDS Awareness Month, Georgia Pecan Month, and Peanut Butter Lovers' Month. Here are some date-specific observances for the month: National Author's Day and National Family Literacy Day (11/1); Sandwich Day (11/3); Young Reader's Day (11/6); Dunce Day (11/8); Forget-Me-Not Day (11/10); World Kindness Day (11/13); Clean Out Your Refrigerator Day (11/15); Occult Day (11/18); National Cashew Day (11/23); Pins and Needles Day (11/27); Square Dance Day (11/29).

November 3

Today's Scorpion acts more like a pussycat, seeming to have at least ten lives. You're agile, fast-acting, irresistibly charming, and able to reinvent yourself on a moment's notice. More amazing still, no matter how chancy things get, you usually come out unscathed, if not better than you started. Thank your Pisces decanate for that. It gives you the insight and sensibilities necessary to judge various situations accurately. In turn, that means being able to have a backup plan and safety net ready just in case.

Your birth number of 5 certainly feeds the adventurous free fall that your life embodies! Five charges ahead with vibrancy and happiness in that movement. In fact, many Scorpios sharing this birthday find themselves hopelessly attracted to jobs that involve some type of movement—be it swinging from a trapeze, dancing, or flying airplanes. And with luck in your back pocket, you make good money while living those dreams. Another excellent path is that of escape artist or magician, as there is a little spark of the dramatic and a craving for attention here.

Your friends had better strap in for an exciting ride (and wear comfortable shoes—you're going to have to move quickly on short notice). And in love—oh my! There is no middle ground, no "kind of" in your love life. Any feelings are shown completely, honestly, and with an intensity that can scare those afraid of deep commitment.

Gift idea: a snorkeling trip.

November 4

You never stop running! Inside you, there's a fully stoked engine that wants to apply all that power creatively, spontaneously, and sometimes wildly. People probably see you as a bit odd, yet they wouldn't want it any other way. Besides, even though you have some untamed tendencies, life's experiences have provided you with some shocking wisdom. In fact, part of what spurs your eclectic behavior is a yearning to uncover those sagacious tidbits in life. It doesn't matter if the path to achieving that goal doesn't even come close to Main Street, USA.

Today's birth number is 6, which gives you an artistic sense for the beautiful things in life. This combines with a Pisces decanate for a somewhat dreamy, hopeful nature. This may translate into lofty humanitarian goals (as is the way of 6) that prove very difficult to manifest. You must learn how to set your sights on what's sensibly achievable within a set framework. This isn't easy, as your heart often leads your head until reined in by harsh reality. And when you come down from that high, it's with a resounding thunk. Loved ones should be ready to pick up the pieces at least for a short while.

As for relationships, whether with a friend or life partner, you move forward hesitantly, having been burned before. You have no desire to feel shortsighted again, or to be made the fool. Nonetheless, eventually your uniqueness and naturalness will win over the perfect partner, who will discover a totally delightful lover.

Gift idea: a pinball machine.

shakes things up. This last designation resonates heavily with your birth number of 9, which already has all that potential built into it.

So how does all this affect love? It can initially scare potential friends and mates. Everyone wants to keep some things private at least for a while. However, your aptitude in the bedroom, and your ability to sense others' needs and desires eventually overcome those lingering concerns. Additionally, you never push for a commitment too soon.

Gift idea: a piece of copper to help channel excess psychic input and ground it out (perhaps a bracelet?).

November 8

If you're celebrating your birthday today, you probably feel like you're constantly struggling with yourself. You've got a very spiritual side, and a very logical side. The one feels, the other thinks. Additionally, there's one side of you that strives toward "all good things," while the other side is continually tempted toward mischief. Which side wins often depends on the situation and how much profit or esteem it can bring you. That means that many acquaintances aren't sure what side you're on at any given time, and they may keep their distance to protect personal interests.

Professionally, you are attracted by curiosities. You might become a thriller author, go off on archaeological digs, or even become an international spy. The challenge here is control: once you commit to a particular allegiance you cannot continue to be swayed by money and power. At some point you must commit and begin building long-term trust. Having a birth number of 1 will help. This number reinforces uniqueness and a competitive spirit that hones focus and improves the chances of success.

Privately you like a naughty partner, or minimally you're attracted to that image at first. You thrill at the chase with someone who feels dangerous. If that's not possible, then an ambitious and strong partner suits. Once the initial spark grows into a well-tended fire, this will be a sensitive and often fun partnering.

Gift idea: a belt buckle.

November 9

This Scorpio has incredibly strong convictions and a warrior spirit to match. Ever bearing a sharpened sword and tongue, you can act very quickly, with confidence and energy. You've got a nose for problems and aren't content to sit on the sidelines waiting for trouble to come. Consequently you're probably attracted to careers in the military and law enforcement.

Today's birth number is 2, meaning that if you share this birthday your courageous endeavors are often aimed at what seems to be a contradiction—making peace! You'll break up a fight between two beefy guys without thinking that one is much larger than you. Likewise, you'll take disruptive problems to the CEO without worrying a bit about your position. People recognize that you only put your time and energy into situations where dilemmas threaten to spiral out of control.

Speaking of control, it's good for you to have regular physical activity to help burn off some of that fire-in-the-belly—a fire that burns in the bedroom too. This Scorpion can go all night long and part of the next day and not be totally satiated. So, if this is your partner, take your daily vitamins!

Gift idea: a sword cane thrills the warrior spirit.

November 10

If you celebrate your birthday today you have Pisces as a decanate, which gives you a truly unique outlook on life. Having lived life by the seat of your pants, your experiences up to this point have taught more than a fair share of solid lessons—lessons that you've integrated into daily reality. Additionally, you have a clever wit—one that helps you cope, but one that also acts as a teacher in difficult circumstances. Use that aptitude to help others when perspective is lacking.

Today's birth number is 3, which of its own accord provides a lot of positive energy, be it for laughter or for personal goals. You are very mature, probably beyond your years, and you can spot potential from a mile away. While others may not see the truth in your advice immediately, more often than not the counsel was spot-on, especially from a proactive viewpoint.

With this in mind, motivational careers are good options for you, or those that help others heal emotionally.

You love to touch, fondle, sit close, hold hands, and hug. Not everyone takes this attentiveness as it's intended, so you choose an inner circle very cautiously, looking for smart, savvy, sensual, and self-actualized individuals who know when to draw close and when to release.

Gift idea: a loveseat.

FACT

Famous November birthdays include Larry Flynt (11/1), Walter Cronkite (11/3), Yanni (11/3), Tatem O'Neal (11/5), Tom Fogerty (11/9), Demi Moore (11/11), Jonathan Winters (11/11), Rock Hudson (11/17), Jodie Foster (11/19), Robert Kennedy (11/20), Billie Jean King (11/22), Harpo Marx (11/23), Boris Karloff (11/23), Ricardo Montalban (11/25), Amy Grant (11/25), Bruce Lee (11/27), William Blake (11/28), C.S. Lewis (11/29).

November 11

The desire to build respectability motivates this Scorpio. You've got a very clear-cut view of how the world works. Gray zones just don't figure into your programming, and you can't tolerate being around people who constantly dance around the guidelines. It's yes or no, stop or go, good or bad—no middle ground, no vacillating allowed. That entire outlook is one that your birth number of 4 celebrates and augments. For you, the construct is every-thing, and there will be no coloring outside the lines. In highly technical fields this is a wonderful aptitude, as you'll always be able to find the faults in blueprints or programming (for example).

You have a Pisces decanate, which inspires an intuition that you can find uncomfortable. That discomfort, in turn, leads to some extremes. At one point you show charity, and at another you're completely without mercy—most often the down side of these swings happens due either to stress or to being blindsided by a trusted acquaintance. Again, this goes back to your Scorpion's black-and-white universe (what you thought was white should not be black and vice versa).

When it comes to relationships, the number 4 becomes a protective box within which you try to nurture love. You love to pamper your mate, are devoted and affectionate, but sometimes it comes across as smothering. Once you learn to relax in love (at least unclench a little) the relationship smoothes out and becomes far more balanced.

Gift idea: monochromatic art pieces.

ALERT!

Scorpions have a rather pragmatic approach to personal interests. They want to have everything necessary to enjoy a hobby, and will take the time to gather each part so it suits personal tastes and the overall media. In particular, culinary arts appeal greatly—whether you bake decadent cookies, decorate amazing cakes, or put together a cultural dish "just so." Scorpios are often collectors of fine things—wine, fabric, art, etc. They want to surround themselves with the images and items that resonate deeply within. If they can get their hands on something every other collector craves, that's the cherry on the sundae. Scorpio loves to compete!

November 12

The darker, moodier side of Scorpio seems to have completely left the building in today's personology report. You and your birthday peers are typically well-adjusted, happy, powerful individuals who have specific ideas on what you want to achieve. You don't see a job as "work" but rather as something through which to reach goals and enjoy the good life. So you approach every morning with a smile, and try to keep it that way.

Today's birth number is 5. This means you're probably very affected by your senses, and want to be able to see, touch, and taste nearly every corner of your reality. That's how you process information and how you relate to the world. Careers in fabric design, art, gourmet food, etc. really appeal to that aspect of your makeup. However, number 5 also craves a little adventure, so whatever you try, it's going to be new and exciting.

There's no lack of friends or hopeful lovers for you. You have a huge presence that attracts attention without even trying. That aura can overwhelm companions if you don't regulate that energy carefully. Additionally, you don't want complex relationships. Simple and sublime is the way to your heart.

Gift idea: gourmet herbs in a French copper cooking pot.

November 13

While you might have a periodic burst of spontaneity, you'd far prefer a good plan, and adequate time to ponder and process. Your birth number of 6 probably has its fingers in the pot here, in that you care so much about how outcomes affect people that you don't want to take any chances. That's an admirable trait, but be aware that sometimes you miss excellent opportunities by waiting too long.

In business, that paced nature serves you well, as does your eye for detail. You'd make an excellent art appraiser, for example, as that's something requiring some artistic sense, some old-fashioned learning, and some patience to determine fakes from the real thing. This is certainly a life path that your birth number of 6 would appreciate—the ability to express the value of beauty! By the way, don't be surprised if the oddest or most amazing things land in your lap careerwise—it's just a way that the ever-whimsical Serendipity works overtime in your life, usually for the better.

Speaking of fate and fortune, your path in love is never anything ordinary. It's not surprising to find you in relationships that don't even come close to the societal status quo, and you like it that way. Pacing is one thing; overlooking the heart is another altogether. Partners should not take this strange setup as a sign of no commitment from you. It's certainly not. Rather it's an acceptance of change as a reality and an honest expression of attraction without judgment.

Gift idea: a hand-carved chess set.

November 14

Those who are born today seem to have an emotional disconnect compared to other Scorpios. You're logical, investigative, watchful, and seem to be able to turn off any type of sympathetic response as the situation requires. You're also very serious, with an uncanny ability to sniff out a lie faster than a dog can find a bone. No one can pull the wool over your eyes (but some will try just for kicks). Your detached nature, however, sometimes gets misunderstood. It's not that you're unemotional, but you know how emotions can blur the bottom line of a matter. Until you find that root, there's no relaxing.

The birth number of 7 stresses that scrutinizing manner, but usually as the lone wolf seeking after clues. Coupled with the circumspect and tactical nature of a Cancer decanate, you could be a very successful PI, spy, or investigative reporter. You can find what others cannot, and make it look easy. That talent may foster some jealousy if you work in a group environment. However, you can allay problems by making sure due credit goes to the right helpful individuals.

While you manage to maintain the boundaries between head and heart professionally, you find it hard to do so in love. Once in a relationship, you feel things very deeply and want very much to have a completely trustworthy partner. Sometimes that manifests as jealousy or possessiveness, which you have to learn to overcome if you want a long-term commitment that's healthy.

Gift idea: a sundial.

QUESTION?

What does November's numerology reveal?
As the eleventh month, there's a certain magic to November. Because of its placement on the calendar, it's a bridge between fall and winter, and a time when it seems as if the unseen world can touch our lives more easily. In modern numerological systems for letters, November equals a 4, a number that reminds us of practicality and common sense (something very useful in planning for harsher weather!).

November 15

You have a very gentle demeanor that endears you to many. Inside that soft presentation, however, rests a backbone of steel. No one should take you lightly, or start overlooking your kindness, unless they're prepared for a big surprise. You know that life is rarely easy, let alone uncomplicated, and you have little tolerance for whiners.

Careers in accounting and research, or even as the CEO of a *Fortune* 500 Company blossom at your hand.

Relationships don't fare so smoothly for you, however. There's a bit of jealousy inherent in today's personology report, as well as a desire to control the relationship so it fits some ideal. People just aren't that perfect, meaning you are often disappointed in friends and lovers until you begin to recognize human limitations and accept them.

Gift idea: a pocket knife.

November 16

You definitely have two distinct sides. The personal side is a little rash, fun loving, and impish. Then there is the more professional side—the one that's logical, sensible, and opinionated. To handle this, you often compartmentalize your life into safe places in which to express those facets fully.

People who know you in both your career and home life find you enigmatic yet incredibly interesting. Somehow you seem to be able to tune into the directions your community is taking way ahead of time better than a police scanner. This is great if you act on those insights by pursuing careers in fields like real estate and promotion. Just be careful that the figurative "compulsive bug" doesn't sink its teeth into you after a few successes. What goes up must come down.

Today's birth number is 9—the number of the muse and prophetic aptitude. It's easy to be forward thinking professionally, but not so easy in love. The emotional sway caused by inner conflict becomes more pronounced in intimate relationships than in any other aspect of your life. In particular you have problems balancing the idealistic relationship against what is realistic, and often put your partner on a pedestal from which that person could easily fall.

Gift idea: a pendulum.

Some pivotal historical events of November: The Soviet Union launched Sputnik II (November 3, 1957); Abraham Lincoln was elected president (November 6, 1860); The great blackout occurred, affecting 30 million people along the northeast coast (November 9, 1965); the U.S. Supreme Court determined that racial segregation on busses is unconstitutional (November 13, 1956); the North American Free Trade Agreement was approved (November 17, 1993); the Cold War ended (November 19, 1990); Prime Minister Margaret Thatcher announced her resignation (November 22, 1990); *On the Origin of Species* by Charles Darwin was first published (November 24, 1859).

November 17

As suits a birth number of 1, you are stubborn, willful, and a political power-house. If people ask you a question, they receive direct, honest answers (no fluff, no sugar coating). Additionally, you're very confident about your place in life, your ethics, and your opinions. Some people find this comes off as arrogant, so take care as to how you phrase things. Delivery counts for a lot professionally and personally.

Typical of a number 1 personality, you want to make your mark on the world, and might be very well suited for careers like law, where your forward-ness is welcome. Nearly any field you try will launch you into a leadership role very quickly; the ever-intelligent Cancer decanate nearly ensures that. Plus, you have an air about you that speaks of authority, and coworkers and employers alike respond to that presence quite naturally. Just take care that you don't let the controlling nature of your personality become overwhelming.

As one might expect, you like strong partners—people who can stand toe to toe with you in a discussion. You also like a good fight periodically (break up to make up). Anyone getting into a long-term relationship with you will come to see this as a regular cycle, and one that passes quickly with great lovemaking afterward.

Gift idea: boffers (spongy sword-like toys).

November 18

You are very physical in nature. You like working out, keeping yourself fit, and probably have at least one intensive sport as a hobby. Be careful not to get so caught up in the body that you neglect matters of mind and spirit. To be a truly whole person, you have to feed the other aspects of yourself too.

The birth number for today is 2, which implies you are a cooperative person who works well in teams (another indication that you may be attracted to sports, even going professional). This number gives you an awareness of other people's needs, yet you are very opinionated as to how to fulfill them. Compromise isn't an easy word for you, meaning that sometimes you miss good opportunities to help just because you've dug in your heels and won't budge. You are someone others will want on their side in a literal or figurative tug of war!

In relationships your physical nature is very apparent. There is no way you can live without companionship, touching, and sensuality for long periods of time. Sexual release is incredibly healthy for you, which is good since you want a lot of it. Any partner will need to be equally lusty, but also have some depth so the relationship doesn't become only about sex.

Gift idea: wrestling sneakers.

November 19

You have a very high rate of success in whatever you undertake. Part of that comes from the birth number of 3 that makes you very appealing to individuals and groups. Your happy demeanor is contagious, especially when coupled with your enigmatic charisma and an ever-versatile Cancer decanate. Don't be surprised if people gawk—your aura enters rooms an hour before you do!

You probably like to talk, which is something that today's birth number supports with keen communication skills. Careerwise, this may manifest in sportscasting, politics, or even standup comedy. On the other hand, you should not allow yourself to limit life options to small stages. You have a huge potential for influencing a bigger picture, and could easily get into global affairs in positive ways. Such ambitions are optimistically supported by the birth number of 3, which also provides a little go-to!

As for love, you want a little bit of a challenge. Lovers should play hard to get . . . just a little. Be mysterious. Pretend you're a secret admirer—this Scorpion will love it! There is plenty of room for whimsy and youthful enthusiasm in this relationship.

Gift idea: flowering plants.

FACT

Carrying topaz supposedly protects the bearer from the evil eye and stomach disorders. It has also been carried to attract wealth, quell anger, inspire happiness, and improve loyalty. Egyptians felt that the sun god, Ra, colored the stone, making it highly protective. Romans similarly assigned the gem to the sun god's (Jupiter's) domain. In Greece people used it for strength. While a lot of topaz is yellow, it also comes in peach, brown, and orange, and some of the rarest gems are red. Topaz is relatively hard, but a strike at the right angle can split it.

November 20

It's a good thing that you have a birth number of 4 to help keep you somewhat out of trouble. You have a huge hunger for mischief, hate when things stay the same for too long, and just want to "get out there" and "do something"—anything! That craving brings many adventures your way, but also a fair amount of problems that could be avoided by a little patience on your part. Yeah, I know—what's patience? Having that Cancer decanate with its lunar influences only generates more restlessness, inspires a gypsy spirit, and creates fluctuating emotion. Whew!

One lesson for you is learning how to sense danger. Otherwise you tend to walk—no, run—headlong into it. It wouldn't be surprising to find you playing wild sports like car jumping, very atypical for a Scorpio. You really love that sense of power and being in the spotlight. Friends, family, and coworkers aren't sure whether to admire your courage or fear for you! This brings us back to number 4, which usually manages to insert some common sense into the picture. That may be just enough to hold you back from the brink of disaster.

In relationships 4 comes to bear again in that you want a long, steady relationship (which is hard to find considering most people aren't good at letting their partners take big risks every day). Additionally, you insist on a cat-and-mouse game during courtship—you adore that time of chasing, as it makes the capture so much sweeter.

Gift idea: a day at the racetrack.

November 21

You have lots of street smarts, and you're also a highly innovative thinker. Your unique perspective combines nicely with a keen mind and a birth number of 5 that loves to experience new things sensually. You are a restless theorist who might well go off globe-hopping while you formulate another concept or ten.

The main problem you've struggled with is how to take a concept from the drawing board into reality. Professionally, you're constantly asking questions that challenge the old ways of doing things, yet may not yourself have found adequate answers yet. With this in mind a career as a blueprint designer, architect, or feng shui consultant might bode well. Here you can express the fundamentals in your own unique fashion, but let others act on them. Meanwhile, privately you do a wonderful job of motivating others to greater things, which always leaves you with a secret smile.

In general, love has been kind to you. You have good friends who share your sense of adventure and curiosity, and who can appreciate those "ah ha" moments, and lovers who are just as adventurous in the bedroom as you wish to be.

Gift idea: frequent-flyer miles.

November 22

Happy birthday Sagittarius! Those born today start out this birth sign on a strong note. You're very wise, probably way beyond your years. It seems that as soon as life presents you with a lesson you integrate it, then dust yourself off and move onward and upward. As a brave, daring, zealous individual, you epitomize the Archer who spies his mark and plans to make certain the aim is true. The place to find some of that certainty is among like-minded people. Those interactions give you the fresh input you need to address things in the best possible manner and hit the target spot-on.

People sharing this birthday have two key numbers to consider in their personology profile: 22 and 6. Twenty-two is a master number that implies great things to those willing to put their best foot forward. Bear in mind, however, that for 22 to work in anyone's favor there must be honest effort applied. Six inspires an appreciation for beauty. This may combine into careers where you can use eye, hand, and heart—creating community art forms, taking family photos, and the like.

In relationships you tend to feel a great deal very early on, which can scare off potential mates. If you can learn to rein in that emotion just a little and go more slowly, you can find long-term happiness.

Gift idea: a satellite dish.

November 23

You speak in a verbal shorthand into which tons of information and wisdom are condensed. Miss a word or two, and you miss most of the conversation! At first this type of wording leaves people feeling like you're antisocial, but nothing could be further from the truth. You just don't like wasting time with excess words where none are necessary (if someone tries to babble on the phone to you, you'll just hang up!).

If you're celebrating a birthday today you're an upbeat person who enjoys a bit of playfulness. Friends can count on you to be completely real with them—there's never a question of ulterior motives or swallowed opinions. However, you do hold those people in your circle to rather high standards. Thankfully you've also chosen all but family by those standards, neatly avoiding confrontations over expectations and limitations.

Relationships for our Sagittarius need to be very balanced and true—no games allowed. As a reward for that, however, you provide your partner with tons of sexy and seductive attention by night, and a fine mind to enjoy by day. Additionally, thanks to a birth number of 7, you can always tell when something's wrong with your partner and will be quick to attend to that situation.

Gift idea: massage oil.

ALERT!

Most people have a distinct image of what the first Thanksgiving was like back in 1621. However, historians offer us a slightly different look at this holiday. First, there's strong evidence that Thanksgiving didn't begin at Plymouth. In fact, it was an English custom known as a harvest festival filled with all manner of food and song—nothing quite so solemn and pious as the Pilgrims had. For the next two centuries, Thanksgiving was observed only periodically. It wasn't until 1777 that the Revolutionary War inspired a national moment of thankfulness. It wasn't established as a recognized holiday until 1863.

November 24

At the moment, this Archer has put down the bow in favor of a party hat. There's little you enjoy more than a good party, especially your own! Like a little kid on Christmas, gifts are the first thing on the list, followed by cake and games, all of which are greeted gleefully. It's your simple, straightforward, fun-loving nature that truly endears you to many publicly. Private life is a little different.

On the home front you're rather down to earth and more subdued. You like your space relatively orderly but comfy. The things with which you surround yourself are meaningful but not ostentatious. Much of this softer side comes from your birth number of 8, which really loves a good construct and strong foundations. Professionally 8 makes a showing as well. Your boss and coworkers regard you as focused, efficient, and dedicated, but certainly not stuffy!

When it comes time for love, you want an adventurous partner with whom to experience the pleasurable moments of life. In some ways, you have a gypsy soul, and look to dance the night away under the stars with a mysterious companion who you can love.

Gift idea: a secret rendezvous.

November 25

You are lead by your heart and pushed back and forth by emotions. Like the ocean, you wax and wane, hot and cold, happy and sad—sometimes over a week, sometimes in seconds! Keeping up with you is nearly as difficult as with a changeable Gemini, but at the same time you're terribly fun loving and really know how to have a good time, so most people who really care will stick it out.

Those sharing this birthday may exhibit warning signs of an addictive personality. Part of this happens because of an overall dissatisfaction with the life you see before you versus what you believe can truly be. That's perfectly normal for the birth number 9, but it's also very dangerous if not kept in check. One way to offset the yearning for unhealthy things is by traveling—see the world and what it has to offer. Go to sacred sites around the globe and come to understand why they resonate with your soul.

In love, you really want a person of depth who will go the distance and not just give up when the road gets bumpy. But that person also has to be one of passion with enough of an adventurous spirit to "come with," be it to Boston for tea (followed by Japan) or to Florida and swimming with the dolphins.

Gift idea: tickets to a sci-fi convention.

November 26

You are a stickler for details. Structure gives you a comfort zone, like black-and-white outlines to which you bring your personal crayons and vision. Oh, once in a great while you color outside the lines just to see what happens, but for the most part you honor the letter of the law, not simply the spirit.

People regard you as somewhat of an example to others, be it in your job or your own backyard. You're smart, know how to really listen to people, and enjoy helping other people achieve potential (as long as it's not quite as much as your own). Ah, that's the pesky birth number 1 rearing its somewhat selfish side—it's okay for everyone to shine, but your star still needs to be the brightest. Try to find a way to feed that aspect of yourself by putting your best foot forward no matter your choice of careers.

As for relationships, you crave a partner who's appealing from head to toe, and in every cell in between. This isn't simply about external beauty, it's about the whole "package"—and it can't be an altered one at that. You feel plastic surgery is rather silly when a decent stylist, makeup artist, and some wardrobe changes can make the worst external "geek" into a prince just waiting for a quest.

Gift idea: a compass.

November's flower is the chrysanthemum. As early as the fifteenth century B.C.E. the Chinese were cultivating it. Around the eighth century B.C.E. it came to Japan where it became the national flower (it even appears on Japan's flag). The name was taken from the Greek *chrys* (golden) and *anthemom* (flower). Many varieties of chrysanthemum are edible, having a biting, tangy edge favored in Asia. As with many other flowers, they have a language all their own: a regular golden variety means friendship, red is for luck, and a white flower is for honesty.

November 27

Dear Archer, breathe! I know it's very tempting to go off with that heated temper of yours, but you really could hurt someone. You've got the physical power behind you to do serious damage if you don't think before acting out. And no matter how righteous the indignation, make sure you're angry with the right parties! One good way to overcome this fly-off-the-handle tendency is by finding an exercise outlet that blows off steam, like using a boxing bag.

People sharing this birthday lean toward being overly defensive and having a knee-jerk reaction when friends and family seem to need protection. This is completely understandable with a resolution-oriented birth number of 2. Better still, this birth number provides a little restraint with that anger, in that it would prefer a peaceful negotiation to outright war any day.

Professionally you would do well in jobs such as PE coach and personal trainer. You also excel in team activities. Personally, you know love is an important element in life, but as with other areas, you act without thinking things through. Some partners find you much too forward at all the wrong moments.

Gift idea: Tai Chi lessons (which also improve focus).

November 28

Your birth number of 3 sets a cheerful tone from the get-go. Threes love to be the life of the party, and are very social animals. Better still, you've got a huge amount of magnetism to accompany that energy. Everyone seems comfortable around you, and no matter where you go you attract a flock. Be aware, however, that not all these people can be counted on as tried-and-true friends. Sort through that bevy of individuals to find those you can trust for a lifetime, not just this moment.

Archers sharing this special day are humorous and charming. They have a good eye for style and in fact might make very good fashion consultants or designers. Your generally optimistic attitude is contagious, and makes everyone in the vicinity feel better, even at the worst of times. So, another possible career path might be grief and crisis counseling. Here, however, that usual levity has to be tamed a bit, and used prudently.

The Archer's friends and family get treated with respect, and are given a lot of liberty. You aren't clingy and don't like people who are overly needy. In love, that outlook continues. You want an easygoing commitment in which both people maintain their individuality and have a fair amount of freedom. You may, in fact, opt for a non-traditional situation.

Gift idea: a carved memory box for special items (remember to put something inside!).

Scorpio

Sign: Scorpio
Date: October 23–November 21
Ruled by: Pluto
Element: Water
Lucky Color: Blue-green, turquoise
Gemstone: Topaz, opal
Keynote: Rebirth
Positive Traits: Charismatic, intense, strong will and convictions
Negative Traits: Jealous, hypocritical, gossip, skeptical
Famous Scorpios include: Prince Charles, Richard Dreyfuss, Goldie Hawn, Katharine Hepburn, Rock Hudson, Marie Antoinette, Pablo Picasso, Kurt Vonnegut, Jr.

The Scorpion's ruling center is the heart, meaning they feel everything deeply. Following instincts diligently while maintaining a certain level of reservation when entrusting others creates an interesting energetic struggle for this sign. Scorpios are terminally curious, motivated, and determined to see through even the most difficult projects until the bitter or blissful end.

In personal territory the Scorpio obsesses about various things, usually a private spot that's "off limits" to all but intimate companions. This is a direct reflection of the Scorpio sense of distrust, as well as a need to refine the self. In an odd dichotomy, Scorpio has a strong sensual side, even wild and wonton. So what happens to the inner sanctum then? Nothing. Scorpios enjoy sex around the house or at a hotel just as well!

In relationships there's no question that the Scorpion has great magnetism, loyalty, and sexual energy. However this doesn't come without a price tag. This is a high-maintenance partner whose demands and stubbornness may sting. Scorpios are also competitive, even with partners, often wanting the last word and definitive win.

This sign's ruling "planet" Pluto creates a dark, secretive cloud that taints even the most wonderful of moments. There's a "tug" toward over-examining things, looking for hidden scenarios, or beating around the bush. The greatest lesson for a Scorpio is that sometimes a rock is just a rock, and sometimes we must tackle our fears head on.

Chapter 14

December

In Roman times December was the tenth month, so indicated by *decem*, meaning 10 (a word that we also use in talking about the decimal system). In 46 B.C.E., Julius Caesar added two days to the month, giving it the 31 days we presently recognize. Sagittarius astrologically dominates the beginning of December, making it a month filled with the energy of change. Come the end of the month, Capricorn joins in, offering far more even-handed vibrations so that we can end the year on a calmer note.

December 1

You are fairly stubborn about your ideals. However, in almost everything else you're willing to find a middle ground with family, friends, and acquaintances. While there's no question you're every bit the opinionated Sagittarian, you've learned to infuse your words with positive energy and good humor so that the core ideas are more easily accepted.

Being vulnerable isn't your greatest attribute, so any career that requires taking down personal barriers simply won't do. Instead, consider looking to the birth number 4 as a guide in jobs. Very direct, no-nonsense positions suit you well—like accounting, where there are rules, defined answers, and clear-cut detachment. Having a rather practical nature, and a birth number that inspires even more expediency, creates a person with strong organizational aptitude to keep any project on track.

So where does the traditional Archer's restlessness come out? In relationships, of course! It takes a long time for you to consider settling down, and you may even prefer dating several people at once. The birth number 4 councils against such risky behavior, but sometimes one's birth sign wins out. It will take quite a creative charmer to turn you into Cupid! Once that happens, however, a more stable relationship begins to blossom, and you are able to show considerable affection.

Gift idea: personalized stationery.

December 2

You like to celebrate your birthdays in style. You love a good gathering of people, and if you can mix a little business with pleasure, that's icing on the cake. You've got a very outgoing personality, and love feeling useful, but within reason. Nearly everything you do has some thought and planning behind it, something your birth number of 5 may try to undermine. Remember that 5 is the adventurous, adaptive, and free-wheeling personality, so when you periodically and uncharacteristically take a leap of faith, don't be too hard on yourself. It's just that pesky birth number exerting its influence, and inserting some excitement into your life.

In careers, you excel at any position that lets your personality shine. You can meet deadlines, but also want some room to create. Why not look into being a writer, a set designer for theater, or the spokesperson for a favorite cause? You have a sound head for business and enough charm to open a lot of otherwise stubborn doors.

In personal relationships you have a healthy appetite for sex, and love spontaneous moments in the bedroom.

Gift idea: a candlelit bubble bath for two.

QUESTION?

How can I spot a Sagittarian?

They ooze optimism. They have a wide variety of interests and open minds, which guides them into diverse hobbies and haunts. Additionally, Sagittarians are usually quite forward with their opinions. Many Archers have a poetic nature and a restless soul. When they're not pondering life's mysteries, they're actively seeking out answers. Some turn that restless energy toward sports or physical outlets like dancing, the latter of which provides another medium for self-expression. Being goal-oriented, Sagittarians engage tasks and life itself very energetically. They meet challenges head-on, and avoid needy or selfish people at all costs.

December 3

You are the explorer of this birth sign. Life is a lovely adventure, and you just can't get enough! This doesn't mean that you're reckless—in fact, just the opposite is true. You think long and hard about many things. From those musings comes a vision, and out of the vision action manifests. Sometimes the outcomes are a little weird (as a wise person once said: expect the unexpected), but overall most of your efforts pan out, even if the results are completely startling.

The investigative nature of those born today naturally inspires career choices like anthropology, archaeology, legal investigator, and researcher. Combine this with the birth number of 6, and most of those choices will be driven by what can best benefit humankind or the world. There's no lack of big thinking here, but it's backed up with honest, concerned action and typically welcomed by many supportive individuals or groups.

Six also expresses itself in the relationship game. Today's Archer sets their sights on beautiful individuals (inside and out). You enjoy an artistic face, romantic hairstyles, artistic clothing—anything that's eye catching and speaks of personal style and flair. You will never be happy with a stoic, bland, and wholly dependable person. You need a little excitement, and love being swept away in a movie-like moment.

Gift idea: champagne breakfast in bed.

December 4

You have tons of autonomy, self-determination, and aggressiveness to go around. Where most Archers speak their mind, you do so with unflinching firmness, and sometimes get a little hot under the collar if the topic is close to your heart. The more pragmatic nature of your birth number 7 will help you a lot here, offering more logic or compassion as a situation requires.

Seven also helps control your risk-taking nature. You often come right to the edge of risking all for an ideal. Periodically the drive may be too strong to stop. However, 7 provides good instincts to recognize the danger ahead. Overall, it wouldn't be surprising to see you in counseling, moderating, or representing individuals or entire groups, so long as you keep impulsiveness in check.

Long-term relationships don't hold a lot of appeal for you. While you welcome company and enjoy intimacy, being tied down makes you very uneasy. If a relationship is to work, it must be altruistic on every level.

Gift idea: roller blades (with a helmet).

December 5

You have a natural mellowness, and even as a child you seemed like a "little adult," with insights and pragmatism far beyond your years. This wisdom is the result of a quick mind and a regulated heart. That doesn't mean you are dispassionate—just even-keeled. You aren't quick to anger, don't laugh too loudly, or love spontaneously. Additionally, the Aries decanate speaks of someone very secure, who has a clear image of goals and how to reach them.

Having a birth number 8, you can do nearly anything to which you apply your mind and hands. You've got enough work ethic for two people, and the brainpower to create wonders. Better still, your brilliance isn't over-whelming—you still know how to talk to the "everyday" person and explain profoundly complex ideas in simple, beautiful ways. Everyone around you naturally trusts that, which in turn thrusts you into leadership roles no matter the career path chosen. In particular teaching would be a great place for your personality and intellect to shine. You would be the teacher everyone remembered fondly.

In relationships people find today's Archer to be as direct as your arrow. You don't like "small talk" and appreciate people who are truthful and coop-erative. As a partner, that aptitude for leading can sometimes come across as being overly authoritarian, but the issue is quickly resolved with a gentle reminder that mates are not coworkers or employees.

Gift idea: a fruit tree.

December 6

December 6 bears the birth number of 9, a digit that speaks of highly devel-oped prophetic ability, or, minimally, truth-seeing. This is the perfect cou-pling for your discerning mind and gentle spirit. You truly want the best for everyone, but realize there are only so many quests to which you can give your whole attention. An Aries decanate provides physical and mental for-titude, but it's not something you squander. Applying effort and energy to hopeless causes isn't something you'll ever undertake knowingly.

Socially you are a bit on the stoic side, sometimes lapsing into long philo-sophical thoughts about what's wrong with the world and how to right it. The solutions you find are typically ones founded in non-aggressive approaches, as there's no question you are a pacifist. The only thing you'll ever use that bow and arrow for is hunting (figuratively or literally). If you need to feed your family, you head to the woods. If you need to feed your spirit, you track after the right group or ideology to fulfill that hunger. And thanks to having luck on your side, somehow the approach works out okay.

In commitments, you are not overly aggressive but very passionate and a bit of an idealist. Thankfully your perceptive nature breaks through any rose-colored fog that comes of love-at-first-sight, and provides a gut level "yes" or "no." So long as you listen to this instinct, typically you find the happily-ever-after scenario you crave.

Gift idea: a night at the symphony.

ALERT!

December dates in history: Monroe Doctrine presented to Congress (December 2, 1823); First heart transplant undertaken (December 3, 1967); Prohibition repealed (December 5, 1933); John Lennon shot and killed in NYC (December 8, 1980); First trans-Atlantic radio signal received (December 12, 1901); Boston Tea Party (December 16, 1773); Nelson Rockefeller sworn in as vice president of the United States (December 19, 1974); U.S. Federal Reserve System established (December 23, 1913); Soviet troops invade Afghanistan (December 27, 1979).

December 7

You love being physical and getting out to "rough it" on a regular basis (hiking is a great pastime to consider). In nature's classroom you often explore your spiritual side. Even though you can't always grasp highly developed philosophies, you feel them to the core of your being.

Socially you love to interact and talk, but can't always back up your ideas with action. It's not lack of honest intent, rather a tendency to get distracted easily. If you can learn to focus, it will improve your follow-through greatly. Your birth number 1 helps here, driving some type of unique achievement in your life—in the best time and space for you. Mind you, that may not be soon enough for family and companions who have Type A expectations. As these people come to understand your nature, however, you'll find a happy middle ground that's not so tense.

When it comes to intimacy you aim your arrow toward finding a soul mate, even though you're not sure such a relationship is realistically possible. Physical touch is very important to you, as is romance, but heavens—

don't talk it to death! More action, less words is definitely this Sagittarian's way in bed.

Gift idea: a trip to a rodeo.

December 8

You're a bit of an extremist, often fueling thoughts and actions well ahead of their time. Once in motion, you support what you've started with a fervent, passionate stance that's nearly as stubborn as a Taurus. Better still, you have the charisma of a Scorpio to back that zealousness up. Throughout life you are highly focused on morals and convictions.

You're not afraid to confront problems or people head-on, and sometimes do so a little too strongly. Additionally, you don't suffer fools or willfully ignorant individuals in the least. Others should not expect any type of tact or compassion in those arenas. The only thing that may soften this trait is the birth number of 2, which offers some tact and diplomacy.

On a personal level, you love a good party as that's your downtime during which stress runs off. In love, you run completely either hot or cold. In heated mode, you like variety, new things, a challenge, or a fight (complete with make-up sex). In cold mode—just leave you alone. With this in mind, an Aries fire might be a perfect fit for your heart.

Gift idea: a date on the firing range.

December 9

Instantaneous—decisions, actions, thoughts . . . today's Sagittarian is very spur-of-the-moment and intense. You have a very strong will, a mind hungry for life, and a passion for "good things" not only personally but also globally.

With friends, you always keep a bit of yourself hidden. The only people who ever get close enough to find those secrets are people willing to really put forth ongoing effort in a relationship. In truth, you prefer a few very trustworthy friends to hundreds who you can barely get to know. This group of chosen people, however, have a very joyful and dependable friend in hand whom they value, thanks in part to the birth number 3's influence.

Socially you probably enjoy travel, the theater, and comfortable social situations. You're not big on noisy places where you can't have a decent conversation, so will usually gravitate to a coffee house over a bar any day. Romantically you want passion and pizzazz—lots of fireworks and all the hearts and flowers that go with it. Look for a partner who has Mars figuring heavily in their chart to help spark that fire.

Gift idea: a camping trip with friends.

There are several places that Sagittarians like to hang out. Their natural interest in other cultures means you can find them frequenting cultural history museums, and art exhibits, attending a variety of spiritual institutions, and enjoying foreign films. Additionally, there's usually a child inside the Archer who enjoys a good magic show, Easter egg hunt, or an afternoon of picking out patterns in the clouds at a nearby park. Watch these spots, and when you see certain folks frequenting them, you're probably on the right track to finding a Sagittarian.

December 10

You are incredibly energetic and zealous, especially about what you perceive as having potential. You have a very optimistic outlook on life and a strong work ethic, both of which blend effectively with the birth number 4 as a recipe for professional success. Careers that require impressive communication skills are doubly apropos—think about being a motivational speaker, for example!

Your birth number implies that you stick to goals like glue, and have the energy to see things through to the end. You love it when you come up against a wall, as that moment inspires fresh ideas. However, at that juncture try to avoid nay-sayers. They can unplug your enthusiasm and put you into a depressive cycle, completely undermining the genius you could otherwise create.

In relationships you provide people with lots of support and positive emotion. You're not usually one to settle down early in life, wanting a certain amount of autonomy to pursue whatever vision lies in your soul. After the age of forty, however, you might settle down with a highly solar person, whose warmth and hopefulness nurture the relationship.

Gift idea: a closet organizer.

December 11

You're a very empathic person, and you use that aptitude to ensure equity in a variety of situations. Other people come first in your life, especially the underdog. Since your youth, you've fought for what was right, even when peers snickered. You've always known who you are, and exactly what ethics guide personal actions, meaning nearly every lost puppy in the universe has at one time or another landed on your doorstep. Unfortunately, some people will misuse your compassion.

Today's birth number is 5, which sometimes confuses issues. On one hand there's a strong pull toward being responsible for others' well-being. On the other, this birth number encourages independent thought, action, and adaptation. You don't always understand why others can't just land on their feet, yet you know intellectually that not everyone is so fortunate. If you can teach your adjustment skills to others, you'll succeed in feeding their kind nature, and the energies of 5.

In long-term relationships you make an excellent parent and role model, and will probably want several children. You are a very nurturing individual, who will give passionately and kindly to the right mate, especially one who has heightened sensitivity (perhaps someone with strong lunar influences in their chart).

Gift idea: a framed photograph of a harvest moon.

December 12

This Archer has a very charitable nature balanced with objectivity. You have incredible effervescence, especially when presented with a challenging situation. However, you don't sit still very well. That nervous energy and a curiosity toward other cultures may lead to globe-trotting or hobbies that "move" (like running or biking). Physical outlets are very helpful to improving your ability to stay on task.

Your birth number is 6, so you love beautiful things, but they cannot be superficially so. You want something lovely to the core—be it a concept or person. This feeling is accentuated by your Aries decanate, which has a highly developed sense of depth and virtue. Six may also manifest in your life as a desire to create beautiful things (or collect them in your travels). There's some inventive energy here, so use it effectively!

Your love of challenges comes home to roost in relationships too. You don't want an easy lover, or someone overly needy (the latter is a huge turn off). The game of cat and mouse, especially when orchestrated by a keen mind, is very exciting.

Gift idea: a collection of stones from around the world.

FACT

Turquoise is December's birthstone. Tradition holds that carrying turquoise protects against injuries in travel. It also inspires bravery, protects against fighting with your spouse, improves friendship, and even gives passion a boost. If there's trouble afoot, this stone is said to change color or shatter as a warning. Turquoise comes in different colors. The darker the blue, the more copper is present in the stone. Green turquoise bears more aluminum, and yellowish turquoise is high in zinc, something that's relatively rare. The markings in turquoise are caused by the rock in which it forms: black is typically iron pyrite, while brown is iron oxide.

December 13

Today's Sagittarian is as changeable as a Gemini. Being somewhat silly and odd, you have a liberal mind and a gypsy soul. The words "normal" and "mundane" will never describe your life. Your calling is to see and do things differently, even if people don't always understand why. Consequently, a 9-to-5 job will never work for you. Seek out freelance jobs or careers that allow you to express your visions in your own time and way (such as an artist).

With a birth number of 7, this differentness is perfectly normal and has been part of the routine seemingly forever. To be honest, you probably wouldn't want it any other way. Being slightly out of step with society means you're in step with other visionaries. This also appeals to your Leo decanate, which loves to shine with self-reliance, anticipation, and a hint of the dramatic.

Love proves highly unconventional for this Archer. You seek a challenging partner with brains, beauty, and zeal who can share the stage easily. No stand-ins will do here. Until you locate that person, being monogamous probably isn't in the cards for you, and in fact you may never really want "marriage" in the conventional sense.

Gift idea: roller blades and a date at the nearest skate park.

December 14

You're creative and talkative, and you want to be sure your message hits home. The only problem is sometimes you forget to breathe and listen, and this makes other people uncomfortable or put off. Your challenge is to learn the art of two-way conversations, and realize you do not have to speak just for the sake of hearing your own voice.

You've got a very hungry mind and may become a perpetual student. You could well work as a spokesperson or announcer, putting that verbose nature to good use. Also consider guest lectures at colleges where you can meet like-minded people. Your dramatic Leo decanate will thrive in that type of atmosphere and help manifest the success you need to continue your personal quests. Additionally, your birth number of 8 won't be happy unless you provide yourself with some measure of security on which to depend when other plans fall through.

Your love life is pretty unpredictable. There's no question you want someone smart, savvy, sexy, and highly creative in bed. However, you are somewhat naïve in thinking that long-term relationships constantly burn at a high flame, and you can easily burn out with the wrong partners (ones who don't temper that passion and nurture stability).

Gift idea: prepaid cell phone minutes.

December 15

You are quite adept at multitasking, and have excellent social skills. You speak clearly and evenly, but also know how to listen and really hear what others are trying to communicate. This is your quieter aspect, while your other side is a bit of a wild child: loving to flirt, and having tons of presence. This leads to having a flock of admirers, especially in a party atmosphere. Watch out here! While all that attention is fun, it can distract from the "main event" and lead to unwittingly hurting feelings.

You truly do enjoy a good party, and may also be an avid dancer. You live here and now, not thinking too much of the future. This rather nonchalant approach clashes a bit with the birth number 9, which tends toward activism and wants to change the world for the better. Such goals are hard to reach when one is rather naive and avoids responsibility when possible. Having that conflict doesn't bode well for careers, unless you fall back on speaking in a light-hearted field like comedy or acting.

In relationships you tend to be a little overly dependent. You want mates to tell you how wonderful you are, and "ooh-ahh" over every creative effort. That puts many potential mates off, who see you as needy. In turn, you might go through lovers nearly as fast as jobs.

Gift idea: disco music and a mirror ball.

December 16

Today's Archer goes from the firing range to the kitchen range. You're a bit of a domestic diva, especially when it comes to cooking up really imaginative meals (do not, however, try baking—it's too precise for that creative spirit). In fact, this aptitude is perhaps the only really pragmatic talent you've acquired. Being run-of-the mill or "normal" just isn't your thing. The more hazardous or difficult a person/situation, the more it attracts you. With this in mind, you might do well to become a ghost hunter or spiritualist, where that instinctive nature and vision can shine. This also feeds birth number 1's thirst for the unusual and unique.

Socially, you love to fix people (forgetting to fix yourself all too frequently). Needy people gravitate like moths to a flame. Privately, you love much too quickly, often ending up with exactly the wrong partner—or worse, trying to fix that person too!

Gift idea: a dream catcher.

December 17

You have a highly refined sense of structure, precision, and patterns, and can use that to your advantage personally and professionally. Where others might buck the rules, you find a way to work inside them and still make things happen. Your birth number of 2 suggests that others respect that aptitude, and often look to you for help where guidelines are called into question. Why not put this to use in a legal career, or in regulatory positions.

Your personology report implies a very strong presence, but one highly restrained (sometimes too much so—unclench once in a while!). You work very well with deadlines and pressures, and you can size up other people very quickly. By applying those perspectives you can motivate very smooth workflows, but will not tolerate slackers. Watch out, that pointed tongue is pretty sharp and holds little back when confronted with a sloth!

What about love? Well, sure . . . um, maybe . . . but . . . . You yearn for a sturdy, dependable partner who revels in constructs as much as you do. Unfortunately, you also love variety, meaning you might stray from the very thing you hope to achieve.

Gift idea: a key chain tape measure.

ALERT!

December's birth flower is narcissus. In Greek myth, the boy Narcissus avoided romantic attentions from everyone, yet was charmed by his own reflection in a pond. He would not leave that spot and was slowly transformed into the flower that bears his name. Narcissus is a spring blossom that loves damp soil (near ponds and rivers). Greeks and Egyptians used the flower as a funerary plant, Europeans saw it as a symbol of death, while Arabic people considered it an aphrodisiac. We know the narcissus by the less fanciful, but no less playful, name daffodil.

December 18

Wow, are you ever a powerhouse! If you find a vision and start following after it, like a dog with a bone, you keep going until the bitter or sweet end. Challenges simply make you more determined and assertive, and you see these moments as learning experiences. Life for you is as much about staying focused as it is living each moment fully—and in fact, that serves you well overall.

Individuals sharing this birthday often love nature, and may find that the outdoors inspires moments of creative flashes or outright genius. Once acted upon, your enthusiasm never wanes, nor does your eye leave the prize. Having a birth number 3 certainly boosts that overall energy level by providing a relatively optimistic perspective and a joyful approach to every day.

Relationships, however, are not quite so sunny for you. You need ongoing assurances of honest affection, touch, and tenderness to feel secure. Additionally, you prefer an alpha role (which is somewhat confusing in light of the confidence issue).

Gift idea: a tent or other camping gear.

December's number is a 1, which implies some endings and beginnings (somehow apt for the end of a year). Another number that figures into the energies for December is 12 (being the twelfth month on our calendar). This represents awareness and fulfillment, meaning now is an excellent time to concentrate on seeding self-development and relationships so those efforts blossom come spring.

December 19

Most people who meet you may think at first you're a Leo. You love the spotlight, and the spotlight loves you! You have a joie de vivre that is absolutely contagious, and may naturally find yourself in fields like advertising, modeling, or acting, where that charisma can pour out liberally.

You've been blessed with a fair amount of good fortune in life, and you don't for a moment take that lightly. To you, luck is something on which no one should depend, but that everyone should appreciate. When something good happens, you're likely to share it and make it grow. Having a birth number of 4 certainly supports that by providing firm foundations on which to build any idea, investment, or project. The only real council in your personology report is not to be so harsh on yourself. There's a secret voice inside that nags you, and isn't always very personally positive. Tell it to shut up and see yourself as others do: warm and wonderful.

So what's in store for you relationshipwise? Well, your road may be a bit bumpy. You have a huge presence and partners might feel swallowed up by it, especially if that partner is somewhat insecure. With that in mind, you might do well to seek out a Leo with similar outspoken pizzazz.

Gift idea: a pool table or pinball machine.

December 20

Those born on the 20th have a birth number of 5, which comes out strong and sure. You depend heavily on emotional and sensual input when exploring and interacting with the world. Your heart definitely leads your head, but thankfully you have enough common sense to know when you're in hot water. Better still, you have very accurate intuitive skills, and if you trust them they rarely lead you astray. Some say you have second sight—and they're not far off. It's what the Icelandic people call "seeing true." There's little others can effectively hide from you. You'll never be caught off guard by a surprise party, although you'll feign surprise so your friends' hard work doesn't seem wasted.

One concern that comes forward in your personology profile is the tendency to focus on other people or situations to your own detriment. You think long and hard about life, seeking answers to the mysteries, which you may well find. However, along that path, if you forget self-nurturing and care you'll miss the mark and burn out.

Your love life is tentative. You are very giving by nature, which has caused a fair amount of heartache. Consequently, you're not going to rush in blindly. Partners need to give you time. If they're being real, you'll know and respond with uncommon passion.

Gift idea: a piece of moldavite jewelry to support and hone the spiritual nature.

QUESTION?

What Famous people were born in December?
Woody Allen (12/1), Marco Polo (12/1), Britney Spears (12/2), Tyra Banks (12/4), Sammy Davis, Jr. (12/8), Flip Wilson (12/8), Kirk Douglas (12/9), Emily Dickinson (12/10), Dick Van Dyke (12/13), Charles Dickens (12/16), Brad Pitt (12/18), Christina Aguilera (12/18), Christopher Columbus (12/21), Mary Higgins Clark (12/24), Rod Serling (12/25), Barbara Mandrell, (12/25), Louis Pasteur (12/27), Mary Tyler Moore (12/29), Ted Danson (12/29), Anthony Hopkins (12/31), Donna Summer (12/31).

December 21

With the energy of Capricorn creeping in, today's celebrants are silly, life-loving, and energetic. You avoid conformity like the plague, yet expect everyone else to do so as well! Hint here: When you demand that others walk your path, you cease being original or unique. Dance to your own tune, and let others do likewise!

Today's birth number is 6, giving you an eye for beauty. You'll target all good things in life, and thirst after things that seem well ahead of their time. Additionally you thrive on compliments. If there's a way to gain public acclaim and interest, you'll go out of your way to make it happen. With this in mind, positions in modeling, fashion design, or as a member of a rock band all fit perfectly. Lady luck also loves you, so there will be some unexpected twists and turns in life that lead to success.

Privately you're a hippy born in the wrong era. Free love, unconventional living situations, and avoiding all the normal constructs is the "norm" here. You do not want to be tied down, especially to a homebody. However, a person who can keep you surprised has a better chance of longevity than anyone else.

Gift idea: bell-bottoms or a tie-dyed shirt.

December 22

Those born today love to tinker, and you're no exception. As a child you probably took apart everything just to see how it worked (much to your parents' frustration). Nonetheless, that curiosity provided you with insights into how things work, and how to take a good idea and make it even better. With this in mind, it wouldn't hurt to consider mechanically oriented careers where you can apply that perspective in a "hands on" manner. This is doubly true when you consider the birth number of 7, which just loves unraveling a mystery.

Those sharing a 12/22 birthday seem totally secure and resolute. They seem to know who they are, where they're going, and how to get there intact. Having a prosperous professional life and happy home life is important to you, but sometimes you overlook personal needs in the process of achieving those two goals. While climbing all those mountains, you need to learn how to relax periodically and have some spontaneous fun.

In relationships, typical of a Goat, you sometimes get overly obstinate. It's just the nature of the beast. Other times you retreat up the hillside into a cave and just want to be alone. Partners are well advised to give this Capricorn the space desired (at least for a short time), as it's very healthy and gives them time to process ideas and lessons effectively.

Gift idea: a family portrait.

December 23

Come to December 23rd and we find ourselves talking about a stubborn Goat. You have a highly refined sense of responsibility, especially toward your job, and are probably working on your birthday unless your boss bans you from the office. There's a fine mind here, very academically honed but rather serious. You love other smart people, but have very little time to enjoy them, so typically you curl up with a good book instead.

At home, you'll find this Capricorn surrounded by tomes and educational tapes. You'll also likely find a private office of some sort where work comes home to roost. Having a birth number of 8 doesn't help ameliorate this focus in the least—it's quite content to put forward the effort necessary for long-term security (even when it appears that security has already been achieved). Needless to say, you need to give more time to play and being wistful, but don't really know how. You find sincere comfort in the routine and ordinary, and may even get frightened off by overly adventurous sorts.

In the relationship arena you aren't terribly aggressive. The busy nature of your professional life combines with shyness to make those opportunities for intimacy few and far between. The best partner for you is someone who can release your inner child, and who also has a well-defined personal life outside the relationship (for those long nights when the Capricorn's at work).

Gift idea: a gift certificate for a bookstore.

December 24

You protect your space and everyone therein in a determined but well-planned way. Yours is not a life of unregulated passion, but rather control and preparation. One doesn't climb the mountain without the proper equipment, and that's pretty much your outlook on life—think, equip, then act! The difficulty here is having the birth number of 9 that's going to whisper "no amount of planning is good enough." Be careful that you don't get mired in negativity or the changes you want to make will endlessly sit on the "someday" shelf in your closet.

You may also seem invulnerable. Your exterior is honed and poised no matter the circumstances. This has come about in part due to a rather clouded past with more than its fair share of pain. So rather than risk, you put up a big wall and proceed very cautiously. Nonetheless, that aptitude for regulation would serve you well in nearly any administrative position, or jobs in time management.

As one might expect, that pattern of caution continues in relationships. It's vital that you find a trustworthy companion, and even then the idea of a long-term relationship scares the heck out of you. As a partner, you will need regular reassurances of love. In turn, you become a very sensitive and loving mate.

Gift idea: a pocket multi-tool.

QUESTION?

What interesting holidays, celebrations, and observances take place in December?

World Aids Awareness Day (12/1), National Pie Day (12/2), St. Nicholas Day (12/6), Pearl Harbor Day (12/7), National Pastry Day (12/9), Ice Cream Day (12/13), National Maple Syrup Day (12/17), Go Caroling Day (12/19), National Flashlight Day (12/21), Christmas Day (12/25), Boxing Day (12/26), Fruitcake Day (12/27), National Chocolate Day (12/28), New Year's Eve (12/31).

December 25

Today's Capricorn has a naturally curious nature. If there's a mystery within ten miles, you're out trying to unravel it. In fact, you'd make a great investigator, historian, or archaeologist because of your refined ability to find things. If that idea doesn't quite appeal, the other alternative is counseling. You really know how to listen (it's part of fact finding) and have a very soothing voice. The dichotomy of head and heart is common to folks born today, but eventually one has to win out for you to be successful in your career path.

The birth number for Christmas babies is 1, implying that you're bound to do something outstanding in your life for which people will remember you. However, timing is everything. Use your insightfulness to know where your time and efforts are best applied to achieve your goals personally and professionally.

In relationships, you have a lot of fantasies but are somewhat hesitant to actually try any of them. Additionally, you have a highly sensual nature. To woo this individual use incense, candles, music, interesting fabrics, and fine food. The more senses you engage, the better your chances.

Gift idea: a potpourri burner.

December 26

Folks born today have a lot of inner fortitude and are more stubborn than most Taureans. Once they lay down a rule, they fully expect everyone to stick to it like glue. There's very little room for compromise in this person's life.

That hard-nosed nature comes out in your work too. You have a very strong sense of duty and responsibility, to the point that you never let up. Be careful—if you don't give yourself downtime and a chance to unwind, you will eventually blow up emotionally (or give yourself an ulcer).

When it comes to friends and family, you hold everyone to the same expectations as yourself, which isn't always reasonable or fair. The thing that may downplay the controlling aspect of your personality is a birth number 2, which seeks out more equity and wants positive interactions with others. Nonetheless, potential mates must understand you have a jealous, regulated nature. It's part of the package. But once you learn to receive from a loved one, you make a very devoted partner.

Gift idea: a punching bag to work off stress.

December 27

You're a physical powerhouse. You probably focus a lot on bodily development—not necessarily being muscle bound, but rather healthy and toned. Organic diets work very well for you, and you enjoy an on-the-go lifestyle that's filled with good energy. In fact, you might do well as a professional trainer or athlete. Teaching others to live better is definitely part of your nature, especially considering the upbeat influence of a birth number 3.

People sharing this birthday do have a stubborn side, but it's one that helps in achieving goals. You also tend to be a harsh self-critic. Friends would do well to regularly remind you to simply "lighten up" and allow for your humanness. If others can get you to step outside the ordinary from time to time, it will greatly benefit your creativity too.

In relationships today's Capricorn doesn't always handle things very well. While you've got lots of passion and the ability to give, you forget about the little things. Relationship maintenance isn't something you will ever excel at, so you do best with a relatively independent partner.

Gift idea: running shoes.

December 28

Today's Capricorn is a real looker. It might not be physical comeliness, however, so much as a presence. You just catch people's eye with your bearing and aura. Additionally, people naturally seem to trust your judgment and organizational aptitude, making you a natural leader and facilitator—and one who's not afraid to get your hands dirty.

The birth number for December 28 is 4, which has strong earth-oriented energy, something that expresses itself most powerfully in personal spaces. Many people sharing this birthday are homebodies and really want a warm, welcoming space to retreat to and unwind. This is a balance point to a success-oriented drive, and a true appreciation for the finer things in life (which require hard work to obtain).

In private, you are very independent. You will never be "owned" by friends or family, and have very little patience for jealousy. Partners, if you love today's Capricorn, set them free. They will come back with tons of appreciation in tow.

Gift idea: gourmet goodies or culinary tools.

FACT

Winter begins officially around December 21, on the longest night of the year. In ancient times, people grew frightened by the waning light, so they offered sacrifices and held special rituals to placate the sun. Mesopotamians celebrated the new year, and Babylonians and Persians had a holiday in which slaves became masters, and masters, slaves. Europeans simply welcomed back the sun and worked magic for protection against any lingering malevolent spirits, especially those of sickness. The Romans called the celebration Saturnalia, which lasted the whole month of December. They used laurel garlands for decoration and lit trees with candles burning brightly.

December 29

You have a psychic, insightful edge. You can see the cycles in your life and the world as a whole. Beyond this, you have an empathic aptitude that you need to be aware of and learn to hone. Otherwise the emotions of others can absolutely drown out your own inner voice and sense of balance. It wouldn't hurt to read a good psychic self-defense book to get a handle on this.

Those sharing this birthday would do well to focus on the present. There's a tendency here to hang on to the past and let it drag down present situations. While learning lessons is great, clinging to them is not. You know full well how to teach other people to release, now you have to apply that awareness to yourself. So doing might be a challenge, but it will please the birth number 5, which seeks after new experiences and usually makes the most of any situation.

Holding on to unneeded things sometimes sneaks into relationships too. You get skeptical and pessimistic, often pushing people away with the negativity. Meanwhile, the heart of a romantic lurks beneath. The partner who learns to tap that will have a truly affectionate companion for life.

Gift idea: an amethyst to help with self-regulation.

December 30

As we near the end of the year, we come to a Capricorn who's filled with life, ambition, responsibility, and an eye for detail. This is a very potent blend that serves you well in life. While there's no question you want all "good things" (your birth number 6 nearly ensures that), you also know the value of hard work.

You want to get out and adventure, but not at any cost. You have a poised, cautious curiosity that's always tempered with practicality. In fact, you have no patience for people who cannot effectively apply the skills they have—it's seen as such a waste, and can lead to a sound scolding. What you need to remember is that people are a combination of many factors, and perhaps by looking deeper, an individual's valuable characteristics can be found.

This need to go beyond the surface occurs in relationships too. Having a birth number of 6 sometimes causes you to focus too much on externals. However, by overcoming that, you can fulfill your need to nurture, teach, and inspire. In fact, you might do well to seek a younger lover.

Gift idea: a trip to New York City or San Francisco.

ALERT!

With winter getting into full swing, some of the most common names for December's full moon include Cold Moon (Celtic) or Long Night Moon (because the moon sits above the horizon for many hours). Other names are Bitter Moon (China), Snow Moon (Cherokee), Oak Moon (Old England), Wind and Rain Moon (New Guinea), and Respect Moon (Hopi).

December 31

We end the year on a very steady note. You're an insightful Capricorn with a strong intellect and a unique ability to stay in focus no matter what chaos abounds. Staying an active participant in life is very important to you—you'll never sit on the sidelines and just wait. In fact, you probably often volunteer to lead or facilitate to make sure the job gets done!

While all this sounds rather logical, you have a spiritual side too. Life is a bit of a quest for you. You can think globally, and see potentials in people or situations that others readily miss. This certainly pairs perfectly with the birth number 7's visionary aptitude.

On a personal level, it takes a while before you bond to anyone, even as a friend. You'll watch from a distance and measure things thoughtfully before acting. You also have some trouble expressing emotions effectively, meaning partners need patience.

Gift idea: a spyglass.

Saggittarius

Sign: Sagittarius

Date: November 22–December 21

Ruled by: Jupiter

Element: Fire

Lucky Color: Sky blue

Gemstone: Turquoise, lapis

Keynote: Adventure

Positive Traits: Curious, idealistic, truthful, upbeat

Negative Traits: Lecturing, intolerant, belligerent

Famous Sagittarians include: Beethoven, Andrew Carnegie, Walt Disney, Patty Duke, Betty Ford, Harpo Marx, , John Milton, Agnes Moorehead, Mark Twain

Sagittarians are among the luckiest people in the world. There is an uncanny bit of serendipity that surrounds the Archer, rewarding even the most spontaneous of ideas with some type of good fortune. If Lady Luck is the friend of the brave-hearted, that would explain a lot. There's little that Sagittarians face where their courage, strength, and a little bit of inner fire can't come out victorious.

The Sagittarian home is bright and unconventional. Not wishing to be tied down to any one place, the Archer prefers rent over mortgages and exotic locations over familiarity. Inevitably, having a "home" takes a back burner to the adventurous soul of Sagittarians, who crave travel and new experiences. The Archer is all about the journey, not the destination. They think big, live big, and dream big (with style!). Better still, the nonjudgmental nature of a Sagittarian allows him or her to feel comfortable and relatively welcome no matter the cultural setting.

In relationships, Sagittarians inspire others to be true to self. They're fun-loving, flirtatious, sincere, honest, and good lovers, but also far more vulnerable than they appear. This can lead to a level of paranoia in the Archer who's afraid to ask questions and clarify. In part this comes from the honest belief that true love is forever, even though their love of the hunt often leads them to many relationships.

THE EVERYTHING SERIES!

BUSINESS & PERSONAL FINANCE

Everything® Accounting Book
Everything® Budgeting Book
Everything® Business Planning Book
Everything® Coaching and Mentoring Book
Everything® Fundraising Book
Everything® Get Out of Debt Book
Everything® Grant Writing Book
Everything® Home-Based Business Book, 2nd Ed.
Everything® Homebuying Book, 2nd Ed.
Everything® Homeselling Book, 2nd Ed.
Everything® Investing Book, 2nd Ed.
Everything® Landlording Book
Everything® Leadership Book
Everything® Managing People Book, 2nd Ed.
Everything® Negotiating Book
Everything® Online Auctions Book
Everything® Online Business Book
Everything® Personal Finance Book
Everything® Personal Finance in Your 20s and 30s Book
Everything® Project Management Book
Everything® Real Estate Investing Book
Everything® Robert's Rules Book, $7.95
Everything® Selling Book
Everything® Start Your Own Business Book, 2nd Ed.
Everything® Wills & Estate Planning Book

COOKING

Everything® Barbecue Cookbook
Everything® Bartender's Book, $9.95
Everything® Chinese Cookbook
Everything® Classic Recipes Book
Everything® Cocktail Parties and Drinks Book
Everything® College Cookbook
Everything® Cooking for Baby and Toddler Book
Everything® Cooking for Two Cookbook
Everything® Diabetes Cookbook
Everything® Easy Gourmet Cookbook
Everything® Fondue Cookbook
Everything® Fondue Party Book
Everything® Gluten-Free Cookbook
Everything® Glycemic Index Cookbook
Everything® Grilling Cookbook

Everything® Healthy Meals in Minutes Cookbook
Everything® Holiday Cookbook
Everything® Indian Cookbook
Everything® Italian Cookbook
Everything® Low-Carb Cookbook
Everything® Low-Fat High-Flavor Cookbook
Everything® Low-Salt Cookbook
Everything® Meals for a Month Cookbook
Everything® Mediterranean Cookbook
Everything® Mexican Cookbook
Everything® One-Pot Cookbook
Everything® Quick and Easy 30-Minute, 5-Ingredient Cookbook
Everything® Quick Meals Cookbook
Everything® Slow Cooker Cookbook
Everything® Slow Cooking for a Crowd Cookbook
Everything® Soup Cookbook
Everything® Tex-Mex Cookbook
Everything® Thai Cookbook
Everything® Vegetarian Cookbook
Everything® Wild Game Cookbook
Everything® Wine Book, 2nd Ed.

GAMES

Everything® 15-Minute Sudoku Book, $9.95
Everything® 30-Minute Sudoku Book, $9.95
Everything® Blackjack Strategy Book
Everything® Brain Strain Book, $9.95
Everything® Bridge Book
Everything® Card Games Book
Everything® Card Tricks Book, $9.95
Everything® Casino Gambling Book, 2nd Ed.
Everything® Chess Basics Book
Everything® Craps Strategy Book
Everything® Crossword and Puzzle Book
Everything® Crossword Challenge Book
Everything® Cryptograms Book, $9.95
Everything® Easy Crosswords Book
Everything® Easy Kakuro Book, $9.95
Everything® Games Book, 2nd Ed.
Everything® Giant Sudoku Book, $9.95
Everything® Kakuro Challenge Book, $9.95
Everything® Large-Print Crossword Challenge Book
Everything® Large-Print Crosswords Book
Everything® Lateral Thinking Puzzles Book, $9.95
Everything® Mazes Book

Everything® Pencil Puzzles Book, $9.95
Everything® Poker Strategy Book
Everything® Pool & Billiards Book
Everything® Test Your IQ Book, $9.95
Everything® Texas Hold 'Em Book, $9.95
Everything® Travel Crosswords Book, $9.95
Everything® Word Games Challenge Book
Everything® Word Search Book

HEALTH

Everything® Alzheimer's Book
Everything® Diabetes Book
Everything® Health Guide to Adult Bipolar Disorder
Everything® Health Guide to Controlling Anxiety
Everything® Health Guide to Fibromyalgia
Everything® Health Guide to Thyroid Disease
Everything® Hypnosis Book
Everything® Low Cholesterol Book
Everything® Massage Book
Everything® Menopause Book
Everything® Nutrition Book
Everything® Reflexology Book
Everything® Stress Management Book

HISTORY

Everything® American Government Book
Everything® American History Book
Everything® Civil War Book
Everything® Freemasons Book
Everything® Irish History & Heritage Book
Everything® Middle East Book

HOBBIES

Everything® Candlemaking Book
Everything® Cartooning Book
Everything® Coin Collecting Book
Everything® Drawing Book
Everything® Family Tree Book, 2nd Ed.
Everything® Knitting Book
Everything® Knots Book
Everything® Photography Book
Everything® Quilting Book
Everything® Scrapbooking Book
Everything® Sewing Book
Everything® Woodworking Book

Bolded titles are new additions to the series.
All Everything® books are priced at $12.95 or $14.95, unless otherwise stated. Prices subject to change without notice.

HOME IMPROVEMENT

Everything® Feng Shui Book
Everything® Feng Shui Decluttering Book, $9.95
Everything® Fix-It Book
Everything® Home Decorating Book
Everything® Home Storage Solutions Book
Everything® Homebuilding Book
Everything® Lawn Care Book
Everything® Organize Your Home Book

KIDS' BOOKS

All titles are $7.95

Everything® Kids' Animal Puzzle & Activity Book
Everything® Kids' Baseball Book, 4th Ed.
Everything® Kids' Bible Trivia Book
Everything® Kids' Bugs Book
Everything® Kids' Cars and Trucks Puzzle & Activity Book
Everything® Kids' Christmas Puzzle & Activity Book
Everything® Kids' Cookbook
Everything® Kids' Crazy Puzzles Book
Everything® Kids' Dinosaurs Book
Everything® Kids' First Spanish Puzzle and Activity Book
Everything® Kids' Gross Hidden Pictures Book
Everything® Kids' Gross Jokes Book
Everything® Kids' Gross Mazes Book
Everything® Kids' Gross Puzzle and Activity Book
Everything® Kids' Halloween Puzzle & Activity Book
Everything® Kids' Hidden Pictures Book
Everything® Kids' Horses Book
Everything® Kids' Joke Book
Everything® Kids' Knock Knock Book
Everything® Kids' Learning Spanish Book
Everything® Kids' Math Puzzles Book
Everything® Kids' Mazes Book
Everything® Kids' Money Book
Everything® Kids' Nature Book
Everything® Kids' Pirates Puzzle and Activity Book
Everything® Kids' Princess Puzzle and Activity Book
Everything® Kids' Puzzle Book
Everything® Kids' Riddles & Brain Teasers Book
Everything® Kids' Science Experiments Book
Everything® Kids' Sharks Book
Everything® Kids' Soccer Book
Everything® Kids' Travel Activity Book

KIDS' STORY BOOKS

Everything® Fairy Tales Book

LANGUAGE

Everything® Conversational Chinese Book with CD, $19.95
Everything® Conversational Japanese Book with CD, $19.95
Everything® French Grammar Book
Everything® French Phrase Book, $9.95
Everything® French Verb Book, $9.95
Everything® German Practice Book with CD, $19.95
Everything® Inglés Book
Everything® Learning French Book
Everything® Learning German Book
Everything® Learning Italian Book
Everything® Learning Latin Book
Everything® Learning Spanish Book
Everything® Russian Practice Book with CD, $19.95
Everything® Sign Language Book
Everything® Spanish Grammar Book
Everything® Spanish Phrase Book, $9.95
Everything® Spanish Practice Book with CD, $19.95
Everything® Spanish Verb Book, $9.95

MUSIC

Everything® Drums Book with CD, $19.95
Everything® Guitar Book
Everything® Guitar Chords Book with CD, $19.95
Everything® Home Recording Book
Everything® Music Theory Book with CD, $19.95
Everything® Reading Music Book with CD, $19.95
Everything® Rock & Blues Guitar Book (with CD), $19.95
Everything® Songwriting Book

NEW AGE

Everything® Astrology Book, 2nd Ed.
Everything® Birthday Personology Book
Everything® Dreams Book, 2nd Ed.
Everything® Love Signs Book, $9.95
Everything® Numerology Book
Everything® Paganism Book
Everything® Palmistry Book
Everything® Psychic Book
Everything® Reiki Book
Everything® Sex Signs Book, $9.95
Everything® Tarot Book, 2nd Ed.
Everything® Wicca and Witchcraft Book

PARENTING

Everything® Baby Names Book, 2nd Ed.
Everything® Baby Shower Book
Everything® Baby's First Food Book
Everything® Baby's First Year Book
Everything® Birthing Book
Everything® Breastfeeding Book
Everything® Father-to-Be Book
Everything® Father's First Year Book
Everything® Get Ready for Baby Book
Everything® Get Your Baby to Sleep Book, $9.95
Everything® Getting Pregnant Book
Everything® Guide to Raising a One-Year-Old
Everything® Guide to Raising a Two-Year-Old
Everything® Homeschooling Book
Everything® Mother's First Year Book
Everything® Parent's Guide to Children and Divorce
Everything® Parent's Guide to Children with ADD/ADHD
Everything® Parent's Guide to Children with Asperger's Syndrome
Everything® Parent's Guide to Children with Autism
Everything® Parent's Guide to Children with Bipolar Disorder
Everything® Parent's Guide to Children with Dyslexia
Everything® Parent's Guide to Positive Discipline
Everything® Parent's Guide to Raising a Successful Child
Everything® Parent's Guide to Raising Boys
Everything® Parent's Guide to Raising Siblings
Everything® Parent's Guide to Sensory Integration Disorder
Everything® Parent's Guide to Tantrums
Everything® Parent's Guide to the Overweight Child
Everything® Parent's Guide to the Strong-Willed Child
Everything® Parenting a Teenager Book
Everything® Potty Training Book, $9.95
Everything® Pregnancy Book, 2nd Ed.
Everything® Pregnancy Fitness Book
Everything® Pregnancy Nutrition Book
Everything® Pregnancy Organizer, 2nd Ed., $16.95
Everything® Toddler Activities Book
Everything® Toddler Book
Everything® Tween Book
Everything® Twins, Triplets, and More Book

PETS

Everything® Aquarium Book
Everything® Boxer Book
Everything® Cat Book, 2nd Ed.
Everything® Chihuahua Book
Everything® Dachshund Book
Everything® Dog Book
Everything® Dog Health Book
Everything® Dog Owner's Organizer, $16.95
Everything® Dog Training and Tricks Book
Everything® German Shepherd Book
Everything® Golden Retriever Book
Everything® Horse Book
Everything® Horse Care Book
Everything® Horseback Riding Book
Everything® Labrador Retriever Book
Everything® Poodle Book
Everything® Pug Book
Everything® Puppy Book
Everything® Rottweiler Book
Everything® Small Dogs Book
Everything® Tropical Fish Book
Everything® Yorkshire Terrier Book

REFERENCE

Everything® Blogging Book
Everything® Build Your Vocabulary Book
Everything® Car Care Book
Everything® Classical Mythology Book
Everything® Da Vinci Book
Everything® Divorce Book
Everything® Einstein Book
Everything® Etiquette Book, 2nd Ed.
Everything® Inventions and Patents Book
Everything® Mafia Book
Everything® Philosophy Book
Everything® Psychology Book
Everything® Shakespeare Book

RELIGION

Everything® Angels Book
Everything® Bible Book
Everything® Buddhism Book
Everything® Catholicism Book
Everything® Christianity Book
Everything® History of the Bible Book
Everything® Jesus Book
Everything® Jewish History & Heritage Book
Everything® Judaism Book
Everything® Kabbalah Book
Everything® Koran Book
Everything® Mary Book

Everything® Mary Magdalene Book
Everything® Prayer Book
Everything® Saints Book
Everything® Torah Book
Everything® Understanding Islam Book
Everything® World's Religions Book
Everything® Zen Book

SCHOOL & CAREERS

Everything® Alternative Careers Book
Everything® Career Tests Book
Everything® College Major Test Book
Everything® College Survival Book, 2nd Ed.
Everything® Cover Letter Book, 2nd Ed.
Everything® Filmmaking Book
Everything® Get-a-Job Book
Everything® Guide to Being a Paralegal
Everything® Guide to Being a Real Estate Agent
Everything® Guide to Being a Sales Rep
Everything® Guide to Careers in Health Care
Everything® Guide to Careers in Law Enforcement
Everything® Guide to Government Jobs
Everything® Guide to Starting and Running a Restaurant
Everything® Job Interview Book
Everything® New Nurse Book
Everything® New Teacher Book
Everything® Paying for College Book
Everything® Practice Interview Book
Everything® Resume Book, 2nd Ed.
Everything® Study Book

SELF-HELP

Everything® Dating Book, 2nd Ed.
Everything® Great Sex Book
Everything® Kama Sutra Book
Everything® Self-Esteem Book

SPORTS & FITNESS

Everything® Easy Fitness Book
Everything® Fishing Book
Everything® Golf Instruction Book
Everything® Pilates Book
Everything® Running Book
Everything® Weight Training Book
Everything® Yoga Book

TRAVEL

Everything® Family Guide to Cruise Vacations
Everything® Family Guide to Hawaii

Everything® Family Guide to Las Vegas, 2nd Ed.
Everything® Family Guide to Mexico
Everything® Family Guide to New York City, 2nd Ed.
Everything® Family Guide to RV Travel & Campgrounds
Everything® Family Guide to the Caribbean
Everything® Family Guide to the Walt Disney World Resort®, Universal Studios®, and Greater Orlando, 4th Ed.
Everything® Family Guide to Timeshares
Everything® Family Guide to Washington D.C., 2nd Ed.
Everything® Guide to New England

WEDDINGS

Everything® Bachelorette Party Book, $9.95
Everything® Bridesmaid Book, $9.95
Everything® Destination Wedding Book
Everything® Elopement Book, $9.95
Everything® Father of the Bride Book, $9.95
Everything® Groom Book, $9.95
Everything® Mother of the Bride Book, $9.95
Everything® Outdoor Wedding Book
Everything® Wedding Book, 3rd Ed.
Everything® Wedding Checklist, $9.95
Everything® Wedding Etiquette Book, $9.95
Everything® Wedding Organizer, 2nd Ed., $16.95
Everything® Wedding Shower Book, $9.95
Everything® Wedding Vows Book, $9.95
Everything® Wedding Workout Book
Everything® Weddings on a Budget Book, $9.95

WRITING

Everything® Creative Writing Book
Everything® Get Published Book, 2nd Ed.
Everything® Grammar and Style Book
Everything® Guide to Writing a Book Proposal
Everything® Guide to Writing a Novel
Everything® Guide to Writing Children's Books
Everything® Guide to Writing Research Papers
Everything® Screenwriting Book
Everything® Writing Poetry Book
Everything® Writing Well Book